Praise for

OUR
DAMAGED
DEMOCRACY

"A Washington insider draws on decades of experience to deliver a blistering critique of the state of American government. . . . Califano is doggedly bipartisan in his criticism, leaving no doubt that there is ample blame to go around for what are ultimately systemic faults that have been building for half a century. . . . The author's concerns about the executive and legislative branches are particularly well informed, persuasive, discouraging, and sometimes frightening."

—*Kirkus Reviews*

"It's hard to argue with [Califano's] analysis."

—*The New York Times Book Review*

"Joe Califano serves up a fascinating and even-handed wake-up call for we the people to understand and act to repair the damage to our democracy. Those who treasure our freedom should read this book."

—Tom Selleck, Actor, Producer

"Joseph Califano delves deeply into the inner workings of Washington and delivers an unstinting look at how power, money, and politics have produced the ugly mess we're in today."

—Karen Tumulty,
National Political Correspondent, *Washington Post*

"Joseph Califano, one of America's true statesmen, makes a powerful case for what has gone so terribly wrong in the country and the role we must all play in reversing that damage."

—Peter Osnos, Founder of PublicAffairs Book Group

"No sacred cows in this well-referenced and documented book. Califano lays it on the line about the present state of American democracy, how we got here, and how we can save it. Couldn't be more timely."

—Senator Tom Harkin (D-IA, Retired)

"In this enlightened, entertaining, and rigorously nonpartisan book, Joe Califano succinctly details the forces that have brought us to this dangerous moment in our democracy, as well as a course of action to restore balance to our government and hope to our politics. If the opposition is an intimately familiar one—in the words of Pogo, 'We have met the enemy and he is us'—then so is the solution. What we have broken, we can mend if we have the will to do so."

—Robert Schenkkan, Pulitzer Prize– and
Tony Award–winning Playwright

"[Califano] turns his seasoned eye toward root causes when he examines our democratic processes and republican structures. . . . [H]e is particularly thoughtful in avoiding the cheap rhetoric of partisanship. . . . *Our Damaged Democracy* is not afraid to step on toes for the sake of finding ways to fix our broken political system."

—*America* magazine

"An insightful and often searing look at how the dynamic among the three branches of government functions today. This book is full of helpful documentation and real-life examples. The arguments are clear and cogently argued. Califano deserves a hearing by those entrusted with the future of American democracy."

—Rev. Edward A. Malloy, C.S.C.,
President Emeritus, University of Notre Dame

ALSO BY JOSEPH A. CALIFANO JR.

OUR DAMAGED DEMOCRACY

We the People Must Act

JOSEPH A. CALIFANO JR.

ATRIA PAPERBACK

New York   London   Toronto   Sydney   New Delhi

ATRIA
PAPERBACK

An Imprint of Simon & Schuster, Inc.
1230 Avenue of the Americas
New York, NY 10020

Copyright © 2018 by Joseph A. Califano Jr.

All rights reserved, including the right to reproduce this book or portions thereof in any form whatsoever. For information, address Atria Books Subsidiary Rights Department, 1230 Avenue of the Americas, New York, NY 10020.

First Atria Paperback edition edition April 2019

ATRIA PAPERBACK and colophon are trademarks of Simon & Schuster, Inc.

For information about special discounts for bulk purchases, please contact Simon & Schuster Special Sales at 1-866-506-1949 or business@simonandschuster.com.

The Simon & Schuster Speakers Bureau can bring authors to your live event. For more information, or to book an event, contact the Simon & Schuster Speakers Bureau at 866-248-3049 or visit our website at www.simonspeakers.com.

Interior design by Jill Putorti

Manufactured in the United States of America

10   9   8   7   6   5   4   3   2   1

Library of Congress Cataloging-in-Publication Data
Names: Califano, Joseph A., Jr., 1931- author.
Title: Our damaged democracy : we the people must act / Joseph A. Califano, Jr.
Description: New York : Touchstone, [2018] | Includes bibliographical references and index.
Identifiers: LCCN 2017045556 (print) | LCCN 2017058764 (ebook) | ISBN 9781501144639 | ISBN 9781501144615 (hardcover) | ISBN 9781501144622 (trade pbk.)
Subjects: LCSH: Political culture—United States. | Democracy—United States. | Political ethics—United States. | United States—Politics and government—Moral and ethical aspects.
Classification: LCC JK1726 (ebook) | LCC JK1726 .C355 2018 (print) | DDC 320.973—dc23
LC record available at https://lccn.loc.gov/2017045556

ISBN 978-1-5011-4461-5
ISBN 978-1-5011-4462-2 (pbk)
ISBN 978-1-5011-4463-9 (ebook)

DEDICATION

For the women and men who give their lives to public service in the nation's capital and in the states, cities, counties, and towns across America.

Throughout legislatures, executive offices, and courts, dedicated public servants devote their talent and energy to designing laws that serve all the people, executing those laws with competence and compassion, and adjudicating cases with justice and mercy. I have been privileged to work alongside thousands of them, and there is no one with whom I'd rather pass, execute, adjudicate, or debate about a law or program than a committed public servant.

—JAC Jr.

CONTENTS

CONTENTS

PART V:
MONEY: THE ROOT OF POLITICAL EVIL

PART VI:
AMERICAN FAULT LINES

PART VII:
WE THE PEOPLE

PREFACE TO THE PAPERBACK EDITION

CONFRONTING THE CHALLENGES IN 2020

This book sets out the awesome challenges we all face to energize our democracy, protect our freedom, eliminate gridlock, and get government in Washington, state houses, and town halls to work with competence, compassion, and common sense for all our people.

It's up to you and me to wrestle with those challenges.

Most immediately, it's up to you to select the man or woman who will be elected to take office as president in 2020. This will be the most important vote you will ever cast, the most solemn political action of your life, an act that deserves your thoughtful attention and preparation.

How can you prepare?

Get informed and get involved.

Today's buffet of media—right-wing, left-wing, all shades in between, and at outside fringes—makes it easy for each of us to watch and read only the news that we agree with. How many of us have heard a friend say (or perhaps said ourselves), "Do you really watch Fox News?" or "How can you watch MSNBC?" or "I don't watch CNN; it's too biased" or "After that editorial this morning I canceled my subscription to the *New York Times* (*Wall Street Journal, Washington Post*)."

Those are the words of the uninformed.

We must resist the temptation to read and view only reporters and broadcasts that tell us what we want to hear and reinforce our opinions. Being informed requires listening to reporters, politicians, and pundits who make us uncomfortable. It is aggravating to hear from those we vehemently disagree with, but listening to opposing views can help us reach thoughtful decisions. Watch all the talking heads, but make up your own mind.

In Gallup/Knight Foundation surveys, most viewers regard cable channels Fox News, MSNBC, and CNN as biased. They are, but much of that bias is in the eye of the beholder. Democrats and liberals are far likelier to consider Fox News one-sided. Republicans and conservatives tend to find MSNBC and CNN slanted. Biased channels have become political quicksand sucking in viewers who want to watch only news and opinion shows that echo their political beliefs. In the cable media's brave new world, viewers need not see or hear any news or opinions they don't like.

The partner of being informed is being curious, finding out for yourself, never collapsing into a I'll-never-understand-that-issue comatose state. Too many of us back off from too many issues saying, "I'll never figure out: what's happening in Yemen, or why President Trump did that, or whether Republicans or Democrats are responsible for the government shutdown, or if former FBI director James Comey or Donald Trump is telling the truth."

Our democracy depends on your being informed and engaged. Such citizens hold the keys to putting in office talented and committed legislators, governors, city council members, mayors, and presidents. Only you can elect national, state, and local political leaders who have the will and integrity to repair our damaged democracy. Only you can install common sense, compassion, and competence in Washington, state houses, and town halls. You do it by selecting and monitoring the people who hold public office.

PREFACE TO THE PAPERBACK EDITION

If you are seeking someone to blame for self-serving, inept, or corrupt elected officials, look in the mirror first. When did you start thinking about and paying attention to possible candidates for president, Congress, governor, mayor, or county council member from your district? Did you wait until a few days or couple of weeks before the election? That's like not getting to the theater until the play's final act has started.

Like most presidents, Barack Obama and Donald Trump began planning their reelection campaigns the day after they were first elected. Senators and representatives start their next campaign the morning after they win their current six- or two-year term in Congress. That's why it makes sense for you to keep an eye on them from that moment on. Don't wait until a few weeks before the next election.

The 2018 midterm elections, presidential tweet tantrums, demographic revolution, and ambitions of ideological billionaires eying the White House and Congress are setting the stage for the nastiest, and most manipulative, expensive, and crucial presidential and political primaries and campaigns in the nation's history.

If this disturbs you, then get involved in the candidate nomination and election process before it even begins. Find out who is going to run for office. There is plenty of news identifying those folks in print, and on social media and television. Tap into Google and use the mass of information and opinion on the internet to help inform your judgment of candidates and their causes. Watch the talking heads. Listen to candidates, assess their public policies and programs. Pay attention to what they say and do, how they say and do it, and with and to whom. Keep an eye on their supporters and opponents. But make up your own mind. You decide whether they are ego-tripping, seeking political power for their own ends, or dedicated to helping all the people.

Note whether office seekers just attack their opponents or

have public policies and programs of their own. Keep in mind one of Lyndon Johnson's political aphorisms, "Any jackass can kick down a barn, but it takes a carpenter to build one." Support the candidate with the saw, not the one with the sledgehammer. Think ahead and try to imagine how the candidate will speak and act if elected. Keep in mind that a candidate who wants to get something done in politics and public policy doesn't tell opponents to go to hell unless she or he can send them there.

Follow the coverage of candidates in the media that support them and media that oppose them. In examining candidates for the Senate and House of Representatives, go for those who seem to display the courage and tenacity needed to make a difference on Capitol Hill and vis-à-vis the president. There is a host of information available online. Tap into it.

Moreover, use your email to let candidates and your senators and representative know how you feel about an issue, a Supreme Court nominee, or a piece of legislation. Get your friends to do the same. Members of Congress and their staffs pay attention to those emails, especially as they accumulate. Big-time lobbyists spend millions of dollars hiring Washington, D.C., firms to generate thousands of "grassroots" emails on issues important to their special interests. They want to protect favorable tax treatment or tap into the potential billions of dollars available in selling marijuana. Take advantage of opportunities to become an active member of organizations in your community: the school board, senior clubs, church or temple, political or candidate organization. You can organize friends and members of your VA and bridge clubs, reading groups, churches, and fellow parents at your child's school. They can send emails or make calls to your city council member, state legislative representative, senator, or representative.

In judging presidents, senators, and other public officeholders, keep your eye on the important public policy issues. Remember that presidents and senators are human beings, just like you. They get angry. You should distinguish between an isolated outburst and a calculated campaign of anger. Harry Truman sent a blistering letter to *Washington Post* theater critic Paul Hume, who had panned his daughter Margaret's performance at the National Theatre. "Some Day I hope to meet you," Truman wrote. "When that happens you'll need a new nose, a lot of beefsteak for black eyes, and perhaps a supporter below!" But Truman gave us the Marshall Plan and desegregated the armed forces. John Kennedy banned the *New York Herald Tribune* at the White House because of its coverage of the Billie Sol Estes investigation, but he started the program to put a man on the moon and inspired thousands of talented men and women to enter public service. Lyndon Johnson said to me that a White House reporter who repeatedly criticized him was "a revolving son of a bitch. That's someone who's a son of a bitch no matter how you look at him!" But Johnson put on the books the Freedom of Information Act and historic civil rights laws. Trump's angry tantrums appear calculated and aimed at undermining the free press and sharpening racial divisions. Effective citizenship requires you to make the distinctions here.

Our society continues to be shredded socially, politically, and culturally by the revolution in communications (notably cable and social media), the tenacity of racial and ethnic tension, economic disparity, and the chasms between middle America and Ivy League elites. You can certainly do something about this. Use the many opportunities to foster a sense of community: your neighborhood, your church, your child's school, a local political campaign, helping serve meals to the poor in your area on Thanksgiving, thanking a local policeman or volunteer fireman for keeping you safe.

As this book predicted, the debasement of our political culture and discourse has persisted. For potential members of Congress, executive branch officials, and presidents, everything is on the table, from drinking in their high school years to any carelessly worded email. Even those who prevail in the scorching heat of anything-goes Senate confirmation hearings, party primaries, and elections are often permanently scarred. The hot coals of politics and public service don't just singe; they burn. You can make it clear that you are not a proponent of unforgiving politics. What you want to see is how well women and men perform their public service. All politicians and public figures are likely to fall at some point on some matter during their careers. What you care about is how they get up and what they do after rising.

The power of social media and cable news has been growing faster than Jack's beanstalk on steroids. This concentrated control of the information that we see and hear is a more serious threat to our freedom than the yellowest tabloid Hearst journalism of the past.

Today those who control Google, Facebook, or Twitter have far more power than the original designers of our democracy, drafters of the First Amendment, and citizens during our first two and a half centuries ever conceived possible. You can tell your representatives in Congress and executive branch employees that you are concerned about such concentrations of power. Email them and ask what they are doing about it. Think about it as you would think about hackers of personal and financial information. Reining in Silicon Valley media giants merits careful and skeptical attention and carefully crafted curbs on the concentration of their power. If this concerns you, email your congressman or senator. You have the power to do something about this.

This is a big order, all this stuff, you may be thinking as you read this. Sure it is, but you can do something about it.

Stay informed and get involved early on, the way you would if someone in your family was competing for a nomination for office.

And vote, not just at the final stage of election, but in the primaries. That's the most effective way to detoxify our politics and curb pernicious and perpetual partisanship. If you think the Senate Judiciary Committee hearings on Brett Kavanaugh were a political farce on either or both sides of the aisle, then get out there and work to have better Senate candidates. If you see Donald Trump as a dangerous narcissist or are concerned that the Democratic candidates are moving too far to the left, then get involved in your party's presidential nomination process before the party convention.

Legendary House Speaker Thomas P. "Tip" O'Neill Jr. used to say that "All politics is local." Today national politics has become local, intimately involved in just about every aspect of your life. You should get just as involved and engaged in the public conduct of your senators, representative, and president.

It's often been said that you get the public officeholders you vote for. You also get the public officeholders you don't vote for, the ones who are nominated or win elections in contests in which you didn't vote. Getting informed and engaged, then voting— that's how to produce a rejuvenated and caring democracy for yourselves and your children and grandchildren. I hope this book encourages you to get informed and engaged. If you do, you will be surprised at the power you have to help your country and yourself.

INTRODUCTION

Our democracy is damaged.

We all know it. Every measure of our people reveals their perilously low confidence in the potential of the presidency, Congress, and the courts to stem the damage to our democracy and repair it.

But we can do it. First we must recognize that while we do have foreign enemies and adversaries, the greatest threats to our way of life come from within our nation. We must also understand how these forces exacerbate the worst and most destructive aspects of each other.

In his *Study of History*, British historian Arnold Toynbee reminded the world that "civilization is not a condition but a movement, a voyage, not a harbor." He concluded that the great civilizations were destroyed by self-inflicted wounds, not by enemies from without, but from within. As he put it, "In all cases reviewed the most that an alien enemy has achieved has been to give an expiring suicide her coup de grace."

Our nation confronts the fierce foreign winds of ISIS, chaos in the Middle East, Russian hacking and meddling efforts to discredit our democratic system, and an ambitious and aggressive China. We face an unraveling European Union and globalization fired up by an unprecedented technological revolution. There are nuclear weapons in the hands of North Korea and perhaps Iran, proliferating beyond our control. Extremists and enemies are capable of terrorism not only with guns and bombs, but also with biological, chemical, and electronic weapons.

These are serious threats to our nation and way of life. But the most menacing lesson of history—one we may repeat if we refuse to learn from it—is that the greatest danger to our democracy is from within, not from without.

You don't need a high school diploma to know that Washington isn't working. Nor do you need a course in history to understand that America today is a far cry from the America of a generation or two ago, much less the adventurous, heroic, and determined population of the thirteen colonies that founded this nation. Our leaders find it much harder to get government to work, to devise and deliver public policy that helps all our people, and to muster solid majorities of Americans behind it. It's become a backbreaking lift to establish and nourish an economic and social environment that helps parents raise their children. We live in a savagely raw political culture. This is an era of double-edged swords like the technological and social media revolution that may be as much a challenge as a boon to our democratic way of life.

Only we the people can repair our damaged democracy. We must understand the various vexing challenges our nation faces and how they affect one another in order to confront and conquer them. This book reveals how and why our democracy is damaged and makes some suggestions for renovation. This nation is yours and mine. We have the opportunity and the responsibility to repair and renew it. I have long believed that once our people fully grasp the problems, they fix them. That's why I wrote this book.

INTRODUCTION

The dysfunction we see today in Washington is not something spontaneous that just happened. Nor is it the fault of one party or one branch of government. Nor of any one president, Congress, or Supreme Court. The damage to our democracy has been accumulating for many years. Any one of us who has exercised power in the world of Washington over the past several decades almost surely has some fingerprints on it.

We face a disproportionately powerful presidency, a gridlocked and distracted Congress, politicized courts, dependent states, and a big-bucks-shaped public policy. At the same time, media, economic, educational, cultural, political, racial, and religious fault lines fragment our society. My concern is that people see these as isolated problems. They are not. This book shows how they reinforce and aggravate the worst elements in each other. The incestuous and corrosive combination of these problems is a far greater danger to our democracy than the sum of their individual parts. It has diminished the ability of our public institutions and leaders to protect and enrich our inalienable right to life, liberty, and the pursuit of happiness.

In Washington the three branches of government have lost their constitutional bearings. Much of their capacity to provide coherent and unifying leadership that serves all our people and maintains our leading role in the free world has been lost.

There is a colossal concentration of power in the American presidency with its palace guard of hundreds of professionals who answer only to the president. Concentration of power in one person or one branch of government amid fragmentation almost everywhere else is a recipe for damaging democracy.

Congress is crippled by a take-no-prisoners partisanship. The House and Senate are pushed and shoved around by all sorts of well-financed commercial, cultural, and single-issue special interests that call compromise a sellout.

The Supreme Court and many lower federal courts are riven by conservative versus liberal politics. This rift begins with politically charged litmus tests that dominate the presidential nomination and Senate confirmation processes. It widens with the blistering rhetoric in so many of the top court's 5–4 decisions and the politically infused rulings of many district court judges.

A malfunctioning Congress enhances the power of the president. The partisanship that dominates Congress and its confirmation process undermines respect for the Supreme Court. For an increasingly powerful executive branch, the checks, balances, and separation of powers designed to protect our freedom can become lines in the sand that are easily breezed away.

As the fifty states grow more dependent on federal funding, they more readily bow to the mandates that accompany those dollars. They need the money to provide education, health care, affordable housing, and infrastructure renewal for their residents. This dependency is atrophying their political muscles. It suppresses their potential as laboratories for creative public policies and more efficient ways to deliver essential services.

The many millions of dollars—billions for wannabe presidents—required to achieve elective office trample the constitutional concept of one person, one vote. Those with enormous fortunes use their deep pockets to dictate federal, state, and local public policies. High rollers with fat bankrolls move from federal to state government, from Congress to state legislatures, from courts and local prosecutors to city councils and town halls, until they get their way. The demeaning conduct often required to raise political money affects the quality of the individuals willing to enter public life.

Campaigns for elective office and public service have become blood sports. The media, social, cultural, ideological, and racial fault lines in our society inhibit the ability of our public leaders and institutions to function for all our citizens. Fewer qualified and outstanding individuals are willing to engage in, or be subject to, anything-goes, anonymous-sourced, social media political combat in order to win an election or become a federal judge or cabinet or subcabinet appointee. First-rate and courageous public leaders are critical to restore faith in public institutions and conquer cantankerous public problems.

The First Amendment is enshrined in our Constitution so that the press can fearlessly speak truth to power and uncover public and private corruption and incompetence. The press has been weakened by the lack of resources to pay reporters, editors, publishers, and broadcasters, whose bosses must show profits. Political correctness and follow-the-pack journalism in Washington often soften the punch that the First Amendment was designed to give to protected speech. Federal law enforcement and intelligence bureaucrats, sworn to keep secrets in criminal justice and national security matters, act like coup colleagues in a banana republic. They see selective leaking to reporters as a way to undermine senior officials they dislike and policies they disagree with. The anonymous internet fosters a kind of mob rule by irresponsible verbal assault as it distributes false news and unsubstantiated personal attacks. Social media provides fertile soil for the fragmentation of our society.

The First Amendment also protects our freedom of religion. Once universally cherished, respected, and appreciated, this freedom has become a source of confusion and conflict. Those who exercise it run into prickly political and cultural disputes instead of inspiring efforts to find accommodating avenues of public policy, individual conduct, and religious practice. The sacred and secular square off against each other in government health programs, lawsuits about the Ten Commandments carved on stone in government parks, and the phrase "one nation under God" in the Pledge of Allegiance.

Ideological intransigence has created a monstrous traffic jam in the public square. America today is among history's most multicultural nations. Unlocking the power and human beauty of its demographic mosaic has monumental potential. Too many white people and members of racial and ethnic minorities continue to live and play on separate sides of the street. Those who try to cross to the other side or reach out to shake hands sometimes get run over.

Income inequality allows the top 1 percent to gobble up the nation's wealth and bunches millions of the neediest Americans in a pit at the bottom. The chasm between rich and poor stokes a resentment poised to morph into despair, then anger, and eventually (and in some situations already) violence. Education inequality is slamming the door shut on upward mobility and cementing permanent elite and lower classes. Political cowardice and self-interest, and related government gridlock, obstruct compromise and innovative public policies. They stanch efforts to unite all our people and give them the opportunity and motivation to be all that God gave them the talent to be.

It's not enough to be mad as hell about the situation. Now is the time to do something about it, and we the people—and only we—can. We need to take a cold and true look at the way that these problems, which damage our democracy, feed on each other, and how and why they do. Then we must mount an *all-fronts* and *urgent* campaign to confront them. *All fronts*, because the many problems that threaten us are so intertwined. *Urgent*, because the longer we wait, the more dangerous the situation will become and the harder it will be to maintain a government of, by, and for the people. The survival and enrichment of our damaged democracy are the stakes.

To do these things, we need to talk and listen to each other in candid conversation—you and I face-to-face; cities and states and the federal government; black, white, and all other skin pigments and ethnicities; religious and nonreligious; old and young; liberals and conservatives; urban and rural; haves, have-nots, and one-percenters.

We do not need to agree, but we do need to trust each other and to be worthy of each other's trust. There are few angels in politics—or in government, business, labor, education, or any other field for that matter. Yet there was a day when a handshake was as much a commitment as a written contract. There was a time when wrenching public policy disputes eventually brought out the thoughtful best, not the raging beast in each side. Those were the days when we judged a political candidate or a party on more than just a single issue.

Such conversations and trust are essential preconditions for accepting finality in most decisions reached to resolve differences, whether those decisions are reached by passing a law, compromise, judicial decision, or election. Exchange of ideas among friends and foes helps develop mutual trust. With such trust, both sides can accept agreements and decisions as an end, rather than as a time-out in a perpetual dispute. Politics is not Ping-Pong, but crude, narcissistic, and street-fighting Democrats, Republicans, and independents would do better to spend their time looking in the mirror instead of spitting and throwing rocks at each other.

Why are self-examination, conversations, trust, and a sense of finality so important? Because without them, we will never be able to resolve the complex crises we face. We may not even bring ourselves to confront them. We will continue to have difficulty recognizing and recruiting individuals of high character, talent, leadership, and dedication to the public's interest for service in politics and government.

Change is always difficult and often disruptive for our nation. Fundamental changes can be infernally tortuous to negotiate. Nevertheless, if we are to confront the challenges our nation faces, our leaders, institutions, politics, and public policies must change. We must change the way we conduct ourselves as citizens and the way political parties conduct themselves. Even Lyndon Johnson, despite fierce pride in his monumental domestic legislative achievements, recognized that his life's work was not chiseled in stone:

> But most of all, the Great Society is not a safe harbor, a resting place, a final objective, a finished work. It is a challenge constantly renewed, beckoning us toward a destiny where the meaning of our lives matches the marvelous products of our labor.[1]

This book is informed by more than eighty-five years of life experience, beginning in Depression-era Brooklyn with loving, middle-class parents. My education came on the streets of Brooklyn and from Jesuits at Brooklyn Prep and Holy Cross, and professors at Harvard Law School. It reflects lessons learned from working for thirty years in the nation's capital. Those years began in the Kennedy administration, working at the Pentagon for Robert McNamara. Then I moved to the White House staff as President Lyndon Johnson's chief assistant for domestic affairs, and served as secretary of health, education, and welfare in President Jimmy Carter's cabinet. My professional years included acting as an attorney for the *Washington Post* and the Democratic Party during Watergate, decades as a Wall Street and Washington lawyer representing clients as varied as the Black Panther Party, the überconservative Peter Grace, the überliberal Daniel Schorr, and Coca-Cola in courts and in the secret tunnels of Capitol

Hill. I have served on the boards of more than fifteen public companies.

I have never been so concerned about the destiny of our democracy. I've never seen the nation's capital so self-centered, fractured by angry partisanship, and weakened by the soft corruption of billions of dollars of political money. Many friends and colleagues of every political and ideological stripe are profoundly troubled about the condition of the capital and the country that we are passing on to our children and grandchildren.

We're the people. You and I. The ball is in our court, yours and mine. If you're ready to play, read on to find out what's broken, why it's broken, and a few ideas on what we must do to repair it. I hope what's written on these pages will spark even more and better ideas from you. Together, we can once again make government work for all our people.

OUR
DAMAGED
DEMOCRACY

PART I

POTUS THE POWERFUL

1

ENHANCING POTUS POWER

POTUS, as White House staffers and Washington insiders call the president of the United States, looms over the political and institutional hierarchies in the nation's capital.

We have always been a Presidential Nation, and Washington works best when presidential leadership is strong, creative, and caring. But with the nation's Congress politically pulverized and bureaucratically hog-tied and the Supreme Court ideologically split and politicized, the executive branch has become more like a giant among pesky pygmies than a first among three coequal branches of government.

Congress is composed of 535 individuals of differing political views, social values, racial and ethnic backgrounds, and religions, from districts and states with diverse economic interests. The federal judiciary is mired in procedural complexity, bogged down by a backlog of litigation, and led by a Supreme Court handing down razor-edged 5–4 decisions. Neither institution is a match for an agile, single-minded president.

The nominally independent states, counties, and cities are acting like supplicant subjects. They knock on the White House doors pleading for funds or for freedom from some executive branch regulation or mandate. The media—print, television, radio, social—feed the voracious appetite of their endless news cycle by dinging or doting on the president and his political and personal coterie. A variety of special interests—hefty financial contributors, lobbyists, and powerful right- and left-wing organizations—visit the West Wing to plead their case. Most presidents try to do the right thing in the national interest. *But for all presidents it's the right thing as they see it.* Their vision is easily clouded by ideological commitment, political ambition, a vision of their place in history, and the human temptation and political need to accommodate their pals and patrons.

Whatever the campaigning candidate, Republican or Democrat, professes, those who win the presidency move to strengthen the power of the office. As a result, the occupant in the White House has come to tower over the legislative and judicial branches and often exercises powers that were once the constitutional prerogatives of those other two.

For decades our people have been sharply divided about presidential candidates; the roles of federal, state, and local governments; the knee-jerk positions of left- and right-wing ideologues; and the rapid multiculturalization of our population. The 2016 candidates Donald Trump and Hillary Clinton, with his lips curling and her eyes rolling, sometimes resembled cartoon characters in their exaggerated clashes on immigration, taxing the Wall Street rich, and a host of social issues. Americans so vehemently disagreed about them, and some of the positions each espoused, that many families couldn't discuss politics among themselves for months after the election.

But there is one concern that Trumpites, Clintonites, Senators Ted Cruz and Bernie Sanders, and those in between or indifferent about politics should share. It is how one newly elected president after another moves to extend the reach and grasp of the office. Witnessing this, Democrats and Republicans, liberals and conservatives, the far left and far right, should reflect on the wisdom of Lord Acton's wake-up call about concentrations of power. We should all heed Daniel Webster's warning that "the contest, for all ages, has been to rescue Liberty from the grasp of executive power."[1]

A defining principle of political power that I learned serving in Robert McNamara's Pentagon, LBJ's White House, and Jimmy Carter's cabinet was this: where one sits determines where one stands. No political disciples observe that bureaucratic axiom more faithfully than incumbent presidents.

In campaigning, presidential candidates typically condemn incumbents and predecessors for abusing their power, exceeding their authority as commander in chief, and playing trick or treaty with the Senate in making agreements with foreign powers. These Oval Office seekers attack incumbents for issuing executive orders that assume legislative powers reserved to Congress and writing regulations that go far beyond laws Congress has enacted. They promise to accept the judiciary's interpretation of the Constitution and laws. They assure voters that if elected they will reverse or ignore their predecessor's unconstitutional and unauthorized actions. Democrat or Republican, these candidates commit to defer to the power of Congress to legislate and appropriate funds.

Until they get elected.

Such campaigning has been common among presidential candidates throughout most of American history and especially since the development of the modern presidency under Franklin D. Roosevelt. Before his election to the presidency in 1964, Lyndon Johnson said that, unlike his opponent Barry Goldwater and the Republicans, "We are not about to send American boys nine or ten thousand miles away from home to do what Asian boys ought to be doing for themselves," and "get tied down in a land war in Asia."[2] During the 1980 presidential debates candidate Ronald Reagan lambasted President Carter for negotiating with terrorists to return hostages from Iran. "There will be no negotiation with terrorists of any kind," Reagan assured voters in Cleveland in 1980.[3] In office, President Johnson sent more than 500,000 Americans to fight in Vietnam and President Reagan pursued secret negotiations with terrorists to exchange weapons for hostages during the Iran-Contra affair.[4]

Candidate Trump blasted President Obama for abusing the use of executive orders. "The country wasn't based on executive orders," he said. "Right now, Obama goes around signing executive orders. . . . It's a basic disaster. You can't do it."[5] In his first hundred days in office, President Trump signed more executive orders than any of his postwar predecessors; these orders established restrictions on immigration, eased offshore drilling activities, and curbed enforcement of a law under which churches forfeit their tax-exempt status if they support political candidates.[6]

When signing laws passed by Congress, presidents often use the opportunity to make signing statements declaring their intention to ignore or amend provisions they oppose. In 1965, when Congress passed a law mandating 120-day notice prior to closing a military base, President Johnson didn't dare ignore it. He vetoed the law claiming it infringed on his power as commander in chief. He worked us around the clock to convince Congress to reduce the notice period to 30 days.[7] Today any president, Democrat or Republican, would simply ignore the 120-day congressional requirement, likely claiming in a signing statement that it infringed on his or her powers as the commander in chief.

When Ronald Reagan signed the 1986 amendments to the Safe Drinking Water Act, he said his administration would not follow its mandatory enforcement provisions because "prosecutorial discretion is an essential ingredient in the execution of laws [and] Congress cannot bind the Executive."[8] Every successive president has used signing statements at one time or another to indicate he had no intention of following a particular section in a law passed by Congress.

As a presidential candidate, Barack Obama attacked President George W. Bush's use of signing statements to ignore laws he disagreed with. "He's been saying," Obama charged, "I can basically change what Congress passes by attaching a [signing statement] saying 'I don't agree with the part. I'm going to choose to interpret it [my way].'"[9] Candidate Obama promised, "I will obey the Constitution of the United States. We're not going to use signing statements as a way of doing an end run around Congress."[10] President Obama repeatedly used signing statements to nullify legislative provisions such as those involving the transfer of Guantánamo Bay prisoners, diplomatic initiatives with Israel, and protections for chaplains whose religious beliefs limited their ministry with respect to gays and lesbians.[11] President Trump in an August 2017 signing statement said that legislation sanctioning Russia encroached on the executive branch's power in foreign affairs.[12]

Such exercises of presidential power are difficult to curb. Republican Darrell Issa of the House Foreign Affairs Committee, commenting on Obama's determination to close the Guantánamo Bay prison in 2016, said, "There is little we can do if this president ignores the law in a timely fashion. Our process is to go to the court. The court is likely not to rule quickly. The fact is it is very hard to stop a president from doing something if he is willing to ignore the law and his oath."[13]

As time passes during the presidential terms, those who hold the office tend to express their frustration with the limits on their power by assuming more power. In his first term Barack Obama repeatedly said that he could not "just suspend deportations through executive order . . . because there are laws on the books that Congress passed. . . . We've got three branches of government. Congress passes the law. The executive branch's job is to enforce and implement those laws. And then the judiciary has to interpret the laws."[14] In his second term, he suspended the deportation of millions of undocumented aliens by executive action. The federal court of appeals for the Fifth Circuit held that action unconstitutional, a decision the Supreme Court upheld by a 4–4 vote.[15]

The *Wall Street Journal* and conservatives singled out President Obama for his "contempt for institutions he doesn't run" and "unilateral executive action."[16] The *New York Times* and the *Washington Post* have leveled similar criticisms at Donald Trump, but in fact Obama's and Trump's presidencies represent a continuum of presidential conduct.[17] Whatever his campaign rhetoric, president after president has marched almost in lockstep to enhance the power of the Oval Office. This steady trek probably began the day after George Washington announced that he would not seek a third term, establishing an informal rule of term limits that lasted until the days of Franklin Delano Roosevelt. FDR was the first president to continue in office for more than two terms. The end of an extraordinary four-term presidency marked the last time the legislature stood up to the president as a coequal branch by passing a constitutional amendment, quickly ratified by the states, to limit future presidents to two terms in office.

2

POTUS THE COMMANDER IN CHIEF

Perhaps the most dramatic assumption of power by presidents has been in their role as commander in chief. Most notably, and with remarkable congressional acquiescence, presidents have sent American military forces into combat since the middle of the last century without a declaration of war.

How many Americans remember, if they ever knew, that Article I, section 8, of the Constitution provides that "the Congress . . . shall have the power . . . To declare War." The Constitution grants that power *exclusively* to Congress. As Alexander Hamilton wrote in the *Federalist* no. 69:

> The President is to be commander-in-chief of the Army and Navy of the United States. In this respect his authority would be nominally the same with that of the king of Great Britain, but in substance much inferior to it. It would amount to nothing more than the supreme command and direction of the military and naval forces . . . while that [authority] of the British king extends to the DECLARING of war and to the RAISING and REGULATING of fleets and armies, all which, by the Constitution under consideration, would appertain to the legislature.

And as James Madison wrote to Thomas Jefferson, "The constitution supposes, what the History of all Governments demonstrates, that the Executive is the branch of power most interested in war, and most prone to it. It has accordingly with studied care vested the question of war in the Legislature."[1]

Why don't most Americans remember this provision in our Constitution? Because few were alive in December 1941—three-quarters of a century ago—when Franklin D. Roosevelt in his dramatic "day of infamy" address asked a joint session of Congress to declare war on Germany and Japan. That's the last time any president went to Congress for a declaration of war.*

Yet since the end of World War II in 1945, some 100,000 Americans have died in combat, and there have been about a million additional casualties. That's about the same number of American soldiers, sailors, and marines who lost their lives in World War I and more than were wounded in World War II. Presidents ordered all these military men and women into combat without any declaration of war by Congress.[2] The two big events were the Korean War, which President Truman euphemistically called a "United Nations police action," during which 37,000 Americans died, and the Vietnam War, waged by Lyndon Johnson and Richard Nixon, during which 58,000 American combatants lost their lives.[3] On numerous other occasions, presidents of both parties sent Americans into combat or the imminent threat of combat in the Middle East, Central America, the Caribbean, Africa, the Balkans, Southeast Asia, and elsewhere without any congressional declaration of war. They often cited Truman's refusal to ask Congress for one as a precedent.[4]

President George H. W. Bush committed nearly 300,000

---

*In 1942 Roosevelt wrote Congress to ask it to declare war on Bulgaria, Hungary, and Romania, allies of the Axis powers.

troops to the defense of Saudi Arabia and its oil fields in response to the threat posed by Saddam Hussein following the Iraqi invasion of Kuwait in 1990.[5] Five months later when offensive actions were imminent, a reporter asked Bush if he would seek congressional approval. The president snapped, "I'll just repeat for the record that there have been a lot of uses of force in our history and very few declarations of war."[6] Later Congress did pass a resolution authorizing military action against Iraq. In signing it, Bush attached this disdainful statement:

> My request for congressional support did not, and my signing this resolution does not, constitute any change in the longstanding positions of the executive branch on either the President's constitutional authority to use the Armed Forces to defend vital U.S. interests or the constitutionality of the War Powers Resolution.[7]

He reiterated this view in a salty comment while campaigning at the Texas State Republican Convention in 1992, saying that "I didn't have to get permission from some old goat in the United States Congress to kick Saddam Hussein out of Kuwait."[8]

Lack of congressional approval did not trim President Bill Clinton's military sails either. When deploying forces to Haiti in 1994, he said, "I would welcome the support of Congress," but "like my predecessors of both parties, I have not agreed that I was constitutionally mandated to get it."[9] In March 1999, during the conflict between Serbs and Albanians over control of the Kosovo region, NATO organized air strikes to support the Albanians. A resolution to approve US involvement failed to pass the House on a tied 213–213 vote. Following the vote, White House spokesperson Jake Siewert said, "The House today voted no on going forward, no on going back and they tied on standing still. We will continue to prosecute the air campaign and to stop the violence being perpetrated by [Serb leader Slobodan] Milosevic." [10]

In 2002, Congress passed a resolution authorizing military action against Iraq in response to the 9/11 attacks. President George W. Bush signed it with this statement:

> Signing this resolution does not constitute any change in the longstanding positions of the executive branch on . . . the President's constitutional authority to use force to deter, prevent or respond to aggression or other threats to U.S. interests. [11]

Candidate Obama stated during his first presidential campaign that "the president does not have power under the Constitution to unilaterally authorize a military attack in a situation that does not involve stopping an actual or imminent threat to the nation." [12] Yet President Obama instituted military action in Libya, and ordered an additional 60,000 soldiers to Afghanistan. [13] More than 1,800 have lost their lives in a conflict that has become the nation's longest war (entering its seventeenth year as this book is published). [14] Without any notice to Congress and within weeks of assuming office, President Donald Trump sent additional troops to Afghanistan. He also unilaterally increased the number and changed the mission of American marines in Iraq. [15]

The number of American casualties in these Middle East conflicts is enormous when those who suffer from traumatic brain injuries, post-traumatic stress, and other clinical psychological disorders like depression and drug and alcohol addiction are included. [16] The costs of medical care and disability are expected to top a trillion dollars when all accounts are in. [17] All these lives have been lost and costs incurred without any declaration of war by Congress.

In 2013, Donald Trump criticized Barack Obama, tweeting, "What will we get for bombing Syria besides more debt and a possible long term conflict? Obama needs Congressional approval."[18] Less than three months in office, President Trump ordered bombing of Syrian targets without seeking congressional approval.[19] White House officials claimed that Trump's legal justification was "very similar" to the precedent Obama had used in 2011 to support intervention in Libya.[20]

With this history of compliant Congresses, the most powerful restraint on a president from ordering men and women into combat is a compulsory draft that distributes the risk of military services across a broad swath of the entire population. The nation had such a draft during World War I. FDR proposed and Congress enacted such a draft requiring military service in 1940, which, following a brief suspension in 1947, remained in place until 1973.[21]

The power of the military draft to ignite resistance to war was displayed vividly, sometimes violently, during the Vietnam War. The draft then in place initially deferred the obligation of military service for students in graduate school. As a result, the burden of fighting in Vietnam fell more heavily on poor and minority young men who could not afford to attend graduate school. President Johnson eliminated graduate school deferments and established a lottery to subject all young men to the same risk of being drafted.[22] A furious fire of opposition erupted from middle-class and affluent Americans. Parents joined antiwar protesters because they did not think the war in Vietnam was worth risking their children's lives. These demonstrations per-

sisted across the nation and on college campuses after Richard
Nixon became president.

President Nixon and his national security adviser, Henry Kissinger, realized that they could continue and expand the war in
Southeast Asia only if the draft were ended. The Nixon tapes
reveal that on April 7, 1971, they decided to do just that. Nixon
said that he was "going to put the military to the torch" in order
to muster its support for an all-volunteer army because "ending
the draft gets us breathing room in Vietnam." He called the members of the military who wanted to continue the draft "a bunch of
greedy bastards, they want more officers clubs and more men to
shine their shoes. Sons of bitches are not interested in this country." Kissinger, just as eager to continue the war, agreed: "Going
to all volunteer in Vietnam is what we ought to do." [23]

They were correct. Ending the draft increased the president's
power to continue the Vietnam War. Protests by students and
others waned. As Kissinger later wrote, "The draft, which had
been at the heart of so much campus unrest, no longer threatened students with Vietnam service. When schools reopened in
the fall of 1972, the student protests ended." [24]

American military involvement in Vietnam ended in 1973.
But the power of presidents to send American troops into combat persists to this day in large measure because of the absence
of a military draft. In the words of former Harlem congressman
Charles Rangel, a Korean war veteran, "There's no question in
my mind that this president [George W. Bush] . . . would never
have invaded Iraq, especially on the flimsy evidence that was presented to Congress, if indeed we had a draft and members of
Congress and the administration thought that their kids from
their communities would be placed in harm's way." [25]

Not surprisingly, no president has called for a reinstatement
of the draft. Since Nixon's time, in the absence of a military

draft, presidents—and Congresses—have been able to assume that members of the American armed forces sent into conflicts around the world were "volunteers." These volunteers, especially in the lower enlisted ranks, are disproportionately composed of Americans from minority and lower-income backgrounds. The children of affluent and articulate citizens and politicians bear no risk of being sent into combat unless they voluntarily decide to enlist in the military.[26]

The unpopularity of the Vietnam War did prompt Congress in 1973 to pass the War Powers Resolution. Congress then overrode President Nixon's veto, calling it an unconstitutional encroachment on presidential power. The resolution intended to curb presidents from unilaterally deploying military personnel in combat.[27] But, as discussed in chapter 9, that law is a congressional whine that presidents have ignored or selectively observed. According to the Congressional Research Service, there have been more than 150 deployments of American troops since the passage of the War Powers Resolution, compared with 19 deployments in the two decades between World War II and the resolution's passage.[28]

The nearest Congress has come to casting votes on these deployments are passage of resolutions in 1991 supporting George H. W. Bush's action against Iraq, in 2001 authorizing the president to use "necessary and appropriate force" against those responsible for the 9/11 attacks, and in 2002 authorizing President George W. Bush's 2003 invasion of Iraq. When politically expedient, presidents have continued to cite these resolutions as showing congressional support for military actions in the Middle East to this day.[29]

3

POTUS THE LEGISLATOR

When the legislative and executive powers are united in the same person . . . there can be no liberty; because apprehensions may arise, lest the same monarch . . . enact tyrannical laws, to execute them in a tyrannical manner.

—MONTESQUIEU, *THE SPIRIT OF LAWS* (1748)

There is an inevitable tension among the power of Congress to pass laws, the power of the judicial branch to interpret those laws, and the power of the president to issue regulations and take administrative actions in order to execute those laws. Administrative agencies escalate that tension to its constitutional breaking point.

Administrative agencies of sorts have been around since the founding of the nation.[1] But it was during the New Deal that Congress created an array of so-called alphabet agencies like the Securities and Exchange Commission (SEC), the Federal Communications Commission (FCC), and the Agricultural Adjustment Administration (AAA). Two historians concluded that the New Deal "radiated a faith in the capacity of the administrative process perhaps exceeding that of any previous administration."[2] More significantly, President Roosevelt understood the enormous power such agencies would give him.

Although administrative agencies exert a measure of independence in the executive branch, they are constitutionally part of it. For the institutions and individuals within their purview, they can craft rules and regulations analogous to legislative statutes. They can hold hearings, impose fines, and issue orders in a manner similar to judicial proceedings. They were established as part executive, part legislative, and part judicial, a creative and controversial initiative to help avoid another Great Depression and come to terms with the world of a dynamic democracy and economy. Despite their measure of independence, these agencies remain under the political thumb of the president, who appoints and can fire the individuals who run them.

In 1946, Congress passed the Administrative Procedure Act to temper the expanding role that these agencies (and through them, the president) were exerting in the lives of Americans. That law was intended to give interested citizens and institutions a fair hearing before administrative and executive agencies issued rules prescribing their conduct.[3] In passing the act, Congress took some heed of James Madison's warning in *The Federalist* that "the accumulation of all powers, legislative, executive, and judiciary, in the same hands, whether of one, a few, or many . . . may justly be pronounced the very definition of tyranny."[4]

With the sweeping 1960s Great Society legislation in health, education, civil rights, housing, social welfare, poverty, consumer protection, and employment came scores of new and expanded executive branch agencies. These agencies assumed regulatory and administrative power over many more individuals and institutions. Pressed by interest groups, Congress passed laws requiring these agencies to undertake elaborate impact analyses of the economic, environmental, social, and other consequences of their proposed rules. The ensuing rule-making processes have often become the object of fierce, well-financed political jousting and protracted litigation.

Despite congressionally imposed procedural protections, the president's hand can form a fist with respect to administrative proceedings. For example, after years of proceedings, the Food and Drug Administration (FDA) found in 2016 that e-cigarettes, cigars, and hookahs should be deemed tobacco products. That finding would prohibit the use of bubble gum and other flavorings that make them more attractive to children and teens, as well as menthol flavoring, which has helped hook many, including most African Americans who smoke. Bowing to tobacco interests, the White House through its Office of Management and Budget eliminated the proposed FDA rule.[5]

Thanks to aggressive and elusive executive branch policies from 1995 to 2012, most agencies' regulations have been imposed without any public notice or comment period.[6] Yale Law School professor Peter Schuck has pointed out that "the [Obama] administration . . . ignored the notice-and-comment process for . . . controversial issues—on campus sexual harassment, and on the legal status of undocumented immigrants."[7]

How can presidents do this? The Administrative Procedure Act's notice-and-comment requirements do not apply to nonlegislative "interpretative rules and general statements of policy."[8] Presidential administrations have used this exception to justify "clarifying" memoranda and guidance letters. In 2013, the Department of Labor issued a directive that "clarified" that enforcement officers could rely on anecdotal as well as statistical evidence to charge a federal contractor with wage discrimination.[9] In 2016, the Departments of Justice and Education directed every public school in the country to provide transgender individuals access to bathrooms and other activities and facilities according to their chosen gender identity rather than the sex indicated on their birth certificates. These departments issued the transgender and campus sexual assault memoranda to "clarify" a school's obligations under Title IX of the Higher Education Act. However well intentioned, this presidential assumption of power to protect transgender individuals and define sexual assault without any time for comment from affected institutions led to severe backlash and angry litigation.[10] Within weeks of his election, President Trump "reclarified" and rolled back the transgender bathroom directive.[11] Reveling in his own power to issue clarifying directives, Trump also had the Department of Justice "clarify" that jurisdictions must assist the federal government in enforcing immigration laws or face the loss of some federal funds. In 2017, Secretary of Education Betsy DeVos announced that she was revamping Obama administration campus sexual abuse regulations.

To appreciate the legislative power that administrative rule making and regulations have vested in the president and the executive branch, consider this: *in 2016, executive and administrative agencies issued over 3,800 rules and regulations, eighteen times the 213 pieces of legislation that Congress enacted.*[12]

Presidents often turn to executive orders to achieve policy aims without legislating. Every president except William Henry Harrison has issued executive orders.

The 1863 Emancipation Proclamation of Abraham Lincoln was an executive order.[13] The internment of Japanese Americans by Franklin Roosevelt was accomplished through executive orders.[14] President Truman's 1952 seizure of steel mills to block a union strike and take control of steel production was an executive order (overturned by the Supreme Court).[15] President Eisenhower signed an executive order to send troops to enforce the Supreme Court's mandate to desegregate schools in Little Rock, Arkansas.[16]

By executive orders presidents direct departments, officers, and agencies of the federal government to take, or not take, some action. Presidents use executive orders to accelerate, delay, or deny the expenditure of federal funds appropriated by Congress. They can direct an agency not to enforce a law. President George W. Bush announced that, despite the mandate in the Clean Air Act, his administration would not regulate carbon dioxide emissions from power plants or carbon emissions from automobiles.[17]

The drawback to executive orders and presidential memoranda (which are executive orders in sheep's clothing) is that they can be undone easily by the next president. Frustrated with Congress's inability and refusal to act on a variety of issues, President Obama issued a host of executive orders relating to immigration, the environment, and other domestic matters. From the moment he became president, Donald Trump issued executive orders eliminating and reversing Obama's.

As Lyndon Johnson's chief domestic aide, I received calls in late 1965 from George Meany, the president of the AFL-CIO, Walter Reuther, the president of the United Auto Workers, and civil rights leaders including Martin Luther King Jr. urging the president to issue an executive order to eliminate discrimination in housing. "They say," I argued to the president, "you can eliminate redlining and other racial housing discrimination with your pen." "And my successor," LBJ snapped back, "can revoke my executive order with his pen. We need a law passed by Congress that cannot be so easily abandoned." In 1966, when Johnson recommended a fair-housing bill to Congress and vicious and voluminous mail against the bill flooded the White House, I knew he was right. It took more than two years, and King's tragic assassination, to get the Fair Housing Act passed. But it is still on the books more than fifty years later.[18]

4

THE FOUR PILLARS OF POTUS POWER

The White House staff is a case study in the expansion of POTUS power.

From the get-go, Congress was disinclined to provide funds for any staff for the president. George Washington hired, apparently at his own expense, a young Harvard graduate, Tobias Lear, to take care of his correspondence.[1] Unwilling to spend their own money, Washington's successors found a way to get the help they needed and project an image of frugality to Congress and their citizens: place their staffers on the payrolls of executive departments.[2]

After ignoring repeated presidential requests, Congress finally appropriated funds for a private secretary, steward, and messenger in 1857. The first presidential secretary paid the household staff, kept the president's private accounts, and answered mail for his boss, President James Buchanan.[3] Subsequent presidents added stenographers, telegraphers, and ushers.[4] In 1898, Congress funded two presidential secretaries, John Porter and George Cortelyou, and a modest clerical staff for President William McKinley.[5] Porter and Cortelyou were the first White House aides to publicly assume responsibilities for policy. They also acted as press secretaries, to help McKinley control the flow of information regarding the Spanish-American War. President McKinley's biographer Louis Gold wrote that Cortelyou "emerged as the prototype for the modern White House staff member."[6] President McKinley's need for additional assistance reflects the growth of the country. When George Washington took office a century earlier, America had thirteen states and four million people. When McKinley took office the country had forty-six states and a population of seventy-four million. Calvin Coolidge, president during the Roaring Twenties, added the first overtly political staffers, one to deal with the Republican Party apparatus and another with Congress.[7]

Franklin Roosevelt opened the door to major-league staff support. At FDR's request, Congress established and funded the Bureau of the Budget, the Civil Service Administration, six executive assistants to the president, whose salaries could not exceed $10,000, and an executive clerk.* That clerk became the nonpartisan institutional memory through many presidencies. FDR had a few notable aides, including his press secretary Steve Early, his speechwriter and counsel Sam Rosenman, and his powerful assistant and adviser Harry Hopkins. Harry S. Truman's staff was also quite modest. It included White House counsel Clark Clifford, who later became a quintessential Washington insider, and Charles Murphy.[8]

Lyndon Johnson persuaded Congress to authorize up to fourteen presidential assistants at a salary of $30,000 per year (including me). Though prior presidents had detailed several staffers from various government departments, LBJ took this concept to a new level. For example, in late 1963 when I was general counsel of the army, I carried on my office payroll Yoichi Oka-

---

*The Bureau of the Budget is now known as the Office of Management and Budget, the Civil Service Administration as the Civil Service Commission.

moto, LBJ's official White House photographer. He remained on the army general counsel's payroll throughout LBJ's presidency at a steadily rising salary. Even so, Johnson's White House staff topped off at about fifty people.[9]

What followed is not surprising. Like any political warriors—as LBJ once said, "Politics is not like war; politics is war"—presidents who wish to maintain and enhance their power need troops. With calculating consistency, presidents since Johnson have been increasing their staff's size—and power. Recent presidents have appointed a chief of staff who is far more important than any cabinet officer and have hired other senior counselors with broad responsibilities. They have established four positions that I consider the Four Pillars of POTUS Power: national security adviser, domestic policy adviser, special counsel to the president, and communications director. In recent years, these political generals have directed a staff approaching two thousand (most hidden on executive department payrolls, many volunteers) who serve at the pleasure of the president and are accountable only to him (or her, as the case may someday be).*

THE NATIONAL SECURITY ADVISER

During Truman's presidency, Congress passed the National Security Act of 1947, which established the Department of Defense. The idea was to provide greater civilian control over the military and curb the appetites of the army, navy, air force, and marine

---

*The numbers used for White House staff personnel throughout this chapter are as accurate as possible based on the available information and my experience, but the games presidents play to make them hard to determine suggest to me that, however educated, my guesses may be low.

corps for independent power and bigger hunks of the military budget. The act also created the National Security Council (NSC), which included the president; the secretaries of state, defense, and treasury; and the Joint Chiefs of Staff. The NSC's mission was to coordinate our national defense, intelligence (spying), diplomatic, and international financial efforts as the nation assumed leadership of the Western world and confronted the Soviet Union in the bitterly frigid days of the Cold War.[10] Over time, the attorney general, the chairman of the Joint Chiefs of Staff, and the director of Central Intelligence were added to the council. Over the years an increasing number of White House aides have attended many NSC meetings.[11]

The NSC was initially staffed with a few career professionals from the State and Defense Departments. Its creation set the stage for the White House to assume enormous and often secretive power over the international activities of the national government.[12] By appointing senior Harvard University dean McGeorge Bundy to be his national security adviser (NSA) and head the NSC staff, President John Kennedy gave the position a stature approaching that of the secretaries of state, defense, and the treasury.[13] Bundy assembled a professional and politically loyal staff of twenty advisers. He made sure that the president got all the options and the pluses and minuses of each, and ensured that presidential decisions were faithfully executed. Responsibility for detailed staff work and operations remained with executive departments. Lyndon Johnson used Bundy, and his successor, the Massachusetts Institute of Technology professor Walt Rostow, much as Kennedy had. Nevertheless, under Bundy and Rostow the direction of national security policy began a steady creep away from the cabinet officers and toward the White House staff.[14]

Under Presidents Reagan and George H. W. Bush, the NSC

staff grew to fifty professionals.[15] Then, like Jack's beanstalk, it sprouted to 100 under President Clinton, 250 under George W. Bush, and more than 400 under President Barack Obama, where it took intimate control and management of foreign policy.[16] Secretaries of State Hillary Clinton and John Kerry spent their time traveling the world. Donald Trump's secretary of state, Rex Tillerson, may be headed to maintaining their pace of a million miles each.[17] Under Obama, the NSC's micromanagement of military matters helped move Defense Secretary Robert Gates to leave his cabinet post. "I received so many calls from NSC staffers saying 'The White House wants,' " he wrote, saying that he would respond, "A building didn't make telephone calls. I said that as a cabinet officer, I expected to be contacted only by a very senior White House person."[18]

Under Obama, National Security Adviser Susan Rice often bypassed the secretary of state to deal directly with, or intentionally ignore, foreign ambassadors and dignitaries. French ambassador Gérard Araud recounted her call to him when the French were contemplating military intervention in Libya. She snapped, he said, during that call, "You are not going to drag us into your shitty war."[19] Secretary of State John Kerry was repeatedly left out in the cold. Rice publicly attacked Israeli prime minister Benjamin Netanyahu with no advance notice to Secretary Kerry. Her NSA deputy Benjamin Rhodes conducted the Obama administration's negotiations with Cuba to lift the US embargo and resume diplomatic relations with that country without informing Kerry.

The relentless growth of the NSC in people and power led Leslie Gelb, a former president of the Council on Foreign Relations, to say, "Since the 1960's there has been a gradual handing off of power from the 'King's Ministers' [Departments] to the 'Palace Guard' [NSC]."[20] Former NSA Brent Scowcroft has said that the instinctive thing for the NSC staff is to "replace Departments," because it thinks it can do a better job.[21] "The controlling nature of the Obama White House and the NSC staff took micromanagement to a new level," Defense Secretary Gates wrote, charging that the surge in Afghanistan "was planned and operated by the NSS [NSC staff]."[22]

Bigger numbers mean a bigger role for the NSC staff and a greater opportunity for political control. But with size goes mischief. It was the NSC staff of Ronald Reagan who conjured up the Iran-Contra weapons-for-hostages deal. They kept it secret from Secretaries of Defense and State Caspar Weinberger and George Shultz, and they circumvented congressional restrictions on aid to the Contras in Nicaragua.[23] George W. Bush's Treasury secretary Paul O'Neill said that the invasion of Iraq and concept of nation building was set in motion and mounted by the NSC staff.[24] The Obama NSC staff helped craft the misleading statement that Susan Rice, then the US ambassador to the United Nations, used to blame the Benghazi attack that killed four Americans on an anti-Islam video rather than on organized terrorists.[25] Benjamin Rhodes bragged to the *New York Times* about how easy it was to mislead the press (and thus the people) that the negotiations with Iran over its nuclear potential involved moderate Iranians, in order to sell the deal in the United States. "All these newspapers used to have foreign bureaus. Now they don't," Rhodes chortled to the *Times*. "They [reporters] call us to explain what's happening. . . . The average reporter we talk to is 27 years old. . . . They literally know nothing."[26]

With the explosion of the NSC staff has come mission gallop. The NSC now has its own chief of staff, press office, and legislative operation. A bevy of NSC personnel has headed a Principals Committee of agency and departmental secretaries, a

Deputies Committee of agency and departmental deputy secretaries, Interagency Policy Committees of agency and departmental deputy secretaries, and Sub-Interagency Policy Committees of agency and departmental deputy assistant secretaries.

An oversize NSC staff entangles the White House in the intricate woods of policies. The danger is that the president may get lost among the trees and twigs of routine decisions better made by departments and agencies and lose sight of the forest. No wonder State, Defense, and CIA officials ranted about an Obama White House so "obsessed with the tiniest of details of the undeclared war against ISIS that decisions that should take an hour or so often take days, even weeks."[27]

While President Trump appears to give his secretary of defense, James "Mad Dog" Mattis, a longer leash, Secretary of State Tillerson seems more intimately controlled by NSA H. R. McMaster and the NSC staff. President Trump's meetings with other heads of state, which have been attended by McMaster and his staff and often not Secretary of State Tillerson, indicate that he intends to use the NSC staff much as Obama did. The NSC staff remains large while Tillerson, almost a year into his tenure as secretary of state, has had only a handful of deputy or assistant secretaries confirmed by the Senate.

Weary of the burgeoning National Security Council staff, Congress attached a rider to the National Defense Authorization Act in 2016 to limit the number of NSC professionals to two hundred.[28] But since the president can direct other White House staffers to perform some NSC staff functions, that provision is likely to have little impact on the number that President Trump and his successors employ for them on national security matters.

DOMESTIC POLICY ADVISER

In 1965, President Lyndon Johnson named me his chief domestic policy adviser, with authority to establish the first White House domestic policy staff. I recruited four individuals.* We worked with the Bureau of the Budget, executive departments, and others on the White House staff. We consulted private-sector experts in a wide variety of fields, from childhood development, immigration, and hunger to water policy, criminal justice reform, civil rights, health, education, the arts, and consumer protection. The result was the social revolution of the Great Society, and why I have written that, "We are living in Lyndon Johnson's America."†

With this explosion of domestic programs and agencies, the president needs a domestic policy group uninhibited by narrow bureaucratic interests endemic to individual executive agencies. Such a team can solicit the best ideas from the finest minds across the country and present options to the president. They can help make sure that when the president makes a decision to propose legislation, mount a program, or execute a law, departments and agencies energetically and faithfully implement his decisions.

Upon assuming office, President Nixon and his top aides John Ehrlichman and H. R. Haldeman said, "There will be no Joe Califano in the Nixon White House," a reference to the role my staff and I played in driving domestic departments (and we did indeed push them hard).[29] But within weeks Nixon had cre-

---

*Larry Levinson, Fred Bohen, James Gaither, and Matthew Nimetz.

†This is the title to the essay at the start of Touchstone's 2015 republication of my book *The Triumph and Tragedy of Lyndon Johnson: The White House Years.*

ated the first formal White House Domestic Council, with a much larger staff.[30] Like the NSC, this Domestic Council, and the White House groups it spawned, steadily increased in size, responsibility, and power with each successive presidency. President Bill Clinton used his wife, Hillary, to oversee a White House staff group of well over one hundred just to draft and promote the Clintons' health plan.[31]

President Obama's domestic policy staff and related offices hovered at around two hundred people or more. His domestic policy umbrella included professionals in the Offices of Public Liaison, Public Engagement, Strategy Initiatives, Intergovernmental Affairs, Political Affairs, AIDS Policy, Faith-Based and Neighborhood Partnerships, Social Innovation, Native American Affairs, and Urban Affairs, as well as a Rural Council Office.[32] Like Clinton, Obama assembled a staff within the White House to draft his health care plan.[33]

Recent presidents have also created a variety of policy directors that some called czars. Anointing a czar is a way the president can flag his high interest in a matter or group to the public and his administration. It avoids the need for Senate confirmation and its attendant hearings, delays, and possible political embarrassment.

President Obama's wide use of czars so irritated Congress that it included in the 2011 Department of Defense Appropriations bill a rider that prevented the president from appointing czars to handle policy relating to climate change, urban affairs, or health care. Faced with this restrictive rider, in his signing statement President Obama called the provision unconstitutional and refused to abide by it. He established czars for auto recovery, climate change, domestic violence, Ebola, energy and environment, faith-based initiatives, green jobs, health, manufacturing, pay, trade, urban affairs, and weapons of mass destruction. They assumed significant responsibilities normally borne by department and agency heads.

Less likely to be responsive to congressional oversight, presidential czars strike a raw nerve on Capitol Hill. West Virginia Democratic senator Robert Byrd complained to Obama, "The rapid and easy accumulation of power by White House staff can threaten the Constitutional system of checks and balances. At the worst, White House staffs have taken direction and control of programmatic areas that are the statutory responsibility of Senate-confirmed officials. . . . As presidential assistants and advisers, these White House staffers are not accountable . . . to virtually anyone but the president."[34] Wisconsin Democratic senator Russ Feingold noted that czars "are put in the place of Cabinet people and really are the key authorities. . . . [Y]ou can't question them," as you can department heads and employees.[35] That's the point, senators!

President Trump has avoided the term "czars," perhaps due to his Russian political problems. But his appointment of senior staffers like Steve Bannon and his son-in-law, Jared Kushner, and the rapid naming of White House staff contrasts with his failure to make timely nominations of subcabinet officials for Senate confirmation.[36] To some extent this failure reflects Trump's inexperience in government. But it also makes clear his determination to maintain his predecessors' short leashes for cabinet and agency officials and to formulate policy in the White House.

SPECIAL COUNSEL TO THE PRESIDENT

In 1793, when war between France and England erupted, George Washington asked the Supreme Court to advise him on the new nation's treaty obligations with France. Chief Justice John Jay responded that the constitutional separation of powers doctrine prevented the court from rendering an advisory opinion to the president.[37]

In view of that decision, presidents have sought legal advice about their powers and responsibilities from their attorneys general. Questions about the scope of presidential power arose frequently in the early years of FDR's administration. That led Congress in 1934 to create in the Justice Department an Office of Legal Counsel to provide opinions to the president about his authority.[38]

This office has shaped the concept of executive privilege, under which presidents have claimed the power to prohibit executive branch employees from revealing confidential advice provided to the president and his staff. The rationale for the privilege is to help ensure that presidents get cold and true advice with the bark off from aides. When my then-boss Robert McNamara, the secretary of defense, wanted to invoke executive privilege to avoid revealing something before the Senate Armed Services Committee, I had to convince Nicholas Katzenbach, who headed the Office of Legal Counsel, to persuade President Kennedy to do this.

For many years presidents relied on the Office of Legal Counsel and the attorney general and employed only one or two lawyers on their White House staffs. FDR had Sam Rosenman; Truman had Clark Clifford and Charles Murphy; Kennedy, Ted Sorensen and Myer Feldman. Johnson had Harry McPherson, Lee White, and Larry Temple, who succeeded White (as well as Supreme Court justice Abe Fortas, with whom he frequently and often inappropriately consulted). Nixon had John Ehrlichman and John Dean. With the Watergate scandal, Nixon added four attorneys and created the first Office of White House Counsel.[39] President Carter had six.[40] With the Iran-Contra revelations, President Reagan increased his White House legal staff to thirteen.[41]

President Clinton upped the numbers of White House lawyers to twenty-five. With the Monica Lewinsky scandal, White House Special Counsel Lloyd Cutler added another fifteen lawyers and the firm of Williams & Connolly for Clinton's impeachment proceedings.[42] President George W. Bush reverted to twenty-five attorneys.[43] Under President Obama, the White House legal staff increased to near forty.[44] Within several weeks of taking office, President Trump named about thirty attorneys to the White House Counsel's office.[45] With the various investigations of Trump's activities, that number increased, and outside law firms and lawyers were engaged.

With the ballooning of the White House legal staff comes roguishness as well as the diminishment of the attorney general and his Office of Legal Counsel. Under George W. Bush, White House lawyers pressured the Justice Department to give a pass to American military and intelligence officials accused of torturing captured Islamic terrorists.[46] White House counsel Kathryn Ruemmler okayed President Obama's invocation of executive privilege to defy subpoenas for information on the Fast and Furious gun-trafficking scandal, a claim overturned by a federal judge in 2016.[47]

When Attorney General Eric Holder's Office of Legal Counsel concluded that under the War Powers Act the president's action in Libya constituted "hostilities" that required withdrawal of American troops after sixty days, Obama sought a second opinion. His White House lawyers delivered the one he wanted. They concluded that the president's engagement did not constitute "hostilities" and thus there was no need to move US troops out of Libya.[48] The White House counsel pressured lawyers from the State and Defense Departments to agree, and the troops were not withdrawn.[49] President Trump's White House lawyers reportedly sought to invoke executive privilege in an unsuccessful effort to block former acting attorney general Sally Yates from testifying before Congress on the president and Russia.[50]

COMMUNICATIONS DIRECTOR

Every president since Franklin Roosevelt broadcast Fireside Chats has recognized that whoever controls the story lines in the media sets the terms, and often the outcome, of public policy debates. So, inevitably, the revolution in technology, with twenty-four-hour cable news channels, the internet, social media, and instant news on cell phones, has led to a gargantuan expansion of presidential communications operations.

Presidents Eisenhower, Kennedy, and Johnson had fewer than ten professional press/communications staffers. In their administrations, the press secretary was regarded as the director of communications.[51] That was pretty much the case for Richard Nixon, Gerald Ford, and Jimmy Carter. Ronald Reagan's White House was the first in which the press secretary and the director of communications were separate positions, each with its own staff. Reagan's administration was quick to recognize that holding daily press briefings for the White House press corps was a full-time job for the press secretary. The Reagan administration also saw the advantage of having a communications director and staff to manage an array of public relations efforts to burnish the president's image and promote his programs.

Subsequent administrations beefed up the communications function: in "official" numbers, forty-seven for Clinton, fifty-two for George W. Bush, and sixty-nine for Obama.[52] The actual numbers are many times the official ones. The communications offices for George W. Bush included five divisions: Press, Communications, Speechwriting, Media Affairs, and Photography, as well as additional media staffers in the Office of the First Lady, Office of the Vice President, and Office of the National Security Council. Academic estimates set the size of George W. Bush's press and communications staff at 150 with a supporting cast of 200 or so media interns, press clippers, speech transcribers, and television and social media watchers. It is fair to conclude, using the same methodology, that President Obama's communications and related supporting staff numbered more than 400.[53] The staff included dozens of individuals devoted to social media such as Facebook, Twitter, Instagram, and the like.[54] Simply keeping up with Trump's determination to dominate every news cycle and the fallout from his penchant for tweeting requires a significant staff.[55]

The White House communications staff exercises central control over the public affairs appointees in all the executive departments and agencies. Marion Blakey, Reagan's public affairs chief, considered it his basic role "to coordinate our spokesmen all over government. . . . From the Ambassador in Mozambique to the undersecretary of Commerce, we make sure they have the same information and are all singing from the same choir book." [56]

Today's media hunger for instant gratification is ubiquitous, and the politics of the presidency and governing require satisfying this feeding frenzy. As an irritated President Obama griped to the *Huffington Post*, "We live in such a 24/7, Twitter-fed constant news cycle, and everything's . . . [e]verything's a crisis . . . everything is terrible, everything is doomsday, everything is—if it doesn't get solved tomorrow, you know, your presidency is going off the rails." [57]

Presidential speechmaking has become a morning, noon, and evening event in order to help fill the space and reduce opportu-

nities for opponents on the twenty-four-hour cable news channels and social media. During eight years in office, Eisenhower
gave 700 speeches; Reagan, 2,500. George W. Bush and Obama
each gave well over 3,000, Clinton more than 4,000.[58] In terms
of media coverage (good and bad), Trump is on course to set
new records. Modern communications operations and expecta-
tions put intense pressure on presidents who wish to control the
perpetual news cycle—and all presidents do, even though media
madness cuts into their time for deliberation and contemplation.

The enlarged size of the White House communications and
technology operations—from Twitter to YouTube to internet
access—has given recent presidents far more control of what
Americans see and read than ever before. White House press secretary's briefings can be live on the internet and often on television. The longtime CBS White House correspondent Bill Plante
compared the Obama White House media operation, especially
its YouTube channel, available 24/7 to anyone with a phone or
an iPad, to state-run media.[59] Indeed, through social media and
the Whitehouse.gov website, the Obama presidency operated its
own news agency. President Trump has the same kind of media
operation. Moreover, with his late-night and early-morning
tweets and world of fake news, at best we are at the end of the
beginning of a brave new world of presidential pronouncements
and publicity that will have Aldous Huxley twisting beneath his
gravestone.

The significance of the White House press corps has diminished faster than its size has increased—from fewer than one
hundred reporters during the Johnson and Kennedy administrations to almost one thousand in the George W. Bush, Obama,
and Trump years.[60] Ideologically amenable cable news channels
and social media outlets permit the president to communicate
directly to the people, discarding the White House press corps

as casually as a socialite sheds a no-longer-stylish pair of shoes. A 2016 *Politico Magazine* survey of White House press corps members found that only a handful had ever conducted a one-on-one interview with President Obama.[61]

Presidential press conferences receive far less attention than they did under Presidents Eisenhower, Kennedy, and Johnson. Rather than solo appearances, recent presidents prefer to do joint press conferences with foreign leaders. There, most of the time is devoted to foreign policy while politically charged questions are less likely to be asked and more easily deflected. At solo press conferences, Trump has often ignored the questions, and Obama often filibustered with lengthy answers to run the clock.[62] Trump even skipped the traditional postelection press conference, instead disseminating a speech on YouTube.[63] With consistently critical mainstream media coverage, Trump has focused his attention on his millions of followers on social media.[64]

The White House press corps recognized its sharply reduced relevance in 2015 by drafting a "code of principles and practices." It beseeched President Obama and his staff to refrain from making announcements via social media: "White House social media accounts should not be used to circumvent the press corps. Live streams and other White House broadcasts are not a substitute for in-person coverage of an event." Do White House reporters think any president believes that? Certainly not Donald Trump and not any future White House resident.

Presidents now choose the relative safety of being interviewed by a friendly cable news channel or pop culture celebrity instead of subjecting themselves to the rigors of a knowledgeable journalist. The *Washington Post* pointed out in June 2016 that Obama had not had an interview with anyone from its paper in over six years. Trump tweets garner widespread attention without any White House press corps filter.

WHITE HOUSE STAFF ADVANTAGES FOR PRESIDENTS

To appreciate the explosion of the White House staff, consider this: *From 1960 to 2014, while the number of federal executive branch employees in the nondefense area increased by less than 80 percent, from 761,000 to 1.35 million, the size of the White House staff has grown by more than 4,000 percent, from about 50 to some 2,000 when detailees from federal departments and volunteers are included.*[65]

Every president since Eisenhower has increased not only the number of White House staffers but also their involvement in the day-to-day operations of the executive branch. It's not simply that presidents, like most ambitious and successful politicians, are control freaks. There are powerful advantages White House staffers offer presidents.

First, White House staffers have single-minded loyalty to the president, who appoints them and can fire them at will. Cabinet officers and agency heads of course shoulder responsibility to the president. But they are also beholden to members of Congress. Their congressional appropriations committees have the power to fund—or not to fund—their departments. Their authorization committees usually have a decisive say in approving—or disapproving—new and expiring programs. These executive department and agency officials must develop and maintain close and critical working relationships with the constituencies they serve or regulate—for example, railroads and truckers, hospitals and physicians, unions and businesses, environmentalists and oil and gas companies. White House staffers in those areas also have relationships with members of Congress and private-sector constituencies, but those relationships are *always* secondary to their responsibility and loyalty to the president.

Second, there is no need for the delays of irksome Senate confirmation hearings, in which shrewd senators can elicit policy promises from a presidential nominee or embarrass the nominee and president. When control of the Senate and the White House is in the hands of different political parties, such delays can last for more than a year. Even when both branches are led by the same party, delays of many months are common. A president can name White House staffers in whom he has confidence immediately, even in circumstances where they would be unable to obtain Senate confirmation. See Susan Rice's fall from grace (or rise in power) as unconfirmable secretary of state nominee to White House national security adviser and President Trump's naming the controversial Steve Bannon, with his checkered past, as a senior adviser.

Third, a substantial staff across the foreign, domestic, legal, and communications spheres gives the president the wherewithal in the era of modern media technology to dominate the political, public policy, and cultural dialogue.

Fourth, perhaps the most important though publicly unheralded advantage of White House staffs is the option to keep their deliberations secret. The president can persuasively invoke executive privilege or claim as a matter of separation of powers that White House staffers will not accept invitations or honor subpoenas to testify before congressional committees.

There are disadvantages to the burgeoning numbers of White House staffers who have the power to say, "The White House wants . . ." Their influence over departmental policies can make it more difficult for presidents to recruit highly qualified cabinet and subcabinet officials. When the White House staff has young aides for each assistant secretary's area of responsibility (Medicare, welfare, the Near East, Central America, public housing, etc.) or lawyers for each area of an assistant attorney general's responsibility, many highly qualified individuals decline presidential invitations to serve in top executive branch posts. Defense Secretary Gates, who quit the Obama administration, was appalled when Obama NSC staffers contacted four-star generals in the field, something he deemed a "firing offense" in previous administrations.[66] The Clinton administration's deputy attorney general Jamie Gorelick warned that the White House was siphoning decision-making power from all executive agencies, saying, "It's not just defense, it's across the board."[67]

The operational meddling of a bloated White House staff is not its only disadvantage. Of paramount concern is that hundreds of national security, domestic policy, communications, and legal staffers tend to bring to the president irritating but relatively insignificant policy and political hemorrhoids better left in the bowels of the federal bureaucracy. As White House staffers become micromanagers, they tend to lure the president into micromanaging. That diverts his time and attention from larger issues.

Edward Gibbon's landmark *History of the Decline and Fall of the Roman Empire*, written in the 1770s and 1780s, is often cited to argue that self-indulgence, sexual permissiveness, and inane violence marked the collapse of the Roman empire. For me, Gibbon's most telling conclusion is another. It is how the power of the caesars overwhelmed the independence of the Roman Senate and the consequent curbs on individual freedom. As Gibbon saw it, "The principles of a free constitution are irrecoverably lost when the legislative power is dominated by the executive." That may be the historical precedent of most concern for our nation's republic.

The president's increased power as a rule and regulation maker, political mega-fund-raiser, and assessor of individual and institutional conduct is a political Mayday for our democracy. This is especially so with a crippled Congress and politicized Supreme Court. As James Madison warned in *The Federalist*, "The executive shall never exercise the legislative and judicial powers, or either of them, in the end that it may be a government of laws and not of men."[68]

PART II

THE CRIPPLED CONGRESS

THE GRIP OF THE GERRYMANDER

For some time, the capacity of Congress to check and balance the rise of presidential power has been in a largely self-inflicted spiral of decline. This dizzying descent of the legislative branch is greased by gerrymandering, 24/7 campaign fund raising, well-financed lobbyists, petty partisanship, the proliferation of committee and subcommittee responsibilities, and an explosion in the number of constituents to be served.

GERRYMANDERING

Gerrymandering—the manipulation of political boundaries to give a political party a numerical voting advantage—is a preeminent cause of congressional crippling. The practice got its name in 1812 from Massachusetts governor Elbridge Gerry, but it's as old as the republic.[1] In 1778, Patrick Henry and the Virginia House of Delegates tried unsuccessfully to gerrymander Virginia's Fifth Congressional District to deny James Madison, a supporter of George Washington, a House seat.[2]

I first came to understand the consequences of gerrymandering while serving in the LBJ White House. I was presenting ideas to President Johnson for the 1966 legislative program. He had often complained about having "to beg for money from folks that all want something." So I urged him to propose public financing of presidential and congressional campaigns. He agreed to recommend public financing of presidential campaigns, but rejected my suggestion about Congress.* "The House will never go for it," LBJ said. "There are about 100 members who run without any serious opposition. If there's public financing they'll all face serious opponents in running for reelection. Forget it."

One hundred safe House seats out of 435 in 1966.

Today there are 402 safe House seats.

Over the past sixty years, the cancer of aggressive gerrymandering has metastasized to make the House of Representatives less representative and to hollow out the Supreme Court's one person, one vote ruling. In 2016, 171 Republicans and 150 Democrats won election by spreads of 20 percentage points or more. Another 55 Republicans and 26 Democrats won by 10- to 20-point spreads.[3] In other words, in the House of Representatives, 402 of 435 seats—90 percent—were held by members who were virtually guaranteed victory in the general election. That's the exorbitant price we pay for clever, hard-nosed gerrymandering by state legislatures—Republican and Democrat—when they design the boundaries of congressional districts after the decennial census. The decisive significance of gerrymandering to control the House of Representatives has vacuumed barrels of national political money into state assembly, senate, and gubernatorial contests. In states where House seats are lopsidedly

---

*Out of this proposal came the legislative compromise in 1971 permitting taxpayers to check a box to direct $1.00 (now $3.00) of their tax payments to fund presidential campaigns. Because candidates who accept this public financing are limited in their campaign fund-raising and spending, major-party presidential nominees no longer participate.

Republican or Democrat, that party likely controls the state legislature and governor's mansion.

Comparing the percentage of Republicans and Democrats voting in a state's 2016 congressional races to the percentage of House members that each party elected to Congress illustrates how gerrymandering distorts our democracy.

Take Pennsylvania: The statewide vote in congressional races split 54 percent for Republicans and 46 percent for Democrats. But Republicans won 72 percent of the House seats (thirteen), Democrats only 28 percent (five).[4]

Or take North Carolina: The statewide vote in congressional races split 53 percent for Republicans and 47 percent for Democrats. But Republicans captured 77 percent of the House seats (ten), Democrats only 23 percent (three).[5]

If you think that's bad, and only a Republican scam, try these:

In Connecticut, Democrats won 58 percent of the statewide congressional vote, Republicans 35 percent. Democrats captured all five of the state's House seats, rendering Republican votes for congressional candidates about as worthless as three-dollar bills.[6]

In Maryland, Democrats won 60 percent of the statewide congressional vote, Republicans 36 percent. But Democrats won 88 percent of the House seats (seven), Republicans only 12 percent (one).[7] A federal judge called one Maryland Democratic gerrymandered district "reminiscent of a broken-winged pterodactyl, lying prostrate at the center of the state."[8]

Republican Party leaders set out to win a majority in as many state legislatures as possible in 2010. The object was to reshape congressional districts and gain control of the House following the decennial census.[9] In 2012, the GOP won a majority in the House of Representatives even though it lost to Democrats in total national congressional popular votes. The 2012 victory was so heady that the Republican National Committee chairman at the time, Reince Priebus, advocated allocating electoral votes in presidential elections by congressional district instead of by the number of votes cast statewide.[10] Under such a system, Mitt Romney would have won the 2012 election despite losing to Obama by five million popular votes.

Widespread Republican success in state gubernatorial and legislative elections has led President Obama to commit some of his postpresidency time to a National Democratic Redistricting Commission. Chaired by former attorney general Eric Holder, this commission aims to win Democratic majorities in state legislatures and governorships and to mount legal challenges to Republican congressional districting.[11]

In the South, Republicans have used gerrymandering not only to maximize the number of districts they win but also to create some districts dominated by minorities who overwhelmingly vote Democratic. African Americans are assured victory in such districts, sometimes with their silent acquiescence or covert cooperation. In 2016, of thirty-eight congressional districts in Alabama, Georgia, Louisiana, Mississippi, and South Carolina, only eight were held by Democrats, all of them African Americans. The other thirty were won by Republicans, all white. Overall, in these elections Democrats received 38 percent of the votes and 21 percent of the seats, while Republicans picked up 62 percent of the votes and 79 percent of the seats.[12]

While African Americans hold 21 percent of the seats in these Deep South states, they comprise 31 percent of the population.[13] By packing them into a handful of districts, Republicans reduce potential black (as well as Democratic) representation in the House of Representatives. This segregation by gerrymander may be a cutting edge of racially divided politics, with Democrats becoming the party of blacks and Republicans the party of whites.

(See chapter 20.) But this kind of gerrymandering is headed for greater scrutiny by federal courts. In 2017, the Supreme Court held that North Carolina redistricting unconstitutionally limited the votes of African Americans by packing them into two districts.[14]

In House districts where Democrats or Republicans have gerrymandered the majority, party primaries are the political contests that count. General elections become sideshow formalities. That pushes Republican candidates to the (often far) right and Democratic candidates to the (often far) left because activist bases of political parties tend to dominate primary voting. As Senator Marco Rubio said to his students at Florida International University, "If you know the only way to lose your seat is to get outconservatived in a primary, you'll never let anyone get to your right. . . . I'm not telling you this is how it should be. But it's how it is." Driving the point home, Rubio added, "This isn't a good-government class. It's a politics class."[15] In the House, the hot water of gerrymandering has ruinously shrunk the political middle. "Compromise," once considered an accolade that facilitated governing, has become a synonym for "sellout" that ensures primary battles for incumbents in gerrymandered districts.

The success of getting Medicare and Medicaid off the ground smoothly in the 1960s was due to compromises that attracted a significant number of the Republicans in Congress to vote for those programs. What a difference in 2010! Barack Obama lacked both the opportunity and inclination to muster bipartisan support for his Affordable Care Act. Republican and Democratic House members on the right and left refused to take any steps toward each other because their feet were shackled to intraparty primary contests in their districts. Republicans insisted that there be changes to cut the costs and coverage of Medicare and Medicaid. Democrats insisted that Medicare be kept as it was and Medicaid be expanded. Each saw compromise as a walk on the wild side that neither was willing to risk. The results: legislation passed by a strictly party-line Democratic vote and inevitable implementation potholes and loud right-wing cries to repeal and replace the law.[16] The casualty of gerrymandering in this case has been our health care system.

For years the Supreme Court has passed on requests that it determine the constitutionality of partisan gerrymandering. But in 2017, the Court indicated a willingness to examine this issue in *Gill v. Whitford*, a case where Democratic voters have challenged the Republican legislature's congressional districting of the state of Wisconsin.[17]

The ideological fires fanned by gerrymandering have spread to the Senate. For the first times in our history, in 2005–06 and since the 2010 election, most sitting senators have sharpened their political teeth in the House. A generation ago, in the 1980s, only a third of all senators had previously been representatives.[18] Now the heightened partisanship of the House has begun to take its seat in the Senate.

For seven of the nine election cycles since the beginning of this century, control of the Senate has been at stake, with margins of just a few votes on either side. The day after each biennial election, the majority and minority leaders and their political party colleagues turn their attention to maintaining or taking control of the Senate in the next election two years hence. Putting control of the Senate in play every two years dashes the vision of the Founding Fathers that the six-year terms of its members would create a deliberative body prone to take the long view. The Senate today acts more like the House, in which the two-year terms established by the Founders were designed to promote a trendier response to voters' wishes.[19]

Why is control even by a one- or two-vote margin so important? The party in control of either body sets the legislative agenda, controls the committees, has subpoena power, and commands the lion's share of funds and personnel. Moreover, in the Senate a 2013 Democratic rule change banned filibusters that had been used to block confirmation of lower-court judges and executive branch nominees. In 2017, Republicans extended that change to cover Supreme Court nominees in order to confirm Neil Gorsuch to the high court.[20] These changes enable the party with a one-vote majority to place its judges on the federal bench. Control also gets its party leaders all sorts of perks: bigger staffs, chauffeured cars, the best offices, the power to determine who goes where on expenses-paid foreign trips, and administrative control. And politicians love such perks.[21]

6

PAY-TO-PLAY CONGRESS

Congress does most of its work through committees and sub-committees, which draft legislation and recommend funding for the executive and judicial branches and themselves. They hold hearings and they investigate public and private executives to discover and expose improper conduct.

In the 435-member House there are 96 subcommittees, 22 full committees, four joint committees with the Senate, and ad hoc committees that may be established during a session. In the 100-member Senate there are 68 subcommittees, 21 committees, four joint committees with the House, and possible ad hoc committees as well.[1] In the 1950s, a House member served on three committees and subcommittees; today a member sits on six or more committees and subcommittees. In the 1950s senators sat on eight subcommittees and committees, they sit on twelve or more today.[2]

The typical House member is scheduled to attend 64 committee or subcommittee meetings a year, the typical senator, 120. Each session, the jurisdiction of committees and subcommittees involves more issues as the scope of the federal government expands. The decision of Republican House members to limit committee and subcommittee chairs to three terms has the (likely unintended) consequence of replacing them just about the time they are becoming fully effective.[3] Overlap among committees is common: the number of committees and subcommittees with jurisdiction for homeland security may be one hundred and for energy and the environment more than fifty.[4]

If these numbers have your head whirling, think of what this system does to members of Congress. But House and Senate committees are where much of the action is.

What does a member have to do to sit on a committee?

That depends on the committee.

Committee assignments are accompanied by fund-raising taxes, euphemistically called party dues. These taxes are levied by the Democratic and Republican leadership to help finance future campaigns of party candidates for the House and Senate. The House Ways and Means and Senate Finance Committees handle taxes and Medicare, and their recommendations have an enormous impact on revenues of Wall Street hedge funds and private equity firms, banks, and those in the health care industry. These deep-pocket organizations and individuals are willing to pay plenty for protection from legislation that could adversely affect their profits. Members assigned to these committees are expected to raise significantly more money for each chamber's campaign committee than members who sit on, say, the agriculture committees.

Leaked documents show the Democratic fund-raising price tags that its members had to pay for each House committee assignment in 2013. Ranking member positions (top minority committee members) were expected to pay at least $500,000 in party dues to the Democratic Congressional Campaign Committee (DCCC). Minority Whip Steny Hoyer was expected to raise $2.5 million for the DCCC while Minority Leader Nancy Pelosi was tasked with raising $25 million. (See Appendix A.) In the first half of 2017, Pelosi raised more than that amount.[5] The DCCC has reprimanded Congressional Black Caucus members for not paying their dues. The Black Caucus fired back that many of its members, and other African American candidates who lost elections, were not getting enough money from the DCCC.[6]

Republicans expect similar amounts from their members. In 2014, the National Republican Congressional Committee (NRCC) announced the creation of a task force to discipline legislators lagging behind in payment of their dues, with harsh verbal spankings for committee chairs who had not paid theirs. Republican congressman Ken Buck of Colorado revealed in his 2017 book *Drain the Swamp* that top-tier committee chair positions cost $875,000 each in party dues.* He added that party dues were $5 million for the Republican whip position; $10 million for the position of house majority leader; and for Speaker of the House, a price tag of $20 million.[7]

No wonder Paul Ryan said in 2015 that he would agree to serve as Speaker only if he were not required to spend his time flying around the country attending fund-raisers for Republican congressional elections. In fact, as he came to enjoy the taste of the House Speakership he traveled widely to raise money, corralling more than $60 million for the National Republican Congressional Committee in the two years following his election as Speaker. Paul Ryan had raised more than $2 million for the NRCC in 2013–14 when he was gunning for the position of Ways and Means chair.[8]

The pay-to-play world of congressional committee assignments fits snugly with the political interest of many members of Congress. Some seek such positions based on their potential

---

*Top-tier committees include Appropriations, Energy and Commerce, Financial Services, Rules, and Ways and Means.

to raise money for their own campaigns rather than any interest in the subject matter within the committees' jurisdiction. One 2012 analysis of this sordid situation reported that a Ways and Means Committee member averaged $500,000 more in donations per year than the average member of the House.[9] Membership on committees with jurisdiction over deep-pocket interests like banks, oil and gas companies, and Silicon Valley giants like Apple and Microsoft have access to significant political contributions from them and their executives.

Armed Services Committee assignments are also top-dollar positions. In 2015–16, defense contractors made hefty contributions to the Republican House Armed Services Committee chair, Mac Thornberry ($393,000), and the ranking Armed Services Democratic member, Adam Smith ($229,000).[10] In 2015, the forty-eight members of the Armed Services Conference Committee selected to iron out differences between the House and Senate Defense authorization bills culled *four times as much money in campaign contributions from defense contractors* as their fellow committee members who were not named to the conference committee.[11]

Shortly after the 2012 elections, the Democratic Congressional Campaign Committee briefed all of its new members on how to allocate their time. It suggested that those members spend *four hours daily* on "call time," that is, on the phone raising money, when in Washington, and *three hours daily* on call time when in their home districts.[12] One former House member, the Virginia Democrat Tom Perriello, says that four hours a day may be "low-balling the figure so as not to scare new members too much."[13]

Breakfasts, lunches, and dinners that members attend to raise money in the capital and their home districts are not counted as "call time." Nor are money-raising excursions members make to cities like New York, Los Angeles, Houston, Chicago, Atlanta, and Palm Beach.[14] Why so many weekend trips to cities outside members' congressional districts? Because, as the legendary crook Willie Sutton said when asked why he robbed banks, "That's where the money is."

Many of these calls, meals, and visits are likely to be with individuals and lobbyists who represent interests that fall within the jurisdiction of the committees and subcommittees on which a member serves. This explains why a member's loyalty and attention often tilts to constituencies and institutions within the jurisdiction of his committee rather than to those within his congressional district.

Whatever the time a member spends fund-raising, it's certainly more than the time he or she allots for meetings with constituents either in Washington or at home, or to committee meetings and floor debates. One bipartisan nonprofit composed of dozens of former House members and other politicians estimated that the 114th Congress (the last two years of the Obama presidency) spent collectively more than one million hours fund-raising.[15]

CONGRESSIONAL CHAOS

While gerrymandering makes it easier for a Republican or Democrat to get (and stay) in Congress, a representative's job is constant turbulence. The congressional system of committees and subcommittees—and the need to serve constituents with myriad problems, recruit first-rate staff, and raise money—creates a climate of chaos that erodes the ability of the House and Senate to fulfill their constitutional responsibility to legislate, appropriate funds, and oversee the proper execution of the laws they pass.

THE THREE-DAY WEEK

Fueling the chaos of legislators' lives is that they are usually in the House and Senate at most three days a week. The House is in session about 140 days a year; the Senate, about 160. These days, usually Tuesday through Thursday, are crammed with votes on the floor, committee meetings, and lots of "call time."[1] The energy given to raising money and the short workweek leave members with fewer occasions to speak and listen to each other. That shows up in increased acrimony and partisanship.[2]

A member is likely to spend time on the floor of the House or

Senate briefly, in the hope of saying something politically pithy enough to get national or local television coverage, rather than to engage in serious debate. The great oratory that marked the floor debates of Senators Daniel Webster, Everett Dirksen, and Hubert Humphrey is an anachronism.

Most members come to Washington on Tuesday morning, some not until evening when congressional leaders can hold off votes till then. They depart on planes to their districts, or some big city to raise money, in late afternoon or early evening on Thursday.[3] Members persuade airports and airlines to provide flights between Washington, where they are chauffeured by a staffer or have special parking privileges, and their district airports at times convenient to their three-day workweek. Airlines allow members of Congress to book multiple flight times (fully refundable) to guarantee them a seat on a later flight if they miss an earlier one.[4] Usually there are no sessions for most of January, August, November, and December, and the weeks around Easter and Passover, and the Martin Luther King, Presidents, Memorial, Independence, and Labor Day holidays.[5] The decline in legislative activity over the years is evidenced in the average number of bills individual House members introduce annually, from fifty in the 90th Congress (1967–68) to fourteen in the 113th Congress (2013–14).[6]

Many senators and representatives don't like to spend—or be seen spending—too much time in Washington. As former representative Lee Hamilton, an Indiana Democrat, has said, "the politics of the country have grown strongly anti-Washington. Members of Congress do not want to be associated with the city. They want to show they haven't been seduced by the lifestyle of the Nation's capital or adopted an inside-the-beltway mindset. They take pride in rejecting the elitism of Washington. . . . Today's politics make it hard to argue that members should be spending more time in Washington."[7]

Is it any wonder that the legislative branch is no match for the executive branch? Think of it: a member is like a political bouncing ball, ricocheting from subcommittee meeting to fund-raising call, to constituent meetings, to fund-raising parties in the evening, to breakfasts, lunches, and dinners with constituents and wealthy contributors, to meetings with lobbyists either from his or her district or with interests in matters before his or her subcommittee or committee, to the airport for a weekend home or fund-raising in a large city like New York or Dallas, to a vote on the floor of the House or Senate, to a room in the Capital Hill Democratic or Republican headquarters or nearby row houses to fulfill his or her "call time" obligations and to raise money to pay dues for his/her committee assignment and his/her next campaign.*

This bouncing ball and money-pandering lifestyle is a good part of the reason why the quality of our political class in the House and Senate seems to be deteriorating. When Steve Israel, a respected member of the House from Manhattan, was asked why he retired in 2016, he said, he could not "spend another day in another call room making another call begging for money. . . . I always knew the system was dysfunctional. Now it is beyond broken."[8] Because of his Manhattan district and his contacts, Israel was charged with raising $10 million for the House Democratic Congressional Campaign Committee in 2014, more than any of the Democratic House leaders except Nancy Pelosi.[9] Louisiana Republican House member Rodney Alexander left the House in 2013 because "raising money . . . [is] the main business [we're in] and it's 24 hours a day."[10] Democratic senator Tom Harkin retired in 2013, complaining that the fun had gone out of being in the Senate "because members spend too much time fundraising."[11]

---

*It is illegal to raise political money on federal property.

Incumbent members, notably senators, amass intimidating campaign war chests to scare off potential primary opponents. There is also a sleight of hand aspect to incumbent fund-raising. A member accumulates excess money that he donates to the campaign of a colleague. He then asks that colleague to vote for a piece of legislation that one of the member's contributors wants.

This distraction from the original purpose of the legislative branch is why politicians like Barack Obama, Ted Cruz, and Marco Rubio see the Senate as a brief stop en route to a campaign for the presidency and a desk in the Oval Office. Offensive as it may have seemed at the time, there is raw truth in Marco Rubio's defense of his lengthy Senate absenteeism during his short-lived presidential campaign. Being on the Senate floor, he said, was not worth his time, because "a lot of these votes won't mean anything. They're not going to pass [a bill] and, even if they did, the President [Obama] would veto it." [12] In 2017, even with Republican majorities in both houses, many senators and representatives consider legislation on most important issues unlikely because of the different views in the Senate and House and erratic presidential leadership.

The 24/7 fund-raising combines with gerrymandering for a one-two punch that knocks out most efforts to compromise. Republicans look over their right shoulders, and Democrats over their left, in order to avoid facing opposition in the next primary. That fear of being ideologically walloped keeps members of the two parties well in the right or left corner. They are wary of the middle of the political ring, where knockout blows can come from business or labor interests, fracking or environmental interests, Donald Sussman or the Koch brothers, or any number of campaign-contributing institutions and individuals who decide to give only when they get. Billionaire Tom Steyer, for example, gave $70 million during the 2014 House and Senate elections and $85 million during the 2016 election only to candidates and super PACs who agreed with his personal environmental views.[13]

The number of bills passed is not the surest measure of how Congress serves the people. But it does reveal how much work gets done. The 89th Congress (1965–66) enacted 1,283 laws; the 99th (1985–86), 664 laws; the 111th (2011–12), 284 laws.[14] In the Senate it takes sixty votes for cloture to end debate and permit a vote on pending legislation. From 1917 to 1992, there were 485 cloture motions to end Senate filibusters blocking votes on bills. From 1992 to 2016, there were 1,292, virtually none of them successful in ending debate and enabling the Senate to vote on the bill under consideration.[15]

Congress lacks the staff needed to maintain a coequal status with the president and the executive branch. Committees and their professional staffs are central to the ability of Congress to function as an equal branch and to oversee the execution of laws and expenditure of monies. From 1980 to 2016, the number of committee staffers has dropped more than 25 percent in the House and Senate, despite increases in the number and complexity of federal programs and international problems.[16] Over the same period, staff levels for individual House members held to 1980 levels, while the nation's population has become more diverse and its size has climbed from 225 million to 325 million. Over that period, the average population of a congressional district has jumped 40 percent, from 517,000 to 735,000.*

Budgets for the Government Accountability Office (GAO)

---

*Every state is entitled to at least one district; all states except Alaska, Delaware, Montana, North Dakota, South Dakota, Vermont, and Wyoming have more than one district. The largest district size is Montana, at almost one million; the smallest, in Rhode Island, at 527,624.

and the Congressional Research Service, key organizations that aid legislators with policy and financial analysis, have been cut sharply over the past few decades.[17] Republican senator Tom Coburn expressed concern about the shortsightedness of this when he estimated that every $1 invested in the GAO saves $90 in federal spending.[18]

Curtailed congressional staffs not only limit the legislative branch's ability to oversee the executive branch, they give lobbyists an upper hand. Lobbyists and their organizations are experts in the areas of their clients' concerns (e.g., tax laws, energy, education, automobile emission, pharmaceuticals, food processing) and legislative procedures and politics. There are 22 registered lobbyists for every member of Congress. That doesn't count the thousands of lawyers, public relations and social media specialists, and other K Street professionals who spend less than 20 percent of their time lobbying so they can evade the legal requirement to register.[19]

In 2015, Congress appropriated $2 billion for congressional staffing while registered lobbyists reported receiving at least $3.2 billion for their services.[20] Congressional staffers often rely on lobbyists for policy ideas and to draft bills, line up cosponsors, and prepare speeches and op-eds for members. Former South Carolina Democratic senator Fritz Hollings warned, "While lobbyists should have influence in the process, they must not control it. . . . These days the denizens of K Street with their generous campaign contributions . . . can often be found drafting legislation and influencing when a vote is scheduled on it. They have too much influence."[21] Lobbyists use experts in social media to generate grassroots campaigns, emails, and phone calls from a member's district or state in order to persuade them to vote for or against legislation their clients favor or oppose.

While committees' and members' staffs have been short-changed, the congressional leadership has swollen their own staffs over the past couple of decades from 79 to 201 for the Speaker of the House and from 49 to 173 for the Senate majority leader.[22] This concentrates more power in the leadership over the rank-and-file members and supplies the muscular nagging needed to enforce fund-raising taxes levied on representatives and senators to gain or maintain control of the House and Senate.[23]

8

CUTTING OFF ITS NOSE TO SPITE ITS FACE

BUNDLING APPROPRIATIONS

The congressional practice of bundling appropriations in omnibus spending bills and continuing spending resolutions further dilutes its power vis-à-vis the president.

Under the Constitution, "all Bills for raising Revenue shall originate in the House of Representatives; but the Senate may propose or concur with Amendments as with other bills," and "no money shall be drawn from the Treasury but in Consequence of Appropriations made by law." [1] These provisions vest the legislative branch with the exclusive power to raise money and appropriate funds for the congressional, executive, and judicial branches.

Years ago, the House and Senate considered funding for departments and agencies on an individual basis and voted over the course of a year on a series of appropriations bills. Then, when necessary after conferences with the other chamber to settle differences, each chamber would pass the same bill and send it to the president for a signature or veto.

Those days of individual reviews of departments and agencies are ancient legislative history. In seventeen of the last twenty-one years, Congress has simply passed an omnibus spending bill or continuing resolutions covering all or almost all of the entire executive branch.[2] These bills have been thousands of pages long and chock-full of legislative provisions members could not conceivably read.

Individual appropriations committees and subcommittees have become sideline observers, witnessing more than influencing the specifics of executive branch spending. With this process, complaints of House and Senate leaders and committee chairs about the reckless and uncontrolled executive branch spending are reminiscent of the story of the old railroad router. Nearing retirement, he stood by while two trains crashed into each other. When asked why he did that, he lamely answered, "I ain't never seen a train wreck before."

There are advantages for incumbent members of Congress in burying so many appropriations, and often substantive provisions, in the pages of omnibus spending bills. Doing so makes a relatively modest demand on their time. Individual members can claim that, although they opposed a particular provision— say, funding Planned Parenthood, or not funding enforcement of prohibitions against selling marijuana—they voted for the omnibus bill because it was the only way to keep the government going. Such bills also make it comparatively easy to protect the anonymity of members inserting politically embarrassing provisions to satisfy commitments to some lobbyist or campaign contributor.

Individual senators and representatives prefer this way of enacting such tailored provisions, as the song goes, "in the wee small hours of the morning." That way, their deeds can be done before most anyone in Congress or the media notices it. This process enabled Wall Street bankers to tack on a last-minute rider (written by Citigroup lobbyists) on the FY 2015 Omnibus Spending Bill loosening restrictions on derivative trading adopted in the wake of the 2008 financial crisis.[3] The FY 2016 Omnibus Act

contained a rider that lifted the prohibition on exporting do-
mestically produced oil, put forth by industry lobbyists.[4] The
May 2017 omnibus continuing resolution included a provision
preventing the Department of Justice from devoting financial
resources to prohibit states from implementing their own "laws
that authorize the use, distribution, possession, or cultivation of
medical marijuana." This avoided any discussion in hearings or
floor debate on the medicinal value of the drug.[5]

Passing these humongous omnibus appropriations bills each
year has the collateral damage of enhancing POTUS power. Critical negotiations are usually left to the last few days of the session, when members are eager to get home for the holidays or to
run for reelection.[6] They take place behind closed doors among
the leaders of the House and Senate and the president. This is a
federal version of the "three in a room" syndrome that has helped
make New York State's government in Albany perhaps one of
the nation's most corrupt (as evidenced by the indictments and
convictions of that state's politicians and gubernatorial cronies).[7]
New York State's assembly leader, Senate leader, and governor
meet privately to cut deals and produce a budget that passes with
few if any members of the state legislative bodies knowing what's
in it. In Washington, the 2015 $1 trillion tax and spending om-
nibus bill was agreed to by the House and Senate leadership and
the White House just before midnight on the eve of the vote and
adjournment.[8] This process lets the president castigate Congress
for failing to legislate on a timely basis and get the funds the administration wants for its programs from members impatient to
get out of town.

In mid-2017, frustrated members of Congress lamented this
process because it undercut the congressional power of the purse.
Republican senator David Perdue of Georgia wailed, "When are
we going to do appropriations? It's going to come down to . . .

an up-or-down vote on the whole thing."[9] Arizona Republican senator John McCain warned, "Everything piles up, we go to the edge of the cliff . . . then we have an omnibus or a continuing resolution where we can vote yes or no. No amendments, no improvements, nothing."[10]

Two other factors reduce the power of Congress to control how the executive branch spends money.

First, 62 percent of federal expenditures are on autopilot for entitlement programs like Social Security, Medicare, Medicaid, Affordable Care Act subsidies, Supplemental Security Income, veterans' benefits, federal employee benefits, and the Supplemental Nutrition Assistance Program (SNAP). Another 8 percent pay the interest on the federal debt. Only the remaining 30 percent is so-called discretionary spending subject to congressional adjustment each year without amending the underlying laws.[11]

Second, tweaking entitlement programs to add or eliminate eligible individuals or to change benefits is likely to come from regulations promulgated by the executive branch, rather than congressional amendments to underlying laws. The president's branch has significant unilateral power. For example, it can modify and clarify the definitions of disability under the Social Security and Veterans Disability programs. It can establish how much to pay hospitals and physicians and which health procedures or pharmaceuticals will be covered under Medicare and Medicaid. It can determine how to calculate the level of income that qualifies an individual for eligibility for food stamps or welfare.

Over past decades, thousands of pages of departmental and agency regulations have been issued. The use of regulatory authority has become a way for the executive branch to silently usurp power vested exclusively in Congress by the Constitution to appropriate funds and specify how they are to be spent. These executive branch regulations have the force of law. Violating them can sometimes bring civil and criminal penalties. Congress has ceded power over expenditures for so many years that its legislative muscles have atrophied in this gray area of what is new legislation and what is an interpretative or implementing regulation.

ENDING EARMARKS

For half a century, congressional leaders and committee chairs used earmarks in order to convince a member to vote on broader, often controversial matters. These earmarks authorized or funded something that a senator or representative wanted in his or her state or district (a dam, school, port, bridge, defense contract, hospital) or for a campaign contributor. These earmarks helped assemble votes for full appropriation bills or major legislation for elementary schools, special education, health care, civil rights, consumer protection, infrastructure like interstate roads, and financial reform. For the Senate and House leadership, and for committee chairs, earmarks were an effective tool to lubricate Congress's legislative cogs. Compromise was easier for a representative who could return home and say, "I may have given in on this bill, but I got us a new federal building [courthouse, senior citizen center] for the town."

Former Democratic Senate majority leader Harry Reid called earmarks "the way we get things done around here. . . . I go home and I boast about earmarks, and that's what everyone should do."[12]

As House Speaker, Newt Gingrich hiked the use of earmarks from $7.8 to $15 billion, and his successors doubled down to $28 billion, still a rounding error for the total federal budget. In a hissy fit of "reform" in 2011, Congress banned their use as wasteful spending in order to gain political points with constituents.[13]

This self-inflicted wound left only one person in the nation's capital with the power to deploy earmarks in order to get something from a member of Congress: the president. The White House and executive departments promptly played earmark poker, anteing up pet project chips to create and reward friendly legislators. So rampant did this presidential practice become that in 2010 one Republican congressman commented (as many believed) that "there always will be earmarks. It's just that the administration runs the earmarks today."[14]

President Lyndon Johnson understood the power of earmarks. He was able to secure the vote of Arizona senator Carl Hayden to help break the filibuster of the 1964 Civil Rights Act by promising him support for the Arizona Water Project.[15] And when Senator Frank Church of Idaho repeatedly pressed Johnson on Vietnam, citing the ideas of Walter Lippmann (then Washington's most influential columnist), the president snapped, "Frank, the next time you want a dam on the Snake River, call Walter Lippmann."[16]

Democratic Illinois senator Dick Durbin blames congressional abandonment of earmarks for a good part of the failure to fund urgently needed national highway transportation projects.[17] In 2016, Speaker of the House Paul Ryan tried to revive earmarks, but he backed off because Republican backbenchers and Tea Party members saw it as a power grab by the House leadership.[18] In a political move that was all about appearances, Congress has ceded to the president one of its most effective legislating tools.

The Senate has found another way to shoot itself in the foot. The angry perpetual partisanship there has led Democratic minority leader Chuck Schumer to use arcane Senate rules to delay confirmation votes on scores of Trump administration nominees. Schumer is adopting a tactic that Republican senator Mitch Mc-Connell used in prior years when his party was in the minority. As the number of lower-level officials awaiting Senate confirmation piled up, Tennessee Republican senator Lamar Alexander pointed out that this "makes the president more powerful and the Congress less powerful, [because] it gives the people less to say into who the president is appointing, and what they are doing and how they conduct themselves." [19]

TRICK OR TREATY

The penchant of members of Congress to avoid unpopular votes, or ones that might bite back in later political life to threaten their careers, has also helped relinquish power to the president.

A telling example is how the Senate has yielded so much of its constitutional authority regarding agreements with other nations. Article II, section 2, of the Constitution provides that the president "shall have Power, by and with the Advice and Consent of the Senate, to make Treaties, provided two-thirds of the Senators present concur."

Over the years, presidents have eviscerated the meaning of the word "treaties" as they have concluded agreements with other nations that the Founding Fathers and early Senates would have considered treaties. This is true of agreements that FDR concluded before and during World War II, as well as Richard Nixon's 1973 executive agreement with South Vietnam committing to respond "with full force" should the North Vietnamese violate the Paris Peace Accords, a promise the United States did not keep. Bill Clinton's 1994 nuclear deal with North Korea and Barack Obama's Paris climate change agreement, which President Trump abandoned, also fit the constitutional standard of treaties.[20]

From 1789 to 1939, 60 percent of all international agreements were executive agreements binding on the United States and not requiring Senate approval. From 1940 to 2015, 98 percent of all international agreements have come in the form of such executive agreements.[21]

The machinations surrounding the 2015 Iranian nuclear agreement reveal the extent to which skittish senators, and their House colleagues, pretzel themselves to avoid a vote that might adversely affect their political fund-raising and careers. Obama agreed to make available to Iran $100 billion in frozen assets and lift economic sanctions in return for its assurance to delay its acquisition of nuclear weapons.[22]

Many senators and representatives—notably but not solely Democrats—were squeezed in a political vise between pressures from the White House to approve the Iranian agreement and pressures from Israel and many American Jewish voters to oppose it. Those voters were reliable political and deep-pocketed supporters of Democratic candidates. Israeli prime minister Benjamin Netanyahu condemned the agreement in an extraordinary address before a joint session of the US Congress.[23]

The White House and Republican and Democratic leaders in the Congress engaged in some procedural Cirque du Soleil artistry in order to avoid painting the Iranian agreement as a treaty that required an unattainable two-thirds Senate vote for approval.

Congress, both houses with Republican majorities, passed and the president signed legislation that provided that any nuclear agreement Obama made with Iran could be voided if a majority of both chambers passed a resolution of disapproval. The president could sign or veto the resolution, and Congress would have the opportunity to override any veto. *To override a presidential veto, each chamber would have to muster a two-thirds vote, a herculean task.* Neither party's leaders had the political muscle—or guts—to try to achieve this.

Senate Democrats did have enough votes pledged to uphold a presidential veto of any disapproval resolution. But facing implacable opposition to the Iranian deal from Netanyahu and American Jewish voters and contributors, they scrambled to avoid casting any recorded vote upholding a veto of a resolution of disapproval. That would have been seen as supporting Obama's agreement with Iran. So, when the Republican Senate leadership attempted to hold such a vote, Democrats successfully filibustered it. That kept in place the controversial Iranian deal without a recorded vote by any Senate Democrat.[24]

WHERE WAR IS NOT WAR

The most appalling evidence of self-serving congressional cowardice is how it has ceded to the president its constitutional power to declare war. As noted earlier, even though the Constitution vests this power exclusively in the legislative branch, the last declarations of war by Congress concerned World War II at the request of President Franklin D. Roosevelt. Prior congressional declarations of war were the War of 1812, the Mexican-American War (1846), the Spanish-American War (1898), and World War I (1917).[1]

Yet since the end of World War II in 1945, a compliant Congress has colluded with a host of presidents to create a make-believe world in Washington in which war is not war. As indicated in chapter 2, millions of Americans have been sent into combat, more than 100,000 have lost their lives, and more than half a million have been wounded in wars waged by presidents but undeclared by Congress—and not called wars by either.[2]

For Truman, it was Korea. For Johnson and Nixon, it was Vietnam. As the Vietnam War escalated and casualties mounted, Americans became concerned about the failure of Congress to restrain President Nixon.* When the public discovered in December 1972 that he had been secretly and extensively bombing Cambodia,† members of Congress pressed to recoup at least some of its power over ordering Americans into battle. The martial music on Capitol Hill was loud, but the dance step Congress took to reassert its constitutional power to declare war was feeble.

In 1973, Congress passed the War Powers Resolution. "In the absence of a declaration of war, in any case in which United States Armed Forces are introduced . . . into hostilities or into situations where imminent involvement in hostilities is clearly indicated," the resolution requires the president to inform Congress within forty-eight hours of what is going on. Within sixty days, the president is mandated to "terminate any use of Armed Forces," unless Congress declares war or specifically authorizes such use.[3] President Nixon vetoed the resolution and Congress overwhelmingly overrode his veto.

Subsequent presidents from Reagan on effectively reinstated Nixon's veto with their assertions that the War Powers Resolution is unconstitutional. They sent troops into combat in the Middle East, Africa, Bosnia, Kosovo, and elsewhere. In all, hundreds of thousands of Americans fought and thousands lost their lives or were permanently disabled. Most presidents found, disingenuously, that the troops they ordered into combat were not involved in "hostilities" as they interpreted that word in the War Powers Resolution. Both Presidents Obama and Trump made such findings with respect to military actions in Libya and Syria, respectively.[4]

---

*Had Nixon not treacherously sabotaged LBJ's peace negotiations just before the 1968 presidential election by assuring the South Vietnamese they would get a better deal with North Vietnam in his presidency, some 25,000 lives would have been saved. See John A. Farrell, *Richard Nixon: The Life* (New York: Doubleday, 2017).

†President Nixon, through his National Security Council, secretly coordinated and executed the carpet-bombing of Cambodia beginning in 1969.

On rare occasions, a member of Congress or a public-interest group has sought to have a court block, as unconstitutional, a president from waging an undeclared war. But judges invariably have found they lacked jurisdiction because a "political" or a "foreign policy" question was involved, or because the case had been mooted by passing events.[5]

By and large, Congress has accepted its humiliation by this presidential usurpation of its war power. Most members are reluctant to cast recorded votes on issues like the Iraq or Afghanistan wars for fear of losing votes in their campaigns. (See Hillary Clinton's political mea culpa during her presidential campaign because of her Senate vote supporting the Iraq War.[6]) Members retreat to the comfort of providing funding to the Defense Department and professing verbal support for "our brave men and women in uniform." Some note that since the nation has no compulsory draft, an "all-volunteer" military is waging our wars. That way, senators and representatives can support the president if the troops are winning and he's bringing them home, or they can attack him if the troops are stalemated or losing and there's no end in sight.

In 2001, Congress passed the Authorization for Use of Military Force to give President George W. Bush the okay to attack the 9/11 terrorists. In 2002, Congress passed a second resolution authorizing military action against the continuing threat posed by Iraq. Presidents Obama and Trump have cited these resolutions as authorization for military action in Afghanistan and to target ISIS and other terrorists in the Middle East and Africa.*[7] Congress—in a tawdry imitation of the cowardly lion in *The*

---

*The reliance on the 2001 Authorization for Use of Military Force was challenged in 2016 by a service member as being an illegal basis to wage war fifteen years later. The federal district court dismissed the case for lack of standing and under the political question doctrine.

Wizard of Oz—has refused to vote on a new authorization of military force against ISIS even after President Obama publicly pleaded for it to do so.[8]

A few members of Congress, including Republican senator John McCain and Democratic senators Mark Warner and Tim Kaine, tried to put some spine into the limp War Powers Resolution in 2014. But their colleagues lacked the courage to shoulder any more responsibility for military adventures.[9] In a 2015 *Washington Post* op-ed, Kaine castigated Obama for waging and expanding the war against ISIS in the Middle East "without authorization from Congress." He even more harshly criticized his congressional colleagues, "vested with the sole power to declare war by Article I of the Constitution [for refusing] to meaningfully debate or vote on the war against the Islamic State."[10] This attitude may be a hangover from the Vietnam War and the political headache of the Iraq War. Many members of Congress who voted to support either of those conflicts have recanted or lost reelections.[11] Congress has thus become a place where most members see no war, hear no war, and speak no war, as it cedes to the president its profound constitutional responsibility to declare war.

THE HIGH COST OF A CRIPPLED CONGRESS

Thanks in good measure to the crippled (and cowardly) Congress, our nation faces the most dangerous concentration of unchecked presidential power in its history. Congressional conservatives claim to oppose the centralization of power. Congressional liberals claim to abhor excesses in the exercise of power. Yet they lock arms in this quiet bipartisan conspiracy to shuck the constitutional responsibility and power of the legislative branch to write laws, appropriate money, monitor the executive branch, approve treaties with foreign nations, and declare war.

Since the middle of the last century, the House and the Senate have looked the other way time and again as presidents have assumed many of their powers and responsibilities. They have accepted their diminished standing vis-à-vis the president with only occasional and isolated murmurs from a few members and institutional leaders. While power in Washington is not a perfect zero-sum game, as Congress gets weaker, the president does get stronger. Unfortunately (with apologies to T. S. Eliot), this could be the way democracy languishes, with a whimpering Congress.

PART III

THE POLITICIZED COURT

10

POLITICAL LABOR PAINS

Politics was present at the creation of the Supreme Court just as it was at the birth of the executive and legislative branches. Today, however, the court's political elbows are far more sharply pronounced because of its profound and penetrating influence on the politics, culture, social mores, religious practices, and personal conduct of Americans. Its decisions mirror the polarization of American society. On hot-button issues individual justices often reflect the views of the conservative or liberal wings of the political parties of the president who selected them and to which they have belonged. As James Zirin titles his thoughtful book, the highest court in the land is "Supremely Partisan."

Every first-year law student (including me at Harvard Law School in the early 1950s) studies *Marbury v. Madison.* In this seminal 1803 case, the Supreme Court established its power to strike down laws passed by Congress and signed by the president whenever it determines that those laws fail to pass constitutional muster. My professor, constitutional law legend Paul Freund, left me with the unmistakable impression that the life tenure of judicial appointments encourages justices to make courageous calls central to our freedom like this one.* Granted, perhaps, but the *Marbury* decision also reveals that the labor pains of assuming power in the judicial branch were as rooted in partisan politics as they were in the White House and Congress.

In 1800, the Democrat-Republican Thomas Jefferson defeated the incumbent Federalist president, John Adams, in his reelection bid, and the Federalist Party lost its majorities in the House and the Senate. In a political trifecta, the Federalists rushed to entrench their influence before Jefferson and his party took office. The lame-duck Congress created a host of new judgeships, Adams nominated political pals to fill the posts, and the Senate immediately confirmed them. Upon assuming office, President Jefferson told his secretary of state, James Madison, not to issue the commissions essential for the individuals named by his predecessor to don their judicial robes.[1]

William Marbury, one of the disappointed prospective Federalist judges, filed a lawsuit in the Supreme Court for a writ of mandamus, a court order requiring Madison to issue his judicial commission. In a unanimous decision, the justices rejected Marbury's request. They found that the section of the Judiciary Act of 1789 that gave him standing to institute the suit in the Supreme Court was unconstitutional. The justices concluded that the Constitution gave the Supreme Court original jurisdiction only in cases involving "disputes between states or those involving Ambassadors, other Public Ministers and Consuls."[2]

Whatever the lasting merits of the *Marbury* opinion, in its contemporary context the aroma of politics could be sniffed on every page. At first blush Marbury's loss might seem like a victory

---

*Freund, once a clerk to US Supreme Court justice Louis Brandeis, declined President Kennedy's request to serve as solicitor general so he could finish his multivolume history of the US Supreme Court.

for Jefferson and the Democrat-Republicans. Quite the contrary: the Federalist Party, not Marbury, was the big winner. The Supreme Court, entirely composed of Federalist Party members, was telling the Democratic-Republican president and Congress that it could overrule them whenever it found their laws or other actions unconstitutional. Chief Justice John Marshall was able to maintain Federalist influence, including this pioneering view of judicial power for another three decades, long after the Federalist Party all but dissolved following the War of 1812.

Over the years since then, political maneuvering has repeatedly shaped the court. In 1863, Congress increased the number of justices from nine to ten. Three years later, in order to curb the influence of Abraham Lincoln's unpopular successor, President Andrew Johnson, on the highest bench, Congress reduced the number to seven.[3]

In 1869, shortly after Republican Ulysses S. Grant became president, his allies in Congress increased the number of Supreme Court justices from seven to nine.[4] This court-packing law enabled Grant, if necessary, to appoint two more justices in order to uphold the constitutionality of the controversial Legal Tender laws, which required creditors to accept paper currency in payment of debt. In 1870, the seven-member court in a 4–3 decision struck down as unconstitutional the application of the Legal Tender laws to debts incurred prior to its passage. Later that same day, Grant nominated, and the Senate promptly confirmed, two new justices likely to uphold those laws, William Strong and Joseph Bradley.[5]

Two days after his nominees had been confirmed, Grant petitioned the court to rehear the case. A year later, in a 5–4 decision, the court reversed itself and upheld the Legal Tender laws in an opinion authored by Grant's new justice William Strong.[6] The *New York Bulletin* railed, "We now have learnt, for the first time, that a President can pack the supreme tribunal of the land, and [apparently ignorant of or ignoring the backstory of *Marbury v. Madison*] its judges can recognize other considerations than those of law and justice." [7]

Half a century later, the battle over Democratic president Woodrow Wilson's nomination of Louis Brandeis ignited a wildfire of Republican criticism. "In all the anti-corporation agitation of the past, one name stands out," the *Wall Street Journal* wrote. "Where others were radical, [Brandeis] was rabid." [8] Former president William Howard Taft expressed disgust that "such a man as Brandeis could be put on the Court. . . . He is a muckraker, an emotionalist for his own purposes, a socialist . . . a man of infinite cunning . . . and, in my judgment, of much power for evil." [9] After a lengthy, politically charged, and often anti-Semitic battle, the Senate confirmed Brandeis.

Franklin Roosevelt faced a problem similar to that of Ulysses Grant, but his attempt to pack the Supreme Court fell short. During FDR's first term, conservative justices declared unconstitutional several New Deal initiatives, including the National Recovery Administration, the Farm Bankruptcy Act, and the Agricultural Adjustment Act. [10] The ideological undertones of these decisions led the liberal justice Harlan Stone to call out his colleagues in his dissent in *US v. Butler* (1936), writing, "Courts are concerned only with the power to enact statutes, not with their wisdom." [11] Roosevelt toyed with amending the Constitution to empower the legislature to override these Supreme Court determinations of unconstitutionality. That idea was a nonstarter politically. His attorney general Homer Cummings insisted that "the real difficulty is not with the constitution but with the judges who interpret it." [12]

FDR then proposed legislation to authorize the president to name an additional Supreme Court justice for any sitting justice who had served ten years and was more than seventy years old.[13] That would have given him the votes to reverse decisions by the conservative justices invalidating New Deal programs. Roosevelt couldn't persuade Congress to pass his bill. After his resounding reelection in 1936, he delivered a stinging Fireside Chat on March 9, 1937. In what sounds like a precursor of the charges leveled by some of today's conservatives, FDR said, "The court has been acting not as a judicial body, but as a policy-making body. . . . We must take action to save the Constitution from the court and the court from itself." [14]

His election victory, his threatening comments, and a Senate Judiciary Committee hearing on his proposal were sufficient to win support from the existing court for New Deal legislation. The signal 5–4 decision upheld a minimum-wage law for women and children, thanks to Justice Owen Roberts's shift to FDR's side.[15] Roberts's change of judicial position led political wags to call it "a switch in time that saved nine." A few months later, Roosevelt was able to replace a retiring conservative justice with the liberal Hugo Black. That solidified the court's support of Roosevelt's programs and policies.

When President Dwight Eisenhower nominated Earl Warren to be chief justice of the Supreme Court in 1953, he had no idea how liberal Warren would be. Warren brilliantly engineered two groundbreaking unanimous decisions. In 1954, *Brown v. Board of Education* struck down segregation in schools (overruling the court's separate-but-equal 1896 decision). In 1967, *Loving v. Virginia* invalidated state prohibitions of interracial marriages.[16] The Warren court enshrined individual rights in the criminal justice system. It held that police officers were required to inform suspects of their right to counsel. What TV crime show and murder mystery fans know as the "Miranda warning" is named after the plaintiff in that case.[17]

The Warren court also built the wall between church and state with its decisions prohibiting prayer and reading the Bible in public schools.[18] It gave the press the constitutional right to make nonmalicious erroneous statements about public figures with impunity.[19] These decisions remain politically controversial and provide fodder for presidential and congressional election campaigns to this day. They reportedly prompted Eisenhower to call his selection of Warren "the biggest damned-fool mistake I ever made."[20]

The case that dunked the Supreme Court up to its neck in American political waters was *Baker v. Carr* in 1962. That decision held that under the equal-protection clause of the Constitution, states were required to have legislative assembly districts of roughly equal populations.*

The court angrily split on whether this case involved political questions inappropriate for it to decide. Justice William Douglas aggressively pushed for the court to get involved. Justice Felix Frankfurter strenuously resisted on the ground that the case presented political questions. These two justices placed furious pressure on their colleagues. Justice Charles Evans Whittaker, a Kansan who ended his formal education at high school, rehearsed oral arguments before farm animals, and had previously served as a federal district and appeals court judge, withdrew from this case and retired from the court.[21] With Warren's help, Douglas eventually hammered together a 6–2 majority to create what was then called the "one man, one vote" rule. The court followed the *Baker* case with decisions holding that federal congressional districts and state senate legislative districts had to be

---

*The case involved Tennessee, which had not redrawn its political election district lines for sixty years. As a result, in terms of electing individuals to the state assembly, a single voter in rural districts was the equivalent of twenty-three voters in urban ones.

about the same size in population to satisfy the one person, one vote standard.[22] Chief Justice Warren considered these cases his most important on the Supreme Court.[23]

In 1968, President Lyndon Johnson nominated Associate Justice Abe Fortas, his intimate adviser and a liberal, to succeed Warren as chief justice. LBJ knew that attacks on his Great Society programs enacted by Congress would move to the courts. He wanted a committed supporter and a progressive majority on the high court to protect them. Unfortunately, Fortas was a nominee with such serious personal flaws that Republicans were able to filibuster his nomination.* Republicans refused to support any other candidate from lame-duck Johnson, who had a few months left in office. They hoped a new conservative Republican president would move the court to the right and undo some Great Society initiatives. Richard Nixon won the election. After bitter battles with Senate Democrats, he was able to name four justices, thus installing a conservative majority. Ronald Reagan bolstered that majority by nominating Antonin Scalia, whom the Senate confirmed unanimously in 1986.

A year later, President Reagan nominated Robert Bork, a lawyer highly qualified but mightily conservative.† Democrats, led by Senator Edward Kennedy, defeated Bork's nomination because they feared he would reverse *Roe v. Wade*, the court's 1973 decision that a woman's constitutional right to privacy included the right to have an abortion. As the Yale constitutional law professor Jack Balkin later wrote, that case "became a central issue

---

*LBJ was politically formidable enough to assemble a 45–43 majority for Fortas, but that fell far short of the 67 votes then needed to end a filibuster.

†Robert Bork rose to prominence as a constitutional law expert. The Connecticut Supreme Court appointed him in 1971 to redraw the state's congressional district boundaries. He later said that he "always opposed the idea of 'one man, one vote,' anyway. . . . There's nothing in the Constitution that requires it."

in judicial nominations, symbolizing not only the issue of individual freedom but also the larger question of the proper role of courts in a democratic society."[24]

When the liberal Thurgood Marshall, the court's first black justice, retired from the Supreme Court in 1991, President George H. W. Bush nominated the conservative Clarence Thomas, also an African American, to succeed him. Weathering nasty hearings replete with Anita Hill's allegations of sexual harassment and relentless opposition from Democrats, Thomas was confirmed by a narrow 52–48 vote. That gave the court a conservative tilt until Scalia's unexpected death in March 2016.

A month later, President, Obama nominated Merrick Garland, a judge on the US Circuit Court for the District of Columbia, to fill Scalia's seat. The Republican-controlled Senate refused to act on the nominee, in order to hold the seat open until after the presidential election at the end of that year. Republican Senate majority leader Mitch McConnell later called this decision one that helped tip the election to Donald Trump. Both Trump and Hillary Clinton had campaigned heavily on the power of presidents to name Supreme Court justices.[25]

Shortly after his inauguration, President Trump nominated federal appeals court judge Neil Gorsuch to the Supreme Court. Gorsuch, an articulate and ardent conservative, carefully tread the hot coals put in his path by Senate Democrats. When those Democrats filibustered to block a vote on his confirmation, Republicans changed the Senate's rules to allow only a simple majority vote to end debate on Supreme Court nominees instead of the previous sixty-vote requirement. This paved the way to confirm Gorsuch.[26]

Four years earlier, Democrats had controlled the Senate. They had changed the Senate's rules to permit a simple majority, rather than sixty votes, to end Republican filibusters that blocked confirmation of Obama's nominees for lower federal court and executive branch posts.[27] Republicans who had opposed as outrageous that earlier action by Senate Democrats cited it fervently to support their rule change so that a simple majority could end the Gorsuch filibuster. Democrats this time opposed the Republican rule change and fought to maintain the sixty-vote standard to end filibusters of Supreme Court nominees.[28] These 180-degree switches by Republicans and Democrats once again demonstrate that in politics where one sits determines where one stands—even when exposed in a blinding spotlight of hypocrisy.

Over recent decades, the Supreme Court has vested with constitutional stature a host of social policy issues such as abortion, same-sex marriage, affirmative action, individual right to own guns, money as free speech. The justices are certain to face even more lacerating questions, including claims of a constitutional "right to die," assisted suicide, partial-birth abortion, and child pornography.[29] Jagged raw-nerve issues like these are freighted with deeply held personal and moral convictions. They thrust the justices into the cultural craters of our society and the often clashing beliefs of its citizens.

In recent years the court has brought rapt attention to its penetrating and lasting influence on our society. Its sharply phrased majority opinions and dissents sound to those who oppose them like fingernails scratching on a blackboard. Americans can see that a president's most enduring power can come from his or her nominations to the Supreme Court. The power of presidents to nominate justices, and of the Senate to confirm them, determines why many citizens vote for or against particular candidates. Former Speaker of the House John Boehner justified his vote for the controversial GOP candidate Donald Trump this way:

> For me the election is pretty simple. The legislative process, the political process, is at a standstill and will be regardless

of who wins. The only thing that really matters over the next four years or eight years is who is going to appoint the next Supreme Court nominees. The biggest impact any president can have . . . is who's on that court.[30]

During the tumultuous 2016 presidential campaign Trump argued in both the third and first person, "If you really like Donald Trump, that's great, but if you don't, you have to vote for me anyway. You know why? Supreme Court judges, Supreme Court judges."[31] The Democratic candidate, Hillary Clinton, fired back, "If you care about the fairness of elections, the future of unions, racial disparities in universities, the rights of women, or the future of our planet, you should care about who wins the presidency and appoints the next Supreme Court justices."[32] The commentaries of pundits and political campaigners calling the 2016 presidential election a "referendum" on Supreme Court appointments reveals how the court is forfeiting any claim to be regarded as a nonpartisan institution.[33]

PARTISAN POLITICAL POLARIZATION

During the FDR years and the tenure of Earl Warren many votes of justices were ideologically driven. During and after the reign of Richard Nixon, many of the justices and their decisions became politically partisan. In recent years, several Supreme Court justices have acknowledged their political roles. Some seem to revel in them. On and off the bench, a number of justices occasionally sound like growling legal pit bulls, echoing the left- and right-wing barks of the Republican and Democratic parties.

Ruth Bader Ginsburg called Donald Trump a "faker," adding, "I can't imagine what the country would be like" if he were elected president. She then tripled down, saying if her husband were alive a Trump election would make it timely to "move to New Zealand."[1] After attacking Trump in different interviews she eventually issued a written statement through the Supreme Court press office ruing the public nature, but not the content, of her indiscreet remarks.[2] The comments of the eighty-four-year-old justice raise questions about the propriety of her participating in cases involving actions of President Trump.

Ginsburg has perhaps been the most egregiously political Supreme Court justice. But she's not the only one. In 1988, Sandra Day O'Connor wrote to the Republican conservative leader and former presidential candidate Barry Goldwater saying that she "would be thankful if George [H. W.] Bush wins. It is vital for the court and the nation that he does."[3] In 2000, during an election-night party, Justice O'Connor said, "That is terrible," when CBS television prematurely (and erroneously) declared Al Gore the winner of the presidential election.[4] Weeks later, she cast the deciding vote in the 5–4 majority that gave the election to George W. Bush.* Many scholars consider the *Bush v. Gore* decision to be the moment when the court's politicization jumped the shark, inaugurating the new era of an overtly partisan court.[5]

Off-the-bench comments by justices about court decisions have become common. Justice Elena Kagan recused herself in a University of Texas case involving the consideration of race in college admissions. Justice Ginsburg said Kagan would have voted to approve them, which would have made the court's 4–3 decision a "5 to 3. That's about as solid as you can get."[6] Did Ginsburg forget the Warren court's unanimous on issues like school desegregation? Or the Burger court's unanimous decision requiring that Nixon hand over the tapes of his Oval Office conversations? Publicly soliciting a second chance after dissenting in a controversial decision, Ginsburg said she was looking for an opportunity to reverse *District of Columbia v. Heller.* That was the 5–4 Supreme Court decision favoring the individual rights of gun owners.[7]

During his time as conservative leader of the court, Justice

Bush v. Gore. This was not the first time Supreme Court justices had a direct say in settling an election. In 1876, with neither candidate obtaining a majority, a commission was formed to award the twenty disputed electoral votes. The commission consisted of five Democrats and five Republicans as well as five Supreme Court justices (three Republican and two Democratic appointees). The commission of eight Republicans and seven Democrats decided by a one-vote margin to award the electoral votes, and the presidency, to the Republican Rutherford B. Hayes.

Antonin Scalia was often loose-lipped about his views. In 2002, the Supreme Court found unconstitutional a state law prohibiting candidates for judgeships from voicing their positions on political or legal issues. Writing the majority opinion, he said that "avoiding judicial preconceptions on legal issues is neither possible nor desirable."[8]

In a lecture at the American Enterprise Institute, Scalia said, "The death penalty? Give me a break. It's easy. Abortion? Absolutely easy. Nobody ever thought the Constitution prevented restrictions on abortion. Homosexual sodomy? Come on. For 200 years it was criminal in every state."[9] Speaking at Georgetown University Law Center, he told students, "What minorities deserve protection? What? It's up to me to identify deserving minorities? What about pederasts? What about child abusers? This is a deserving minority. Nobody loves them."[10]

The partisan political split on the Supreme Court is analogous to those on the left who watch only MSNBC or CNN versus those on the right who watch only Fox News. A 2016 analysis of outside appearances by justices found that no currently sitting liberal justice had spoken at the annual (conservative) Federalist Society National Lawyers Convention and that no currently sitting conservative justice had spoken at the annual (liberal) American Constitution Society National Convention.[11]

Moonlighting has become a common sideline by justices to supplement their $214,000 yearly salary. A number enhance their income and nourish their egos by making public speeches and writing books. The justices take the position that they are not bound by rules they impose on lower-court judges because they are the court of last resort. They feel free to engage in all sorts of activities that would not be permitted by those serving at lesser levels of the judicial branch. But their outside activities like speaking, writing, and appearing on radio and television shows increase the danger of revealing political as well as legal and constitutional biases. That in turn reduces respect for the fairness of their judicial opinions.

Off-the-court public speeches and interviews by Supreme Court justices have soared over the years. During the 1970s, Supreme Court justices made 91 such appearances; in the decade ending in 2014, they made 744, an 830 percent increase.[12] Not all of these have been paid. Nevertheless, such public events hike the risk of comments and ad libs that reveal judicial prejudices, preconceptions, and political positions. That can lower the respect of the public for the court. As a result, fewer Americans believe that the justices will cast their votes on the merits of the particular case before them. More believe that justices vote on personal or political leanings and loyalties.

With a perennial parade of abortion issues marching to the Supreme Court, Justice Ginsburg, lecturing at the University of Chicago in 2013, criticized the reasoning in *Roe v. Wade*. She expressed her fear that basing the decision on the right to privacy gave detractors an avenue to attack the court's reasoning and "stopped the momentum that was on the side of change."[13] At a Federalist Society dinner in 2012, Justice Samuel Alito reiterated his support for the court's controversial decision in *Citizens United v. FEC*, which gave corporate and union treasury money First Amendment rights.[14] Justice Ginsburg, on the other hand, has said she'd "love to see *Citizens United* overruled."[15] During his 2010 State of the Union message, President Obama criticized the decision, saying, "last week the Supreme Court reversed a century of laws that, I believe, will open the floodgates for special interests, including foreign corporations, to spend without limit in our elections." Sitting in the audience on the floor of the House of Representatives, Alito shook his head and mouthed the words, "Not true." It was the last Obama State of the Union that Alito attended.[16]

For Supreme Court justices, writing books can be a lucrative sideline. While some, like Antonin Scalia and Stephen Breyer, have written books on the law, others, like Clarence Thomas and Sonia Sotomayor, have crafted memoirs. Memoirs can be quite profitable. Justice Thomas made at least $1.5 million on his, *My Grandfather's Son.*[17] Justice Sotomayor made $3 million on hers, *My Beloved World.*[18] Whether legal tome or personal memoir, these books invariably provide insights into the politics of the justices who write them. By expressing in her memoir admiration and gratitude for the affirmative action policies that enabled her to go to Ivy League schools, Justice Sotomayor cast doubt on whether she can or should adjudicate challenges to the constitutionality of affirmative action facing the court.

Book-writing justices often rely on right- and left-leaning media in order to promote their publications. Though he went a decade in court without asking a question during oral arguments, Thomas did numerous interviews promoting his book. He spent ninety minutes on the quintessentially right-wing political broadcast *The Rush Limbaugh Show.* To sell her book, Sotomayor appeared on the left-leaning programs *The View, The Daily Show*, and *The Colbert Report.* To hawk his, the liberal justice Stephen Breyer appeared on the liberal stations MSNBC and CNN.

Supreme Court justices routinely ignore conflict-of-interest limits they place on lower-court judges about vacationing on luxurious trips. The legal ethicist Stephen Gillers worries "about the public perception of gratitude, even if there is no effect on your behavior. And the greater the luxury, the greater the risk of public suspicion."[19] Scalia, a frequent traveler, hunted with Vice President Dick Cheney while the court was reviewing a lower-court order that Cheney make public the deliberations of his energy task force. Returning to Washington, Scalia voted to support the vice president's refusal to reveal those deliberations.[20]

Statements of presidents and senators about the importance of judicial experience are now code for how Supreme Court nominees will vote on particular issues. Are they pro–women's right to choose abortions or pro-life? For or against racial preferences in college admissions? Pro-labor or pro-business? For enhancing or restricting religious freedom? For or against the court's decision in *Citizens United*? The 2016 presidential candidate Bernie Sanders trumpeted a commitment to reverse this decision as his litmus test for Supreme Court nominees.[21]

By limiting Supreme Court nominees to individuals with judicial experience, presidents have no need to shrewdly interview candidates in the discreet quiet of the Oval Office. Nor do potential nominees have to coyly suggest how they would vote on politically charged subjects. Usually those who have served on lower courts have decided and written enough for presidents to know their views before they walk across Pennsylvania Avenue to enter the gates to the White House.*

Senators pretend to ask questions to assess the legal qualifications of judicial candidates, but by and large they are well aware of the nominees' positions on political hot-button issues like abortion, campaign financing, freedom of religion, affirmative

---

*President George W. Bush's 2005 failed Supreme Court nominee, Harriet Miers, was opposed by conservative senators largely because she had no appellate court judicial experience and thus had no track record of her stances on certain issues such as abortion.

action, and gun owners' rights long before those nominees raise their right hand to be sworn in to testify. Every Supreme Court nomination is a political decision for the president, the members of the Senate Judiciary Committee, every senator voting, and every nominee. Senate confirmation hearings feature gotcha games, political theater, sometimes even show trials. Berkeley law professor Melissa Murray, discussing the unanimous Senate vote confirming Scalia in 1986, remarked shortly after his death:

> The confirmation process has become so incredibly politicized in a way that it wasn't when [John Paul] Stevens was nominated, when [William] Brennan and when these older Justices were nominated. Like now it's such a political event. The litmus tests about abortion, about gun rights, I mean, I think it's hard to kind of un-ring that bell at this point.[22]

Such litmus tests virtually guarantee that battles for a majority on the court will be political fights with switchblade knives and brass knuckles. They share characteristics of contests between candidates of the two major parties when control of the House, the Senate, or the presidency is at stake. To paraphrase the Prussian military theorist Carl von Clausewitz, the struggle for control of the Supreme Court, and often the work of the court itself, has become the continuation of political war by other means.

The partisan politicization of the Supreme Court has been dramatic in recent years. Political scientists Neal Devins and Lawrence Baum found that from 1801 to 1937 there were seventy-five "important" cases that had at least two dissenting justices.*

---

*Devins and Baum classified cases as "important" per David Savage's *Guide to the U.S. Supreme Court*, 5th ed. (Washington, DC: CQ Press, 2010).

In only one were the votes along political party lines. From 1937 to 2009, not one of the 322 cases deemed "important" with at least two justices dissenting was split along party lines.[23]

Since then, however, important 5–4 decisions with eight of the justices split along political party lines have been rampant; for example, those establishing a constitutional right to gay marriage, striking down some of Obama's Clean Power Plan, finding Article V of the Voting Rights Act unconstitutional, allowing lethal injection by a drug used in botched executions, ruling that voters could change state redistricting procedure through ballot measures, giving money First Amendment rights, upholding the University of Texas's affirmative action practices in college admissions.*

About 20 percent of Chief Justice John Roberts's court cases have been decided by 5–4 votes. In two-thirds of those cases, eight justices have split 4–4 along Republican-Democratic lines. Justice Anthony Kennedy has been providing the swing vote.[24] The notable exception was Roberts's support of Obamacare in 2012.[25] President Obama had publicly positioned the court as the institution that might take away health insurance coverage from millions of Americans by declaring his health care bill unconstitutional. So Roberts's vote seemed politically motivated to protect the court from a vast and angry public outcry.

With controversial cases decided along party lines by a one-vote margin, Chief Justice Roberts's concern, expressed at the start of his tenure, has become a self-fulfilling prophecy:

I do think the rule of law is threatened by a steady term after term after term focus on 5–4 decisions. I think the Court is

---

*The affirmative action decision was decided 4–3 owing to Justice Scalia's death and Justice Kagan's recusal, with a 3–3 partisan political split and Justice Kennedy, as usual, the swing vote.

ripe for . . . refocus on functioning as an institution, because if it doesn't, it's going to lose its credibility and legitimacy as an institution.[26]

From 2000 to 2016, the proportion of Americans who approve of the way the Supreme Court has handled its job has plummeted from 62 percent to 42 percent. For the first time since Gallup began this polling, more Americans disapprove than approve of the way the Supreme Court is doing its work. The Pew Research Center reported in July 2015 that seven in ten Americans believe that, when making decisions, Supreme Court justices "are often influenced by their own political views."[27]

With key court decisions by one-vote margins, presidents look to ideology as the primary, if not the determinative, consideration in selecting Supreme Court nominees. They want their nominees to follow the party line. They well remember how the liberal Earl Warren had disappointed Eisenhower. They saw Associate Justice David Souter as turning against Republican principles and George H. W. Bush. Indeed, when President George W. Bush considered nominating his attorney general Alberto Gonzales to replace Souter, conservative Republicans feared that Gonzales might drift to the left. They coined the slogan "Gonzales is Spanish for Souter!"[28]

With the ideological homogenization of each party, justices have become more "reliable" in their voting. A recent analysis of the ideological rankings of all Supreme Court justices since 1937 found that three (then-current) members of the court (Thomas, Scalia, and Alito) were among the ten most conservative justices in the modern era, and three (Sotomayor, Ginsburg, and Kagan) were among the ten most liberal.[29]

The partisan politicization of the Supreme Court has inflicted serious collateral damage on the lower federal courts. Both Presidents Obama and Trump have had orders they issued promptly stymied as a result of the legal forum-shopping that results from this politicization. Conservative groups moved to halt Obama's Deferred Action for Parents of Americans (DAPA) immigration program. They filed suit in the Brownsville Division of the US District Court for the Southern District of Texas. There were only two judges in that division. One, Judge Andrew Hanen, was assigned the case. He had previously criticized the Obama administration's immigration policies.[30] He issued a nationwide injunction blocking the program.[31]

Plaintiffs opposed to President Trump's executive order to ban immigration from certain Muslim-majority countries filed suits in federal district courts in Washington and Hawaii.[32] Reliably liberal judges there prohibited the enforcement of the order nationwide. To block Trump's order calling for federal funds to be withheld from "sanctuary cities," plaintiffs filed suit in federal district court in California where the liberal Democratic judge William Orrick granted the requested injunction.[33]

The involvement of the federal courts in social issues has turned the process of presidential nominations and Senate confirmations, even for lower court nominees, into a walk across a political minefield.

In 2012, President Obama nominated Elissa Cadish to the federal district court in Nevada. Years before the contrary Supreme Court decision, Cadish had said that the Second Amendment did not create an individual right to bear arms. Nevada Republican senator Dean Heller exercised his home state senatorial courtesy prerogative. He objected to the nomination and blocked any Judiciary Committee hearings on the nominee.[34] In 2017, Senate majority leader Mitch McConnell advocated ending this prerogative to prevent Democratic senators from blocking consideration of Trump judicial nominees.

In 2017, President Trump nominated Amy Coney Barrett for a seat on the Seventh Circuit Court of Appeals. Barrett, an eminently qualified professor at Notre Dame Law School and a conservative Catholic, faced questions and comments about her faith. Illinois Democratic senator Dick Durbin asked her if she was an "Orthodox Catholic." California Democratic senator Dianne Feinstein told the nominee that "the [Catholic] dogma lives loudly within you, and that's of concern when you come to big issues that large numbers of people have fought for years in this country."[35] Presumably both committed pro-choice senators were focused on protecting women's constitutional right to abortion, a litmus-test political issue.*

As Sheldon Goldman, a political science professor at the University of Massachusetts Amherst, explained:

> Partisan obstruction and delay in the confirmation of lower court judges gained steam when Senate Democrats objected to several Reagan nominees, and ramped up during the presidencies of Republican George H. W. Bush and (especially) Democrat Bill Clinton and Republican George W. Bush. . . . [And delay reached] unprecedented levels under president Obama.[36]

President Obama was able to secure the confirmation of only forty-nine circuit court judges in eight years. That's seven fewer

---

*The comment of Senator Feinstein drew a blistering letter from the president of Notre Dame. He called her words "chilling," and added, "I ask you and your colleagues to respect those in whom 'dogma lives loudly'—which is a condition we call faith. For the attempt to live such faith while one upholds the law should command respect, not evoke concern." Barrett was confirmed in October 2017.

than the number of circuit court judges President Jimmy Carter was able to get confirmed in four years.[37] Remarkably, and despite overwhelming Democratic opposition, Donald Trump and Republican Senate leader Mitch McConnell have been able to get eight federal appellate judges confirmed in 2017. The political and constitutional influence of these judges is likely to be enormous. Federal appellate courts issue thousands of decisions annually, compared to less than a hundred for the Supreme Court.

The politics of delaying confirmation of lower court judges over several administrations has savaged the federal court system. In 2017, the Judicial Conference of the United States deemed twenty-eight understaffed federal district and circuit courts to be in a state of "judicial emergency," up from twelve when Obama took office.* Some federal district courts have an average of nearly 1,200 filings per sitting judge, double the recommended limit.[38]

As I've written, some odor of politics has always been in the air around the Supreme Court. So, you may ask, what's different that's damaging to our democracy today?

For the most part, the tilts of the court in the past have been ideological, not persistently politically partisan. FDR was angered by the court's narrow ideological interpretation of the commerce clause of the Constitution, but many Democrats supported that interpretation. Eisenhower was infuriated with the Warren court's ideologically infused decisions, but many Republicans supported them. Even more to the point, many of the Warren court's biggest and most controversial ones were unanimous.

Since then, however, we have seen the merger of political par-

---

*The Judicial Conference of the United States is a congressionally created conference of sitting federal judges who develop policy guidelines for the effective administration of the federal court system.

ties and ideologies. In the presidency and in the House and Senate, down into town halls and city councils, conservatives control the Republican Party and liberals the Democratic Party. Both impose ideological litmus tests for leadership positions. Perhaps it shouldn't surprise us, then, that Supreme Court justices, and many lower federal court judges, have doffed their black robes for the garb of political parties. In recent decades, most Supreme Court justices have cast party-line votes. Eight of the nine justices on the court today repeatedly vote along the lines of the party of the president who nominated them.

Presidents see the Supreme Court and the lower federal courts less as institutions devoted to equal justice under the law than as instruments that can support or stunt their programs and policies. Senators with responsibility to provide "advice and consent" cast their votes depending on whether they see judicial nominees as supporters or opponents of their party's positions on key issues like abortion, gun rights, or religious freedom. The selection and confirmation process and the ensuing conduct of Supreme Court justices have become nakedly partisan experiences, part and parcel of the presidential and congressional election process.

Today the laws and regulations of the legislative and executive branches affect our lives—from birth to death, in cities and farmlands, in preschool education and on college campuses, in discrimination on the basis of race, ethnicity, or sex, in cultural conduct and religious practices, in the air we breathe and the water we drink. Inevitably, the Supreme Court finds itself adjudicating the constitutional standing of hosts of contentious issues. Interest groups and individuals, and their attorneys, see the federal courts as places that can deliver victories on political issues lost in the executive or legislative branches, or a state or city.

Supreme Court justices are seen as casting politically predictable votes that echo the sharp partisan split in the major political parties. As a result, the court becomes more vulnerable to political attacks. President Trump has shouted and tweeted against many judges and the legal system itself.[39] President Obama attacked the court's decision in *Citizens United* in a State of the Union address. As political party polarization jaundices decisions of the Supreme Court and lower federal courts, presidents will find it easier to circumvent decisions they dislike, and to erode public trust in the judicial branch.

PART IV

THE SUBJECT STATES AND CITIES

12

MONEY MAKES THE RULES

The Constitutional Convention of 1787 replaced the unraveling Articles of Confederation with a constitution that more tightly tied the states together with the national government. The new compact vested more power in the federal government, and notably with the president, but it was careful and politically shrewd enough to treat the original thirteen states as full partners.

Whatever the Founders thought in 1776, I doubt they could have conceived that there would someday be fifty states or of the ways in which technology would ignore state lines. Despite the concerns they expressed during those debates in Philadelphia, they surely did not anticipate the power of the central government in the twenty-first century. Some 250 years later, the states and most cities have become supplicant subjects of the federal executive and the crippled Congress. Today the executive and legislative branches of the federal government control critical resources. They set most of the rules in the nation, many of whose problems—environmental, public safety in an age of terrorism, transportation in a world of airplanes and automobiles, education, science, communications, and technology in a world of revolutionary change—refuse to honor state lines and municipal boundaries.

Thirty-one states derive about a third of their revenue from federal government grants.[1] Mississippi and Louisiana get 40 percent of their revenue from such grants. States now look to the federal government to pay the salaries of almost a third of their employees, and state employees' organizations lobby in Washington for more. Above and beyond that, military installations and defense contracts account for at least 5 percent of the gross domestic product of a number of states, and a higher percentage in some cities.[2]

In life there is no free lunch; in politics and government, there are no free crumbs. The federal government, particularly the president and the executive departments, dots the i's, crosses the t's, and punctuates and parses the sentences that tell the states how to spend the money it gives them. Much of this federal funding and concomitant control is essential to our freedom and human development, and to the quality of life of our people: civil rights; assuring education for special-needs children; Medicare and Medicaid, to provide health care for the elderly and the needy; environmental and consumer protection. But the immense power that administering those funds gives to the president and his appointees imposes a heavy obligation on Congress and the courts to fulfill their watchdog responsibilities to monitor the exercise of POTUS power in order to protect our freedom.

How did we get to the point where the fifty states and their governors, and a multitude of cities and counties across the country, find themselves coming to the White House and Congress on bended knee? They beg for money needed to feed, educate, and provide health care, transportation infrastructure, housing, and police protection for many, if not most, of their residents.

Early in our nation's history, federal involvement in domestic affairs was quite limited. Domestic matters were left to the states while the nascent federal government handled foreign affairs. The national government did not have the money to do too much else. Tariffs accounted for more than 90 percent of federal revenue, and those funds had to be committed to national defense and the payment of foreign debts.[3]

It wasn't until the American Civil War (and the absence of delegations from Southern states) that Congress turned some serious attention toward domestic matters. In 1862, the federal government passed what has been called the "progenitor of federal grant-in-aid programs," the Morrill Act.[4] That law gave federal property to states in order to establish land grant colleges to provide agricultural and mechanical instruction. In 1879, the federal government made its first continuing nonmilitary financial grants to states to develop instructional materials for teachers of the blind. Signaling that enforceable conditions would accompany future grants, the law gave the secretary of the treasury the power to withhold these funds from states that did not use them as directed.[5] In 1890, in the wake of the Civil War, the Morrill Act was amended to provide that "no money shall be paid out . . . to any state or territory for the support or maintenance of a college where a distinction of race or color is made in the admission of students, but the establishment and maintenance of such colleges separately for white and colored students shall be held to be a compliance with [this provision]."[6]

By 1902 there were only five multiyear federal grants to the states, comprising 1 percent of federal spending and 0.7 percent of all state revenue.[7]

Then came the game changers.

13

THE GAME CHANGERS

The first game changer came in 1913: the permanent federal income tax.[1] With this money, the national government could now give cash to states and localities for infrastructure, education, and public health. In the 1917 Smith-Hughes Act, Congress offered funds to states for vocational education in rural areas that needed high schools and replacements for skilled workers in the military during World War I.[2] The law prohibited using its funds to pay a teacher who also taught mainstream classes like history and geography. The idea was to encourage the establishment of vocational education as a separate academic discipline. This law was the paradigm of the "use of the grant as a 'stimulating' device" to entice states to take actions or adopt policies, a technique widely deployed in the Great Society programs of the 1960s.[3] To facilitate the transportation of military supplies during World War I, Congress stepped up federal grants to states for railroads and highways and maintained the subsidies throughout the next decade. Nevertheless, by 1932, federal grants amounted to little more than a rounding error in most state budgets.[4]

The second game changer was the New Deal. Using the expansive view of the Constitution's commerce clause powers adopted by FDR, the New Deal played an aggressive role in economic and social welfare. The states slipped into the role of junior partners to the federal government.

From 1932 to 1938, under laws passed by Congress and guidelines established by the executive branch, federal grants to states more than tripled, to $800 million.[5] With these grants states were required to administer federal programs to assist individuals who were physically disabled, unemployed, elderly, and poor, and to support housing for low-income families and public works. The Social Security Act of 1935 created the first federal welfare program, Aid to Families with Dependent Children.[6] While the states administered this program for poor mothers and children, the federal government provided a third of the funds and regulated in detail how they were to be disbursed.[7] Today the federal government pays more than half the costs for welfare, which states administer in compliance with volumes of detailed regulations.[8]

In an effort to jolt the nation out of the Great Depression, emergency relief assistance to states for income security and job creation constituted 90 percent of all federal grants in 1937.[9] With the onset of World War II in 1941, they dwindled to less than 1 percent. But their lasting impact was instituting the concept, widely replicated today, of allocating funds by a prescribed formula based on the economic situation in a particular state or locality with detailed executive branch instructions on how to spend the money.[10]

The end of World War II brought the GI Bill, which paid the college tuition of returning veterans.[11] President Eisenhower's Federal Highway Act of 1956 funded grants to the states to build the modern interstate road system.[12] To this day, states and municipalities rely on this program to subsidize the maintenance and expansion of the nation's highways. Two years later, fearful of falling behind in a technological race with the Soviet Union after the launch of the *Sputnik1* satellite, Congress passed the National Defense Education Act. This law provided grants for math, science, and foreign-language programs in secondary and higher education and for training teachers to educate those students.[13] With big assists from the explosion of motor vehicle transportation and the Cold War, the Republican Eisenhower administration normalized the concept of federal funding for state activities to be conducted under executive branch regulations and the watchful eyes of the president's men and women who administered these grants.

The third game changer—the most sweeping one—was Lyndon Johnson's Great Society. LBJ inherited an executive branch that operated fifty domestic programs. With his Great Society, he left one operating five hundred such programs. As LBJ's chief White House domestic policy adviser, I was an integral part of this social justice enterprise. Johnson's commitment to civil rights for African Americans, the war on poverty, health care, consumer protection, employment, public broadcasting, the arts, and the environment engaged the federal government in domestic activities once left largely to the states, cities, and private institutions. From 1964 to 1969, the vast expansion of federal grants came with accompanying rules and regulations. With grants to the states for job training, education from Head Start to graduate school, nursing homes, housing, mass transit, clean air and water, and upgrading local law enforcement came more instructions from the president's branch.

The 1954 Supreme Court case *Brown v. Board of Education* declared segregated schools to be unconstitutional. But it was the passage of the Civil Rights Act of 1964 that gave the federal government potent and timely instruments to desegregate state and local schools. Following the *Brown* decision, school districts could be compelled to desegregate only if lawsuits were filed against them and a federal court order obtained. This was a cumbersome and often dangerous process in the days of a southern culture that intimidated civil rights attorneys, equated segregation with states' rights, and encouraged resistance at every stage of the judicial process.

The 1964 act gave the executive branch the power to prohibit discrimination by those receiving federal funds.* A year later, the Elementary and Secondary Education Act offered local schools buckets of federal dollars, but only if they did not discriminate on the basis of race.[14] With these funds and the power to deny them to noncomplying schools, the president and his administration in relatively short order desegregated elementary and secondary schools across the nation. Medicare, created as part of the Social Security Act Amendments of 1965, provided federal funds for the treatment of elderly patients. Once enacted, hospitals and health clinics across the country that received Medicare funds had to desegregate. "With one stroke," as one health care expert later wrote, "more than 7,000 hospitals were subject to civil rights regulations set forth in . . . the Civil Rights Act."[15] And it worked. Medicare regulations required hospitals to have "all patients . . . assigned to all rooms, wards, floors, sections, and buildings without regard to race, color or national origin."[16] Medical residency programs could not discriminate in the admission of students on the basis of race.[17]

The Great Society fine-tuned the concept of attaching mandates to federal grants in order to achieve policy initiatives. Prior to the 1960s, there was a tendency to eschew imposing federal

---

*Title VI provides that "no person in the United States shall, on the ground of race, color or national origin, be excluded from participating in, be denied the benefits of, or be subjected to discrimination under any program or activity receiving Federal assistance." Title VII prohibits employment discrimination based on "race, color, religion, sex, or national origin."

mandates on state and local governments and institutions. In the 1960s era of civil rights, however, the national government distrusted most southern and border states. Governors like Ross Barnett in Mississippi and George Wallace in Alabama (whom President Johnson called "a runty little bastard" and "just the most dangerous person around" with a "powerful constituency") were ardent segregationists.[18] These governors spearheaded the opposition of southern states to desegregation. The Johnson administration's distrust of state governments on civil rights undoubtedly, if unintentionally, contributed to the suspicions of executive branch departments and agencies. That seeded detailed regulations. Meticulous monitoring and enforcement were needed to ensure that states and localities—north, south, east, and west—faithfully administered federal laws.[19] Successive presidents came to appreciate the power of federal funds to buy and enforce compliance with bureaucratic demands from Washington. This inevitably led to increased federal control over state and local government and institutions, and enhanced POTUS power.

The 1960s also witnessed a sweeping economic shift as local banks, pharmacies, and grocers were replaced by national financial institutions, drugstore chains, supermarkets, and manufacturers. States and localities had limited ability to protect their citizens faced with these changed circumstances. To confront these corporate behemoths, the Great Society generated and Congress enacted an array of consumer protection laws in food safety, personal financing, auto and highway safety, consumer product safety, and environmental protection. These laws placed responsibility and power for their day-to-day enforcement on the president's branch.[20]

The expansion of the role of the federal government was also prompted by the recognition that many public needs in social and economic development and health cut across established governmental boundaries. These needs could no longer be met by a state, city, or county acting alone within the borders of its jurisdiction. Air and water pollution were prime examples: the air we breathe and the water that flows in our rivers knows no state boundaries. Mass transportation, with commuters moving in and out of central cities and across state lines, is another example. National travel—by air, rail, or on interstate roads—meant that infectious diseases could spread overnight from New York to San Francisco.

Different public needs required different groupings of states, cities, or counties, or all three. The state and local units that join together to confront air or water pollution might not be the same combination needed to deal with the problems presented in transportation, economic growth, urban development, public health, or law enforcement.

What happened in federal-state-local relations?

The feds stepped in.

POTUS and his people spearheaded efforts to deal with these problems, often by using funds to require all states to meet certain needs in the same way.

Over the decade of the 1960s, the amount of money in federal grants for regional development rose by 1,700 percent; for health care, by 1,800 percent; for income security, by 220 percent. Total grants for states and localities increased by 340 percent.[21] By 1970, federal grants accounted for 20 percent of states' revenue. Spending on federal grants to states and localities doubled in the following five years, as new programs were introduced such as those to develop urban areas and guarantee all disabled children the right to a mainstream public education.[22]

During this period, the states were making a pitch for legislation to get a share of federal funds. They won such a share from 1972 until 1986. Revenue sharing provided all states, and thousands of localities, federal dollars based on income levels, population, and tax base.[23] The grants had few strings attached, for example, paying at least the federal minimum wage if funds were used for construction projects, and prohibiting the use of funds when racial discrimination was involved. Recipient states and localities had the discretion to put the funds to all sorts of purposes: education, police, public works, even to stave off a government liquidity crisis. One-third of a state's allocated amount went to the state treasury; the rest was sent directly to localities within the state. After 1980, all the funds were provided directly to local governments.[24] On average, the grants received by medium- to large-size cities accounted for 2 to 4 percent of their annual budget. The short term of the program and the relatively modest amounts it disbursed indicate that federal money with so few strings is not likely to be offered again.

The 1990s saw federal grants to school districts to subsidize the cost of internet connections and to provide health insurance for needy children ineligible for Medicaid.[25] The 2001 No Child Left Behind Act, a Republican initiative, increased spending for elementary and secondary education and put the federal government deeply into local schools with a national testing scheme.[26] The 2009 American Recovery and Reinvestment Act saw federal grants in 2010 jump 30 percent for a couple of years to assist in the recovery from the 2008 financial crash.[27] The 2010 Patient Protection and Affordable Care Act (Obamacare) increased health-related payments to the states and ballooned Medicaid dollars to becoming a majority of all federal grants to states.[28]

By 2016, more than a third of all states' revenue came from federal grants wrapped with strings tied by lilliputian bureaucrats. Some 1,700 federal grants are available to states and localities (and 160 to educational institutions).[29] Federal grants account for 17 percent of all federal spending, $660 billion, including $368 billion for Medicaid. They constitute 3.5 percent of the national gross domestic product, up from 1.3 percent in 1960.[30]

The federal government is the single largest provider of funds, including grants to students for tuition, to public and private colleges and universities. These funds come with obedience mandates. More than 90 percent of local public school districts receive federal funds under the Elementary and Secondary Education Act (now called Every Student Succeeds Act). These funds are especially important when a state supreme court has found, as some have, that the level of school funding provided by its state legislature is unconstitutionally discriminatory or inadequate.[31]

The federal government provides $60 billion a year for transportation, about 25 percent of state and local spending on infrastructure, including grants for airport improvement and mass transit.[32] Disbursement of these funds is freighted with presidential political power and discretion.

State constitutions and laws require at least forty-five states to balance their budgets every year.[33] An unintended consequence of these provisions renders many states more dependent on the federal government, to which they must plead for funding in order to avoid raising state taxes or cutting popular programs. Such budget-balancing laws, as Harvard economist Edward Glaeser warns, "have turned state governments into mendicants," pleading for support from the president and Congress.[34]

Many cities and localities, including New York and Los Angeles, receive at least 10 percent of their budgets from Washington, turning them into supplicant cities. Chicago got more than $1.3 billion in federal grants in 2016, 15 percent of its budget.[35] These amounts do not include the money localities receive through federal grants to their states. Cities look to the national government for support for community development, mass transit, school, police, and prosecutorial budgets. Funding for programs such as these can give the federal executive branch significant influence over the economic and social development of many cities. President Obama's administration promulgated a rule in 2015 that conditioned Housing and Urban Development grants on building public housing in more affluent areas.[36]

Congress includes mandates in its legislation and appropriations, but most are spelled out in executive branch rules and regulations, presidential executive orders and memoranda, and departmental directives. Of course, there is plenty of political and policy wrangling, but the president and the feds have the funds, and in this case possession is nine-tenths of the law. An administration's interpretations of the requirements of legislation and appropriations are powerful weapons in the president's political armory. The president can achieve broad policy initiatives by attaching a requirement loosely related to the purpose of a grant, sometimes something never originally contemplated in the law Congress enacted.

Fear of losing federal funds is a powerful incentive for states. In 1984, Congress mandated that states pass a law establishing a drinking age of twenty-one or forfeit 10 percent of their federal highway funds.[37] Even though this federal money amounted to only 2 percent of the average state's total highway funding, all states promptly enacted laws prohibiting the sale of alcohol to individuals under twenty-one years of age.

President Trump has threatened to eliminate federal grants for cities and states that refuse to cooperate with federal efforts to enforce immigration laws.[38] Several localities have bowed to Trump's demands and threatening tweets regarding this. Miami-Dade County mayor Carlos Giménez changed existing policy by instructing local authorities to work closely with federal officials to enforce immigration laws.[39] Michigan's capital city of Lansing voted to rescind its sanctuary city status in response to the threatened loss of federal funding.[40] The 2017 application for the Department of Justice community policing funds conditions such grants on jurisdictions sharing the immigration status of criminally detained individuals with federal enforcement officials.[41]

Yet, as states well know, what one president or department head imposes administratively can be changed or revoked by the stroke of a pen by a subsequent one. Secretary of Education Betsy DeVos announced that on her watch she would leave to the states the determination whether a private school receiving federal funds was discriminating against LGBTQ students. With that, she reversed the Obama Education Department's administrative ruling that the federal government would make such determinations.[42]

14

PRESIDENTIAL PREEMPTION AND PREROGATIVES

Presidents have another potent method to tell states what to do: preemption. Preemption is the invalidation of a state law that conflicts with a federal law. This is based on the supremacy clause of the Constitution (Article VI, clause 2):

> This Constitution, and the laws of the United States which shall be made in pursuance thereof . . . shall be the supreme law of the land; and the judges in every state shall be bound thereby, anything in the Constitution or laws of any State to the contrary notwithstanding.

With this power, the federal government can negate state laws contrary to its policy aims. Historically, Congress was the branch of government that preempted state laws through its legislation. The Voting Rights Act of 1965, for example, preempted state laws that restricted a citizen's right to vote. Although aimed at protecting African Americans in the southern states, the law applied to all citizens in all states.

More recently, presidents have used preemption to negate state laws based on a specific authorization of Congress or an inherent or claimed executive power. They do this through rules and regulations promulgated by executive branch departments and administrative agencies to interpret and implement federal legislation. The George W. Bush administration, through the National Highway Traffic Safety Administration and Consumer Product Safety Commission, preempted state laws that had permitted tort claims against products that met federal safety standards.[1] In the Obama administration, the Environmental Protection Agency issued regulations to preempt state laws that contradicted its finding that a particular chemical presented an unreasonable risk.[2] In 2017, the Trump administration, via the Department of Energy, floated a proposal to preempt state laws that required utility companies to derive a prescribed portion of their energy from renewable sources.[3]

PRESIDENTIAL PREROGATIVES

Presidents also have the ability to direct into particular states a significant portion of billions of federal dollars. Although Congress appropriates the funds for specific programs, the president often has the last word about where the money is spent. This can be determined through rules and regulations interpreting laws and implementing policies and through specifying how and where contracts and grants are awarded.

The economic significance of modest amounts of federal dollars is enormous. They can easily make or break a state or local economy.[4] They can determine whether a state or city will go bankrupt, or be required to slash public services or raise taxes significantly to maintain them. For example, the North Carolina Department of Commerce analyzed the importance of $10 billion of defense spending in the state in 2014. The direct and indirect economic impact, including salaries, pensions, contracts, and local revenue, amounted to $34 billion and supported more than 500,000 jobs.[5] That spending alone accounted for about 10 percent of North Carolina's economy.

With so much more money to sweep up in the corridors of power in the nation's capital, it's not surprising that more than one thousand states and localities have representatives lobbying the White House and Congress.[6] States and localities reported spending $640 million on registered federal lobbyists from 2009 to 2016.[7] If the time of others who lobby and prepare registered lobbyists to make the case to the White House, executive branch appointees, and congressional staffers is included, the actual figure certainly exceeds a billion dollars. Lobbying for federal funds with as few strings as possible tends to be job number one for many states, cities, and counties. And the president and his executive branch departments and agencies have the most to say about how long, thick, and taut those strings will be.

I write this section not as an attack on federal spending and mandates. They are generally necessary, sometimes innovative, and usually essential to ensure the fair and effective delivery of often desperately needed services. I am proud to be considered one of the architects of the Great Society social and economic programs. When executed properly, such federally initiated and supported programs can allow states the leeway to be, as Supreme Court justice Louis Brandeis wrote, "laboratories [for] . . . social and economic experiments."* This can be seen in the waivers included in the initial 1965 Medicaid law. These waivers have allowed states to experiment with different initiatives that "are likely to assist in promoting the [program's] objectives." Similar

---

*Dissent in *New State Ice Co. v. Liebmann*, 285 U.S. 262 (1932).

provisions to encourage state experimentation were incorporated into President Clinton's welfare reform and President Obama's health care acts. Such provisions preserve a state's obligation to fulfill its responsibility under these laws, but with the freedom to seek more cost-effective and caring ways to provide services for the needy in health care, social services, welfare payments, and public and low-income housing.

I write this section as an alert for citizens that the extent of federal funding of state and local government activities leaves these jurisdictions singularly susceptible to POTUS power and discretion, and to changes in the federal budget. I hope you see this chapter, and this entire book, as a call for citizens to carefully select and monitor individuals seeking and winning federal, state, and local offices and political party leadership posts. Whatever a citizen's tilt—right or left, liberal or conservative, middle-of-the-road or libertarian—and whether we admire or abhor those in public office, all eyes should be sensitive to the centralization of power. We must monitor such centralization both vertically—federal, state, and local, as set forth in this part—and horizontally: executive, legislative, judicial, as set forth in the first three parts. We the people are responsible to ensure that power is exercised with compassion and competence.

The next part exposes how money is diluting the potency of your vote, which is the source of your power to fulfill that responsibility.

PART V

MONEY: THE ROOT OF POLITICAL EVIL

DAY OF POLITICAL INFAMY

Elective politics has always been something of a money game, whether played at the federal, state, or local level.

In the 1896 presidential campaign, the eventual winner, William McKinley, raised more than $3 million in corporate campaign contributions, six times the haul of the defeated populist William Jennings Bryan, who had charged that his opponent would "crucify mankind on a cross of gold." After Bryan's defeat, his campaign manager said, "All questions in a democracy [are] questions of money."[1] Lyndon Johnson complained repeatedly how demeaning it was for presidents to solicit big donors for campaign contributions. Jesse Unruh, the legendary California Democratic leader, quipped that "money is the mother's milk of politics," never mentioning how rancid much of the milk is.* Eventually a few reforms found their way into the Federal Election Campaign Act of 1971 and subsequent amendments passed in the wake of the Watergate scandal. But politicians have long regarded them as more loophole than law.[2]

---

*When he was California State Assembly leader, Unruh did tell colleagues, "If you can't take their money, drink their booze, eat their food, screw their women, and vote against them, you don't belong here."

Then came January 30, 1976, a date which will live in political infamy. That was the day the Supreme Court gave money First Amendment rights. The high court rendered its decision in *Buckley v. Valeo*, the lawsuit filed a year earlier against Francis Valeo, the secretary of the Senate and an ex officio member of the newly created Federal Election Commission. Among the several plaintiffs were James Buckley, a US senator from New York, a hawkish member of the Conservative Party, and the brother of the right-wing icon William F. Buckley; US senator Eugene McCarthy, an antiwar activist and a leftist democrat from Minnesota; the mightily liberal American Civil Liberties Union; and the mightily conservative Libertarian Party.[3]

In concluding that political money is a form of free speech protected by the First Amendment, the Supreme Court struck down three amendments to the Federal Election Campaign Act. They had imposed limits on total spending—by a candidate's campaign, by a candidate out of his or her own pocket, and by individuals or groups independent of the candidate. With this decision the highest court sowed the financial seeds that grew into the tree of political evil.

Removing any limit on what a candidate could spend on a campaign fertilized a relentless drive to raise money. By eliminating the lid on independent expenditures, the court plowed the political field for its 2010 *Citizens United* decision, which spawned rows of "independent" super political action committees (super PACs) spending hundreds of millions of dollars on federal, state, and local election campaigns. In 2016 federal campaigns alone, about $6.5 billion were spent.[4] Some $4.1 billion were spent on House and Senate races. Another $2.4 billion were put into the presidential race, in which one of the general election candidates spent only $350 million.[5] That $6.5 billion is more than the entire 2017 budget of Delaware, Mississippi, New

Hampshire, South Dakota, Vermont, or the National Cancer Institute.[6]

The daunting dollars needed to mount a successful political campaign place immense influence in the hands of the few with fistfuls of cash. Raising big political bucks forces aspiring politicians to pucker up to wealthy individuals and institutions, or to fund their own campaigns, something only the rich can do. From the contest for the highest office in the land down to races for seats on city councils or local school boards, private political contributions matter.

The quest for political money may grease the way for a candidate to get to Washington, but it clogs the gears needed for functional government and distorts policies, whether conservative or liberal. That quest consumes time that might otherwise be spent working with colleagues. It often requires senators and representatives to walk on eggshells in order to avoid upsetting some special interest that can help fund an opponent in an upcoming primary or reelection campaign. A president's power to raise money for members of Congress can be a Godfather-like offer to lock up a vote, far more persuasive than any sound policy argument.

Campaign spending is just one head of the money monster. After first contributing to candidates, deep-pocket institutions and single-issue mavens also hire lobbyists to ensure they get a return on their investments in those who win elections. The thousands of lobbyists and related professionals employed by large corporations and wealthy individuals in our nation's capital outnumber the staffers that serve senators and representatives. Former members of Congress and Capitol Hill aides can triple and quadruple their income by joining K Street lobbying firms. Indeed, many see jobs on Capitol Hill as springboards to careers at those firms. True believers in particular policies can join think tanks funded by affluent individuals and organizations that span the political spectrum from left to right to libertarian, such as the Brookings Institution, the Urban Institute, the American Enterprise Institute, the Heritage Foundation, and the Cato Institute. They can sign up with privately funded single-issue organizations like Planned Parenthood and right-to-life groups that promote causes by influencing public opinion through social media, grassroots organizing, and advertising campaigns.

All these branches of the political money tree in the nation's capital have made the Washington, DC, metropolitan area into the wealthiest in the nation.[7]

THE MONEY GAME

Thirty years ago, donations from individuals in the top .01 percent of political donors accounted for 15 percent of all money contributed to federal campaigns, political parties, and outside groups. Today those individuals' donations account for 40 percent of such contributions. This does not include the many millions more that these individuals give to so-called dark money groups, which need not reveal the identities of their donors.[1]

DIRECT CAMPAIGN FUNDING

With the $5,400 Federal Election Commission limit for individual contributions to a candidate's political campaign, how can a single donor fork over a few hundred thousand dollars to a presidential candidate?

For years there was a limit on the total aggregate amount an individual could contribute to national parties and federal candidates during a two-year election cycle. In 2014, the Supreme Court struck down that aggregate limit in *McCutcheon v. Federal Election Commission*. But the $5,400 cap on what an individual could contribute to a candidate's political campaign remained.

With that cap in place, how can George Clooney and Barbra Streisand and a host of other Hollywood celebrities pay three or four hundred thousand dollars to have dinner with Hillary Clinton? Or a group of conservative fat cats like Charles Koch and the Houston Texans' owner, Bob McNair, put up similar amounts for dinner with Donald Trump?[2]

Here's how:

An individual may donate up to $5,400 directly to a candidate's campaign fund, $2,700 each for the primary and general election.[3]

That same individual may donate $10,000 to each of the fifty state political parties and $33,400 to a national political party.[4]

State party committees can then transfer unlimited amounts to national party committees, which may use such funds for a presidential candidate.

Thus a presidential candidate can hold fund-raisers at which an individual can fork over several hundred thousand dollars for a seat at a dinner table or a place to stand at a cocktail reception. See the footnote, for example, for an illustration of an event in which thirty-two states agreed to transfer $10,000 donations they received to the Democratic National Committee for Hilary Clinton's campaign.* The Republican Trump used a similar system for his high-roller fund-raising events.[5]

---

*Hillary Clinton money pyramid.

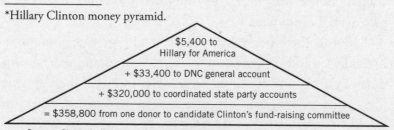

$5,400 to Hillary for America

+ $33,400 to DNC general account

+ $320,000 to coordinated state party accounts

= $358,800 from one donor to candidate Clinton's fund-raising committee

Source: Chart similar to one from the Sunlight Foundation, based on data from the Federal Elections Commission.

In 2014, after the Supreme Court decision in *McCutch-eon*, Congress attached a midnight rider to its adjournment-eve omnibus bill. That rider increased to more than $100,000 the amounts that an individual may contribute to each party's national convention fund, and each party's Senate and House campaign committee's legal and building funds.* Members were quick to take advantage of this midnight rider. In early 2017, Wisconsin Republican and Speaker of the House Paul Ryan asked individuals for checks totaling $247,700 and set forth the breakdown in the fine print of his request: $5,400 to his campaign committee, $5,000 to his Leadership PAC, $33,900† to the National Republican Congressional Committee (NRCC), $101,700 to the NRCC legal fund, $101,700 to the NRCC building fund.[6] More than half of the $17 million Speaker Ryan raised in the first quarter of 2016 came in checks of $50,000 or more.[7]

This situation allows big-money donors to play the campaign finance laws like a game of political three-card monte—with the average American voter as the sucker.

SUPER PACS

Political money spent by individuals or super PACs is considered "outside" or "independent" spending. The Supreme Court decision in *Buckley* lifted the statutory lid on such spending. Millions of dollars have since been deployed to create "issue ads," which do not require a candidate to express support for their message or explicitly state, "Vote for Candidate X." Most of these ads have

---

*All amounts increase with inflation.

† The amount an individual can donate to the national party committees in 2017.

been negative, like the notoriously effective 1988 Willie Horton TV ad. It was about a convict who raped and murdered a young woman. He committed the crime when free on a weekend state furlough, a program established by the Democratic presidential candidate Michael Dukakis while governor of Massachusetts. Republican presidential candidate George H. W. Bush's campaign team created this ad, but its broadcasting costs were paid by an independent group.[8]

To curb the use of money for such "issue ads," the 2002 Bipartisan Campaign Reform Act limited independent expenditures to support candidates in federal elections.[9] In 2007, the Supreme Court found such limits unconstitutional. In 2010, the Supreme Court, in *Citizens United v. FEC*, gave nonprofit and for-profit corporations, as well as unions, First Amendment rights to spend unlimited amounts from their corporate treasuries to influence elections, as long as these organizations did not coordinate directly with a candidate.[10] In his 5–4 majority opinion, Justice Anthony Kennedy, writing that expenditures independent of the candidate "do not give rise to corruption or the appearance of corruption," sprinkled First Amendment baptismal water on super PACs.[11] *Citizens United* opened the way for subsequent judicial and Federal Election Commission decisions to remove all limits on amounts that individuals can spend on independent efforts to influence federal campaigns.[12]

In 2010, in the first few months after *Citizens United*, super PACs spent $62 million on federal elections.[13] In the two-year 2011–12 election cycle, they spent $609 million.[14] In the 2015–16 election campaigns, super PACs spent $1.1 billion of the $1.7 billion they raised for federal election campaigns.[15] *More than $500 million of this total was raised from just sixteen individuals and their spouses. The top one hundred individual and* *institutional donors put more than $1 billion into super PACs in 2016.*[16]

On paper, the claims of these super PACs to be independent of any candidate was central to the Supreme Court's rationale for vesting their unlimited spending with First Amendment rights. In fact, most if not all super PACs are ideological intimates and covert colleagues of the candidates they support. When a candidate is contemplating a run for office, one of her or his first actions is to create a supportive super PAC—often headed by a former aide so that the "possible" candidate can overtly control the super PAC until he or she formally enters the race. Politically hip office seekers like Governor Jeb Bush delay their official announcement in order to keep soliciting big donations before giving their super PAC its independence.[17] The candidate's campaign committee posts B-roll footage from filming sessions online for the super PAC to use in order to create campaign ads. The committee also puts the candidate's schedule online so that the super PACs can help gin up crowds at speeches and other candidate events.[18] Super PACs host their own fund-raisers and conference calls with the candidate appearing as a special guest. Some super PACs place the results of expensive polling data on Twitter accounts known only to campaign aides of candidates they support.[19]

Ideological super PACs tend to pull candidates to the outlying edges on issues and to demand they take no-compromise positions. A candidate may personally be moderate on gun control or pro-choice on abortion, but he or she will not risk upsetting the National Rifle Association or NARAL by exhibiting any flexibility, especially in primaries. In such situations, the big money committed to one side of a particular issue tramples over the grass in the middle ground. Eventually, the middle ground is barren.

DARK MONEY

Super PACS are required to disclose names of their donors. But for those who want to lurk in the darkest alleys of our political system there are "dark money" organizations, which also can raise and spend unlimited amounts but do not have to disclose their donors. Since 2011, more than three-quarters of a billion dollars in dark money has been spent on federal elections.[20]

A loophole in campaign finance rules exempts certain non-profit organizations from disclosure requirements. This includes 501(c)(4) groups, which are technically classified as "social welfare organizations," 501(c)(5) organizations (unions), and 501(c)(6) (trade associations like the Chamber of Commerce).[21]

These organizations are allowed to spend unlimited amounts on advocacy.* They can purchase ads that voters will see but have no way of knowing who funded. Dark money groups can donate funds they've raised from anonymous sources to super PACs. In this maddening political maze, the super PAC can then purchase an advertisement, but anyone who tries to identify that super PAC's dark money donors will run into a dead end.

A TV ad arguing that climate change isn't a serious problem loses some credibility when a viewer sees "Paid for by the National Coal Association." But when it is broadcast by a dark money organization named "Americans for Fresh Air," viewers can easily be misled. Dark money is an ideal way for anonymous donors to finance down-and-dirty ads and material. Ironically, in the Supreme Court's *McCutcheon* decision finding limits on aggregate amounts an individual could contribute to political campaigns unconstitutional, Chief Justice John Roberts wrote,

---

*501(c)(4) groups may devote only 50 percent of their total spending on political activities.

"With modern technology, disclosure now offers a particularly effective means of arming the voting public with information."[22] Perhaps he didn't know about dark money.

WHERE DOES ALL THIS MONEY GO?

Forty-two percent of the money spent by all major-party presidential candidates during the 2016 primary and general election went to purchase media time, largely on television but also on radio and the internet, and in print publications.[23] In their campaigns, Hillary Clinton and Donald Trump each devoted nearly 60 percent of their campaign spending to ad buys.[24] In 2012, Obama devoted 71 percent of his spending to advertising, Romney 39 percent.[25]

Political spending on television ads has soared from about $2.6 billion in 2008 to $4.4 billion in 2016.[26] In 2008, half of all campaign ads were negative. In 2012, 85 percent of ads paid for by super PACs and other outside groups were negative.[27]

Hillary Clinton devoted 20 percent of her money for staff salaries. Trump used the same percentage to hire high-priced political consultants. For travel, Clinton spent 6 percent; Trump, 13 percent.[28]

Super PACs with big bucks purchase expensive donor lists and likely voter registries. They buy state-of-the-art voter identification networks, which gather slews of data about individuals and pinpoint those likely to vote for the candidate who takes the position held by the funder. Targeting such individuals with phone calls and canvassers enables candidates to stick to their funder's position and garner the support of a relatively thin slice of voters.

Senator Bernie Sanders did not depend on fistfuls of super PAC money. Indeed, he attacked the influence of big-money donors. He tapped into the internet to raise millions of dollars in small donations and enlist an army of tech-savvy young voters. Trump used his ability to command incessant media coverage in lieu of political ads. Future presidential candidates will learn from the experience of these two, but so will the media. Coverage is not likely to be as lopsided as it was in terms of the time given to Trump's antics and rallies. Social media will not be so youth oriented or dominated by one or two candidates in terms of fund-raising and communications.

CONCENTRATION IN SWING STATES

Raising large amounts of money from a limited number of donors helps presidential candidates amass the resources and save the time to concentrate campaigns in the highly competitive battleground states where elections are won or lost. In 2016, the presidential race was fought in fourteen states where 35 percent of all eligible voters live. In the general campaign, 99 percent of all presidential TV spending and 95 percent of all campaign visits were in those states. In four—Florida, North Carolina, Ohio, and Pennsylvania—71 percent of TV ad money was spent and 57 percent of candidate appearances occurred.[29] In 2012, there were similar concentrations of campaign TV spending and presidential candidate appearances in the battleground states.[30]

PRESIDENTIAL FUND-RAISING

Presidential fund-raising begins the day after the election to his or her first term. It starts with soliciting money for the inauguration, and big corporate and individual donors stand in line to contribute.

For his 2009 inauguration, President Obama established a $50,000 cap on individual donations and refused to accept donations from corporations, although he did take money from corporate executives and lobbyists. He raised $4.5 million, 10 percent of the total collected, from the financial services industry, which was lobbying to shape the Wall Street reform legislation percolating on Capitol Hill.[31] After four years in office and a successful $1 billion reelection campaign, President Obama lifted the limits for his second inauguration. For his 2013 inaugural festivities, he increased the cap on individual donations to $250,000 and accepted unlimited corporate amounts. President George W. Bush set individual and organization caps at $100,000 for his first inauguration in 2001, $250,000 for his second.[32]

For inauguration bragging rights, President Donald Trump placed no limits on individual or corporate donations and raised more than $100 million, including twenty donations of at least $1 million and a $5 million haul from the Las Vegas casino magnate Sheldon Adelson.[33] Trump doubled the previous record for inauguration fund-raising and quadrupled the amount President Bill Clinton had raised just twenty years earlier.[34]

After assuming office, presidents continue raising political money to boost their own campaign coffers as well as to help the down-ballot candidates of their party, particularly senators and representatives. With razor-wire partisanship, ideological polarization, and rocketing campaign costs, presidents, like members of Congress, have been committing more time to fund-raising, inevitably at the expense of policy making. President Ronald Reagan attended 80 fund-raisers for himself, his party, or another candidate during his first term in office. That number has risen with every subsequent president. During his first term, George

H. W. Bush attended 137 fund-raising events; Clinton, 167; George W. Bush, 173; Barack Obama, 310.[35] The two-term record goes to Bill Clinton, who attended 638 fund-raisers during his tenure, but Barack Obama is close behind.[36]

THE HIGH COST OF RUNNING FOR CONGRESS

Why do congressional candidates need to raise so much money?

Television and, increasingly, digital media advertising costs are enormous and rising. Outside money can be beneficial in purchasing advertisements, but a candidate needs direct donations to his campaign to pay campaign staff and consultants, rent headquarters, conduct polling, purchase merchandise, hire canvassers, cover travel costs, and host events.

In 2016, the average winning candidate for a seat in the House of Representatives spent $1.5 million in campaign funds, which comes out to raising almost $15,000 a week, every week of the two-year term. The average victorious Senate candidate raised $10.5 million, more than $30,000 a week for an incumbent, every week during the six-year term.[37] For incumbents, those are big chunks of time that might otherwise be spent focusing on issues. For all candidates, it's a definite distraction.

The hefty sums needed for Senate and House campaigns push candidates to solicit money from super PACs and other independent, single-issue organizations, usually beyond their states and districts. For incumbents and those newly elected to office, that fund-raising may make them less responsive to the needs of their voting constituents and more responsive to interests with deep pockets. This is especially true in the Senate, where control is in play just about every two years. In the Pennsylvania Senate race between the Republican Pat Toomey, who was reelected, and the Democrat Katie McGinty, $168 million was spent to determine the winner. Some $120 million, or almost three-fourths of the money spent, came from super PACs and other independent institutions.[38] In the state of New Hampshire (population 1.3 million), more than $125 million was spent on its 2016 senatorial election. Almost three-fourths was from super PACs and independent committees, most of it from out-of-state sources. In Nevada, 75 percent of the $120 million invested in the 2016 Senate election was from big-money sources, most pouring in from out of state.[39]

Races for seats in the US House of Representatives are not as costly. Nevertheless, the lion's share of funds in these contests often comes from independent committees and dark money groups. For example, the races for representatives in the Minnesota Eighth and Virginia Tenth Districts each saw $22 million spent in total, 71 percent and 65 percent respectively from super PACS and similar sources, largely from out of state.[40] Of the $50 million spent on the 2017 special election in Georgia's Sixth District (the most expensive House race ever), half came from super PACs and similar sources. Seventy percent of large individual contributions came from out-of-state donors.[41] The amount of money flooding the district led one local Atlanta-area station to add an additional nightly news broadcast in order to have more ad slots to sell to the campaigns and outside groups.[42]

Party caucuses seeking control of the Senate and House have turned the Capitol into a congressional fund-raising pressure cooker, where wealthy donors and super PACs provide a relatively high return for the time and attention of candidates seeking political money. In a scathing speech during a 2016 forum at the University of Pennsylvania, Trevor Potter, a former commissioner of the Federal Election Commission, said:

The system we have has made [Congress members'] real job raising campaign funds for their own campaign committees, leadership PACs, super PACs, and party committees. What Senator [Tim] Wirth calls their "part time" job is serving as members of Congress—researching and understanding legislation, attending committee hearings and markups, working with fellow members. It is the time for these activities—central to the job of legislating—that has been robbed by the current world of almost full-time fund-raising. And our democracy and legislative process are the losers.[43]

MONEY OPENS DOORS AND EARS

For the political contributor, money ensures better access to politicians, more time, and a more timely ability to "make the case" on a piece of legislation or for a presidential favor. More subtle than the flat-out bribe or the quid pro quo favor, money can assure ready access for wealthier individuals and institutions to whisper in the ear of an attentive officeholder.

People with access to politicians can influence the way a bill is drafted, the questions asked during committee hearings, and the public speeches of a senator or representative. They can suggest language in a committee report that might be used to determine the meaning of an ambiguous clause in a statute. They can ask a member to insert into the *Congressional Record* a floor speech about legislation that attorneys can later use in court or before administrative agencies drafting implementing regulations. In short, access can rig the system against those who have none.

Senator John McCain admitted during floor debate on his Bipartisan Campaign Reform Act in 1999 (eventually passed in 2002):

I have personally experienced the pull from campaign staff alerting me to a call from a large donor. I do not believe that any of us privileged enough to serve in this body would ever automatically do the bidding of those who give. I do not believe that contributions are corrupting in that manner. But I do believe they buy access. I do believe they distort the system. And I do believe, as I noted, that all of us, including myself, have been affected by this system.[1]

Both Democratic and Republican leaders in the House and Senate offer increased access to top party leaders like committee chairs and ranking members in return for political contributions. In a dissenting opinion in 2007, Supreme Court justice David Souter expressed concern about the "pervasive distortion of electoral institutions by concentrated wealth, the special access and guaranteed favor that sap the representative integrity of American government and defy public confidence in institutions."[2]

The National Republican Senatorial Committee sent out flyers in 2017 offering certain levels of donors the chance to interact with GOP senators and their "Chiefs of Staff, Leadership Staff, and Committee Staff."[3] Democratic House and Senate leaders offer the same kind of special access. On the presidential level, leaked emails from the Democratic National Committee in 2016 showed communications between large donors and committee officials in which donors sought access to Obama administration staff, often reminding the committee how much money they had raised for the party. The committee kept extensive dossiers on large donors. These dossiers included the amount of money it could still draw from them as well as their particular policy interests.[4]

INFLUENCE OF INDIVIDUALS ON ELECTIONS AND POLICY

The top individual spenders on the 2016 federal elections, the conservative Sheldon Adelson and the liberal Tom Steyer, each contributed more than $80 million to candidates, political action committees, and super PACs. For 2016 state and local elections, the prize goes to the Koch brothers, who invested millions in candidates' campaigns.[5] These donors give to candidates who support their positions on particular issues.

The proliferation of big-money individual and PAC donors with personal agendas increases the number of candidates and their longevity in primary campaigns. A wealthy angel can finance primary candidates no matter how low they are in the polls or unlikely to win a nomination. Twelve Republican candidates took part in the 2016 Iowa caucuses.[6] The month before the caucuses, super PACs underwrote 96 percent of TV ads supporting Jeb Bush, John Kasich, and Chris Christie. Governor John Kasich spent none of his campaign funds on ads in New Hampshire, yet super PACs bankrolled some $10 million of ads supporting him.[7] Sheldon Adelson funded Newt Gingrich's 2012 anti-Romney campaign, including a timely $5 million donation just before the South Carolina primary to bolster Gingrich's dwindling coffers.[8]

Thanks to this bevy of wealthy political angels, the wake-up call for presidential primary positioning comes earlier and earlier. Candidates hunt down well-to-do donors years before the first vote is cast. Some insiders call this hunt "the Adelson Primary" and "the Koch Primary." Upon launching his long-shot bid for the 2016 GOP presidential nomination, South Carolina moderate Senator Lindsey Graham admitted, "the race for billionaires, it's changed everything."[9] Candidates tailor their pitches for money to the interests of potential givers.

BIG UNIONS AND LARGE INDUSTRIES

On one level, the Supreme Court was correct in *Citizens United*: big labor unions and large industries know how to make their voices heard on Capitol Hill.

Big labor unions have both money and campaign workers to put muscle behind their words. New Jersey Democratic senator Cory Booker offers a glimpse of the power of the National Education Association and American Federation of Teachers to humiliate, if that's what it takes, in order to corral a vote they want. In this case, it was a vote against the confirmation of Trump's secretary of education nominee, Betsy DeVos, a strong supporter of school choice, charter schools, and school vouchers. As Newark mayor, Booker sat on a pro–school choice board chaired by Ms. DeVos. He publicly touted his record promoting "real school choice," like charter schools. But Senator Booker chucked his support of charter schools and school vouchers when he cast his vote against confirming DeVos in order to position himself as a candidate for the Democratic presidential nomination in 2020. Humble political pie was easy to eat when flavored with the money and campaigning potential of teachers' unions for Booker's presidential ambitions.

Lee Drutman, in his book *The Business of America Is Lobbying*, estimates that in 2015 businesses accounted for 80 percent of the $3.2 billion in *reported* federal lobbying activities. He writes that unions and public-interest groups spent one dollar for every thirty-four business dollars.[10] Some individual business entities have more than one hundred registered lobbyists prowling the corridors of Congress. Business interests also accounted for the lion's share of the $1.5 billion reportedly spent that year on lobbying state and local governments.

Shortly after Tom Donohue became president of the US Chamber of Commerce in 1998, he wrote:

> My goal is simple—to build the biggest gorilla in town—the most aggressive and vigorous business advocate our nation has ever seen. I want to reach the point where each time our policymakers are prepared to act, they stop themselves and say, "Wait a minute. I wonder what the Chamber would think about this?" [11]

And that is what he did.

From 1998, when Donohue became president, to 2016, the Chamber of Commerce has spent some $1.4 billion on lobbying, more than triple the next-highest spender, the National Association of Realtors.[12] The US Chamber of Commerce is technically a 501(c)(6) "business league/trade association," and thus its towering dark money operation is not required to disclose its donors. The Chamber can serve as a proxy for companies that wish to hide the fact that they are lobbying for or against a certain proposal. This shrewd tactic enabled the Chamber to use small-business members, in Donohue's own words, as "foot soldiers, and often the political cover, for the issues big businesses want covered." The Chamber put on this mask as it became involved in opposing the Justice Department's litigation against tobacco industry giants like Altria/Philip Morris.[13] It also wore this mask in lobbying against the Affordable Care Act for certain health industry interests and against environmental regulations on behalf of the oil and gas industry.[14]

Individual industries are big-money lobbyists. Oil and gas companies and associated trade organizations spent $250 million on lobbying from January 2009 to June 2010 to kill the American Clean Energy and Security bill. That's more than $735 per legislator per day.[15] The American Petroleum Institute alone paid at least $40 million in TV advertisements to oppose the same legislation.[16]

With a larger percentage of the oil and gas industry's political donations going to Republicans, its members in Congress have treated the existence of climate change with greater skepticism. From 2000 to 2015, the share of congressional campaign contributions from the oil and gas industry to Republicans increased from around 50 percent in a year to almost 90 percent.[17] Over that same time period, the number of Republican members who advocate legislative action to tackle climate change has decreased.[18] This, even though internal party polls show that two-thirds of registered voters believe climate change should be addressed.[19]

The tobacco industry has continued to wield considerable influence despite the declining public opinion of smoking. The last cigarette tax increase occurred in 2009. In the 2013, 2014, and 2015 negotiations between the House and Senate budget committees, proposed increases in the federal cigarette tax were eliminated, thanks in good part to the industry's $145 million lobbying effort.[20]

STATES, JUDGES, AND THINK TANKS IN THE POLITICAL MONEY MIX

STATE AND LOCAL ELECTIONS

State legislatures have been a political playground where wealthy individuals invest to promote pet projects and ideologies. Over the past five years, the environmentalist Tom Steyer has contributed millions to state legislative candidates who share his views on climate change.[1] The billionaire Ken Griffin donated $20 million to the reelection campaign of Illinois governor Bruce Rauner and several more million to the Illinois Republican Party treasury in an effort to get Republicans elected to the state legislature.[2]

The guys with deep pockets are pumping money into local races, which had for a long time been relatively free of outside dollars. In 2015 and 2016, George Soros donated millions of dollars to elect local prosecutors around the country who supported his version of criminal justice reform and to promote some form of drug decriminalization.[3] In May 2017, Soros put about $1.5 million into a super PAC supporting a like-minded Philadelphia district attorney candidate.[4] In 2015, Walmart heirs Jim and Alice Walton of Arkansas and Eli Broad of California poured $650,000 into a Louisiana super PAC to elect pro–charter school and pro–school voucher candidates to local school boards.[5] Trump's education secretary, Betsy DeVos, has contributed millions in many states to elect pro–school choice candidates in local elections.[6]

STATE BALLOT INITIATIVES

Individual wealth is also used to promote policy goals through ballot initiatives and other state and local measures. Former New York City mayor Michael Bloomberg has dedicated millions to support gun safety measures in various states. In 2016, he spent some $18 million to help pass soda tax initiatives in San Francisco and Oakland.[7] In 2014, the Las Vegas resident Sheldon Adelson spent almost $6 million to defeat a medical marijuana proposal in Florida. Two years later, he put $4 million into killing recreational and medical marijuana legalization proposals in Florida, Massachusetts, and Nevada.[8] The casino owner billionaire has claimed to be "willing to spend whatever it takes" to defeat state ballot initiatives to legalize online gambling, which competes with his casinos' interest.[9] On the other side, the tech sector billionaire Sean Parker donated millions to support California's marijuana legalization ballot initiative in 2016.[10]

POLICY IDEA CENTERS

In their quest to shape public opinion, some of the top one-percenters fund their own think tanks and policy institutes to perform studies and write articles to support their views. The conservative Cato Institute was originally funded by the Koch family, while George Soros has established his own liberal think tank, Open Society Foundations.[11] Some billionaires use their foundations to develop material to support legal challenges they wish to mount to policies whose merits they dispute.

Even the most prestigious think tanks can be influenced by substantial donors, particularly the interests of large corporations. Google and other corporate enterprises often contribute to think tanks of various political shades. The Brookings Institution, the Urban Institute, the Aspen Institute, the Heritage Foundation, and the American Enterprise Institute often select topics for research and discussion that are designed to appeal to big corporate and individual donors, or to challenge or support certain conservative or liberal positions. They hire professional staff with expertise in areas of contemporary public policy and political interest.

JUDICIAL ELECTIONS

Elections of one kind or another for judges are held in thirty-nine states. During their campaigns, judicial candidates express views that signal their leanings in litigation that might come before them if elected. They might say they'll be tough on crime, pro-LGBTQ rights, or severely punish sexual offenders to protect women. Opponents of incumbent judges can win by charging that the incumbent was soft on a drug dealer, murderer, pedophile, or rapist. Candidates and incumbents indicate they may favor protection of corporations from class actions by plaintiffs' attorneys, leniency for addicted drug offenders, or longer sentences for certain crimes.

Spending on state judicial races hit an all-time high in the 2015–16 election cycle, which saw $20 million in TV ads alone by outside groups, up more than 40 percent from the 2013–14 cycle.[12] Most of these ads were purchased by interest groups and individuals outside the state and were overwhelmingly negative. Former White House press secretary and political commentator Bill Moyers stated in 2010 that "there's now a crooked sign hanging on every courthouse in America reading 'Justice for Sale.'"[13]

In the bitter 2016 North Carolina race for a judicial seat likely to ensure control of the state's supreme court, the two competing candidates' campaigns purchased a combined $100,000 in TV ads. But that was chump change compared with independent groups, which spent $2.8 million, about evenly divided between the conservative North Carolina justice Robert Edmunds and the liberal challenger, Judge Michael Morgan, who won.[14]

More than a century ago, Harvard Law School dean Roscoe Pound warned in a speech to the American Bar Association, "Compelling judges to become politicians in many jurisdictions has almost destroyed the traditional respect for the bench."[15]

Almost?

That may be the understatement of the twentieth century.

As former Mississippi Supreme Court justice Olivier Diaz Jr. explained, "Judges who are running for reelection do keep in mind what the next 30-second ad is going to look like."[16] Supreme Court justice Sandra Day O'Connor wrote in a 2003 concurring opinion, "Elected judges cannot help being aware that if the public is not satisfied with the outcome of a particular case, it could hurt their reelection prospects. . . . The cost of campaigning requires judicial candidates to engage in fundraising. Yet relying on campaign donations may leave judges feeling indebted to certain parties or interest groups."[17]

Can the public expect a judge to rule on the merits of a gun rights case when the pro- or antigun control group bankrolled much of his or her election campaign for the judicial seat? In West Virginia, a mining executive, whose company was appealing a $50 million judgment against it, donated $3 million to support one of that state's supreme court candidates, Brent Benjamin, who won. When later faced with the company's appeal of a judgment against it, Benjamin cast the deciding vote to overturn the judgment. The US Supreme Court in a 5–4 decision ruled that Benjamin should have recused himself.[18] That decision leaves open these questions: How big a campaign donation requires an elected judge to recuse him- or herself? Does the amount vary depending on the size of the state, city, or county? Do you have to trace the identities of dark money contributors?

The mere presence of advertising affects the judiciary. Repeated ads accusing judges of being "soft on crime" affect their decisions. Judges facing reelection have been found more likely to impose tougher sentences and less likely to rule for the defendant. There are lives at stake here. A September 2015 Reuters article reported, "In the 37 states that heard capital cases over the past 15 years, appointed judges reversed death sentences 26 percent of the time, judges facing retention elections reversed 15 percent of the time, and judges facing competitive elections reversed 11 percent of the time."[19]

Sadly, the big-money world of ideological manipulation may now taint the US Supreme Court. Through social media or television ads nationally or in the states of marginal senators, special-interest money can be used to shape the public's or a senator's view of a presidential nomination for the Supreme Court and the lower federal courts. Large corporate donors like the Chamber of Commerce can be enlisted to support conservative Supreme Court nominees. Liberal funders like big labor unions and pro-choice groups like NARAL can be signed up to support left-leaning nominees. The 2017 confirmation battle over Neil Gorsuch saw interest groups on the right and the left, and with opposite cultural and religious views on abortion and gun control, spend millions, sometimes through dark money groups, to influence both public opinion and the votes of senators.[20]

It's time for the Supreme Court to scrap as mistaken and bad law the decision in *Buckley v. Valeo*, and its progeny like *Citizens United*. Giving money First Amendment rights has generated a steady rise in soft and hard corruption, fed a decline of trust in government, and made a mockery of the court's one person, one vote decision.

Over the years, Republicans and Democrats have accused each other of blocking campaign finance reforms. There's ample evidence to indict members of Congress in both houses and on both sides of the aisle, as well as every White House, for perpetuating the sordid state of money and politics in federal elections. But the criminal masterminds are the justices of the Supreme Court who have made it impossible for the legislative branch even to consider reforms.

In the worst way, the Supreme Court has the money = speech equation right: money speaks persuasively to politicians who make public policy and enact and execute laws. It's true that the candidate who raises the most money can—and often does—lose the election. But when that candidate wins, the people who were his or her big bankrollers have special access unavailable to the individual voter. By blessing unlimited political contributions, the court has given special interests and single-issue individuals the power to buy that access and undermine the value of the individual citizen's vote.

PART VI

AMERICAN FAULT LINES

THE MEDIA FAULT LINE

The social and media environment in which our national government and federal-state system function creates fault lines that make smooth traveling demanding and treacherous. The depth and breadth of these fault lines calls for creative, robust, and respected leadership to restore and maintain a political landscape of trust.

Trust among institutions and individuals is a sine qua non if political and public policy losers and winners are to believe that their positions have been fairly and fully aired. In such circumstances, all sides are likelier to accept finality in an election, the passage of a law, or a Supreme Court decision, and to move on. Lack of trust among our people deepens and widens fault lines and hikes the risk of permanent fissures in our democracy. It sets the stage for incompetence, corruption, and exploitation by narcissistic political leaders determined to achieve their ends by any and all means.

Once upon a time in America—so long ago that most citizens probably don't know it—commercial television and radio broadcasters were subjected to a federal code of conduct. They had to abide by a fairness doctrine that required them to cover opposing political positions fairly. When they broadcast a president's speeches, they had to give the opposing party equal time to respond. All commercial broadcasters—even top-twenty rock stations—were required to give a certain amount of attention to news.[1]

Ben Bradlee at the *Washington Post* and Abe Rosenthal at the *New York Times* realized that even the most professional reporter might not be objective. But those legendary editors insisted that the news stories in their papers report facts. They limited opinions to their columnists and editorial pages. News chiefs at radio and television networks made sure their reporters stuck to the facts.

The *CBS Evening News* anchor Walter Cronkite was revered because he was seen as fairly reporting hard news. That's why it was such an unusual journalistic moment when Cronkite expressed his opinion that the Vietnam War was a serious mistake. Immediately after he heard it, LBJ said, "When we've lost Cronkite, we've lost the American people." Those were the days when virtually all of us in public life recognized, as New York senator Daniel Patrick Moynihan remarked, that in America "everyone is entitled to their own opinion, but not to their own facts."

Those days are long gone.

There is no Walter Cronkite today.

Now we have a variety of twenty-four-hour cable "news" channels that measure "news" cycles in minutes if not nanoseconds and frame them with combative talking heads. On these channels viewers rarely have to see anything that doesn't mirror their viewpoint. They listen to a cable news station that echoes what they agree with or want to hear. On the right, Fox. On the left, CNN. On the further left, MSNBC.

Pew Research Center researchers and polls reveal the political tunnel vision that has ensued. Forty-seven percent of people who consider themselves consistently conservative say their main source of news is Fox News. Forty percent who consider themselves consistently liberal cite CNN, MSNBC, or National Public Radio as their main source of news.[2] The sorry self-reenforcing consequence is that these organizations market news like a product. They play to the audience that surveys tell them watch their broadcasts and buy their newspapers—or are likeliest to do so. They see their daily viewers and readers as loyal, often lapdog, customers, not conscientious citizens.

These news organizations have moved beyond the understandable Rashomon effect in which reporters, like most witnesses to the same event, genuinely see it from different vantage points. Some may see that as media bias. But today's media bias fault line comes from what stories are chosen for coverage, reporting facts from an angle perceived as likeliest to appeal to targeted viewers, and providing commentary that will reflect and reinforce what its viewers want to see and hear. Watch back-to-back (as I have several times while writing this book) Bret Baier's *Special Report* on Fox News at six p.m. EST and Erin Burnett's *OutFront* CNN broadcast at seven p.m. EST. The stories they cover seem calculated to appeal to and bolster the opinions of conservative (Fox) or liberal (CNN) viewers. On some evenings so few, if any, common events are covered that a visiting newcomer might think they are reporting on two different days. These broadcasts often seem designed not simply to tell viewers what to think about, but how to think about it.

A 2017 study by the Shorenstein Center on Media, Politics, and Public Policy at Harvard University's Kennedy School of Government found that these outlets, CNN and Fox News, differed strikingly in their coverage of President Trump's first one hundred days in office. On CNN, 93 percent of the Trump stories broadcast had a negative tone; on Fox News, only 52 percent had such a tone.[3]

Trump also fared poorly among major-network media. Even before his inauguration, Trump declared war on the national newspapers and television news broadcasts, and they fired back. When looking overall at the seven outlets analyzed for the study, a negative tone existed in 80 percent of the stories run on Trump during his first one hundred days in office, compared with 41 percent for Barack Obama, 57 percent for George W. Bush, and 60 percent for Bill Clinton.[4] Whatever bad press Trump merited and however biased journalists, his assault on the integrity of reporters inside the Washington Beltway intensified their follow-the-pack mentality in the political stories they covered and how they covered them.[5] Trump never forgave the mainstream media for writing him off as not a serious presidential candidate, and the Washington press corps had trouble grasping how the rest of the country could have elected him. Trump's relentless attacks on the media may be stirring a partisan political reaction to the media. In May 2017, the Pew Research Center found that 90 percent of Democrats believe that media criticism "keeps political leaders in line"; only 42 percent of Republicans believe that.[6]

The big three national networks, ABC, CBS, and NBC, which decades ago covered the same facts, find themselves in today's world of declining viewers competing for eyeballs not just with each other, but with PBS and the Fox network, social media, streaming, and instant news on iPhones and desktop computers. This often leads them to prefer sensational headlines or human-interest stories during much of their evening news broadcasts. Most viewers are already aware of the hard news.

Social media offer individuals anonymity, from where they

can post all sorts of charges, countercharges, and YouTube snippets, and create "facts" that attract susceptible partisans. If "fake news" tweeted or published on the internet goes viral, millions of people fall prey to believing it, especially when it fits snugly with their preexisting political positions. Such news can come from domestic or foreign governments as well as the independent media.

The confabulation of these reports—especially from cable news and social media—has created a world in which we can each have our own facts. Indeed, millions of Americans feel entitled to their own facts. They exercise their right to believe what they see on Fox and not what they see on CNN, or vice versa. To keep the shows lively, producers for these cable news stations book potential guests who will express conflicting views and often bring their own facts. Political leaders, policy makers, and even some scientists and academics (or pseudoscientists and pseudoacademics) see their appearances as opportunities to craft their own version of events to bolster their positions. The power of distortion that this atmosphere gives telegenic politicians, pundits, and political celebrities with the loudest trumpets and the most vivid images is enormous. Cole Porter's lyrics in "Anything Goes" capture this make-your-own-facts political world of cable news and social media:

The world has gone mad today
And good's bad today
And day's night today

Presidents have always had a leg up on dominating the news, but modern technology, social media like Twitter and Facebook, and cable news have given them an unprecedented opportunity to promote their own facts, to fake their own news. Donald

Trump's colorful and sometimes abrasive use of tweeting and social media to put forth and promote his alternative facts has introduced to political public relations a tool that future campaigns and White House occupants may find too tempting to resist. More and more senators, House members, and governors are taking to Facebook and making their own posts to amplify their political and public policy positions.

With its First Amendment rights, the press carries the responsibility to call out all presidents when they lie, the ones it likes as well as the ones it can't stand. The press has nailed Trump when he tells whoppers, such as when he said the murder rate in early 2017 was "the highest it's been in forty-seven years" when in fact it was very low, or "Obama released 122 Guantanamo prisoners who returned to the battlefield" when in fact George W. Bush set 113 of them free.[7] Yet the press let Barack Obama's false claims that with his Affordable Care Act "if you like your own doctors, you can keep them," and "if you like your own [health care] plan you can keep it," go virtually unchallenged until well after the health bill had passed.[8] The failure of the press to hold all presidents to the same standard diminishes its credibility.

There are two important things I learned from thoughtful professionals in this field that are critical to understanding the world of communications and reporting today.

The first was a comment by CBS chairman and CEO Leslie Moonves that I heard at the network's 2017 Upfront Presentation at Carnegie Hall: "Everywhere we turn, norms are being redefined and rules are being bent, if not broken," he said. "But one thing is clear. In this fragmented world, the social and economic value of any medium with the power to bring people together is more important than ever." Unfortunately, and intentionally or not, the three cable news channels have used their national platforms to attract and maintain each one's politically narrow slice of viewers and keep them separate and politically apart from the others.

The other comment was from Peggy Noonan in her 2017 commencement address at Catholic University in Washington. She was appalled at the ignorance of history displayed by reporters and office seekers whom she talked and worked with during the 2016 campaign. These reporters and candidates, college graduates in their twenties, thirties, and early forties, she said,

> Got most of what they know about history and the meaning of things through screens. They've seen the movie and not read the book. They've heard the sound bite and not read the speech. They read the headline on *Drudge* or the *Huffington Post* and then jump to another site with more headlines. Their understanding of history, even recent history, is superficial.[9]

The demise of local news harbors another threat to our democratic government. In the decade since 2006, more than one hundred local newspapers have folded, and the number of local newspaper reporters has plummeted from 55,000 to less than 30,000.[10] Without local newspapers to keep their eyes on the hands in local political cookie jars, the experienced newsman Bob Schieffer has warned, "We're going to have corruption at a level we've never experienced because there's nobody there to reveal it."[11] In its final season, the hit HBO show *The Wire* concentrated on the demise of local newspapers. Later the show's cocreator and researcher, former *Baltimore Sun* reporter David Simon, warned that without them it will be "a halcyon era for state and local political corruption . . . one of the great times to be a corrupt politician."[12] Local television stations are not likely to fill the vacuum. To attract viewers, they have long broadcast under a when-it-bleeds-it-leads standard. They feature violent and other attention-grabbing, the-more-bizarre-the-better-the-rating incidents. TV coverage of local elections and local politicians has always been scarce to nonexistent until after the polls close.

The shock of Trump's unexpected victory may well be attributable in good measure to the loss of political coverage by local newspapers and broadcasters. The national, perhaps more accurately, coastal broadcast and print news came from overwhelmingly pro–Hillary Clinton enclaves like Washington, DC, New York, Boston, San Francisco, and Los Angeles. More than 70 percent of the 200,000 internet news employees live and work on the East and West Coasts.[13] Together these sources provided virtually all the national news heard and seen about the presidential election. There was little political news available from local reporters and broadcasters. This local news might have given a sense of the support Trump was assembling in the fly-over middle of America. As Thomas Patterson, the Harvard University Bradlee Professor of Government and the Press, put it:

> Journalists would also do well to spend less time in Washington and more time in places where policy intersects with people's lives. If they had done so during the presidential campaign, they would not have missed the story that keyed Trump's victory—the fading of the American Dream for millions of ordinary people.[14]

RACIAL AND CULTURAL POLITICAL PARTY FAULT LINES

The racial fault line between the two major parties is wide and deep enough to threaten a societal earthquake.

For more than half a century, no Democratic presidential candidate has been able to win a majority of the white vote. Lyndon Johnson was the last one to do so, in his 59 to 41 percent landslide victory over Republican senator Barry Goldwater in 1964. Humphrey came close in 1968 with 48 percent of the white vote, but since then Democratic candidates have been struggling to hang in with percentages in the 30s and low 40s. In every presidential election since 2000, the Republican candidate has captured more than 50 percent of the white vote, nudging 60 percent since 2004.[1]

Johnson was also the first postwar Democratic presidential candidate to win more than 90 percent of the black vote.[2] Since then, Democratic candidates have won more than 80 percent, with Walter Mondale, Al Gore, and Obama capturing 90 percent or more. The African American vote for Republican presidential candidates has been stuck below 20 percent, sometimes descending into single digits.[3]

For Democratic presidential candidates, the turnout of minority voters is crucial. A Brookings Institution analysis of voting in the 2004, 2008, and 2012 presidential elections found that both the percentage won and the turnout of African American voters was the cornerstone of Barack Obama's election. African American turnout was the highest among all racial voting blocs for the first time in 2012. If minority and white turnout had been at 2004 levels, Obama would almost certainly have lost his reelection to Mitt Romney.[4]

In his concession call on election night in 2012, Romney told President Obama that he "really did a good job of getting out the vote in places like Cleveland and Milwaukee." When Obama relayed that comment to his aides, he added, "In other words, black people. That's what he [Romney] thinks this was all about."[5]

If Romney was thinking that, he might have been correct.

Hillary Clinton's loss and Donald Trump's victory in 2016 are largely due to her failure to attract black voters to turn out and vote for her. His shrewd tap into the latent prejudice and frustration of struggling whites who felt like forgotten Americans encouraged high turnout and votes from millions of white men and women. President Trump's cunning political strategy has aggravated the racial political fault line in the nation. The American National Election Study reported that the racial attitudes of white Republicans who voted for their party's candidate and white Democrats who voted for their party's candidate had never been so far apart. Stanford and Michigan University researchers concluded that white Republicans and white Democrats who voted for Donald Trump were motivated by racial bias at least as much as any other factor.[6]

What a contrast from the 1964 presidential campaign! That year, President Lyndon Johnson had driven through Congress the Civil Rights Act prohibiting discrimination in public accommodations and employment. Senator Barry Goldwater had strenuously opposed and voted against it. Then, in a private meeting at the White House three months before the election, Johnson and Goldwater agreed that they would refrain from injecting racial issues into the presidential campaign. In a taped conversation the day after their meeting, Johnson told an aide, "[Goldwater] came in, just wanted to tell me that he was a half-Jew, and that he didn't want to do anything to contribute to any riots or disorders or bring about any violence; because [of] his ancestry, he was aware of the problems that existed in that field, and he didn't want to say anything that would make them any worse."[7] Goldwater recollected in a later oral history interview that "I told [Johnson] I wanted to discuss the racial problem, that I thought it would be wise not to be pushing it. Those were hot days, you know. And he agreed with me."[8]

The contemporary political racial divide poses a persistent and widening fault line in our damaged democracy. Over the quarter century from 1992 to 2016, the white share of Democratic voters fell from 76 percent to 57 percent, while the white share of Republican voters slipped only slightly, from 93 to 86 percent.[9] Democrats experienced a 19-percentage-point decline in white voters, compared with a 7-percentage-point drop for Republicans. This has led one Democratic writer, Steve Phillips, author of *Brown Is the New White*, to urge his party to double down on African American and minority voters and not squander its money on trying to woo back whites who supported Trump in the 2016 election.

After passage of the Voting Rights Act, LBJ repeatedly urged black leaders to "move from protest to politics," from the streets into the voting booths. As African American voters have moved into the Democratic Party, middle- and lower-income white voters have departed for the Republican Party. No wonder that for so many Republicans the equation is black = Democrat. That's a big part of why they jam African Americans into majority-minority districts in states and localities they control.

The ensuing racial disparity between the parties is vividly displayed in the composition of the quadrennial party conventions. In 2016, of the Democrats' 4,766 delegates, 25 percent, or 1,182, were African American; of the Republicans' 2,472 delegates, less than 1 percent, only 18, were black.[10] The makeup of the conventions also exposes a stark difference in Latino representation: 16 percent of Democratic delegates, 5 percent of Republican delegates.[11]

The racial difference is also apparent on the floor of the House of Representatives. In the 2017–18 Congress, a quarter of Democratic House members, 46 of 194, were African American. Less than 1 percent of Republican members, 2 of 241, were black.[12] If the Democrats had controlled the House after the 2016 election, at least six of the twenty standing committees would likely have been chaired by a black member. With a Republican majority, all twenty standing committee chairs are white.[13] For years, African American congressman Jim Clyburn of South Carolina has been a key member of the House Democratic leadership; the leadership has been consistently all white on the Republican side.

A yawning party preference gap also exists for Latino, Asian American, and LGBTQ voters. In 2016, Hillary Clinton captured two-thirds of the Latino and Asian American votes. Donald Trump garnered just 28 percent of the Latino vote and 27 percent of the Asian American vote.[14] With racial political support split so drastically between parties, there is little incentive for either party to compromise on an issue on which these groups have chosen a side, for or against.

Exit polls from the 2012 election reported that gay, lesbian, and bisexual adults voted for Obama over Romney by 76 percent to 22 percent, a three-to-one ratio.[15] It was an even wider gap in the 2016 election, with 77 percent of self-identified LGBTQ members voting for Hillary Clinton, compared with only 14 percent for Trump, a more than five-to-one ratio.* Although only 3 percent of the population, LGBTQ individuals constituted 5 percent of voters in 2016. The non-LGBTQ vote was split evenly between Trump and Clinton, 47 percent each.[16]

THE IMMIGRATION AND RURAL/URBAN DIVIDES

The changing demography of America is provoking racial and ethnic tension and nasty political skirmishes between Democrats and Republicans about immigration policy.

In the late nineteenth and early twentieth centuries, the migration of Irish, Italians, and Eastern European Jews prompted the passage of a national origins quota act.[17] From the mid-1920s to the mid-1960s, that law largely limited immigration to the English and northern Europeans. The 1965 immigration reform act opened the nation to Central and South Americans, Asians, Africans, Pakistanis, Indians, and Middle Easterners.[18] The racial, ethnic, and religious composition of immigrants flipped. In 1965, 85 percent of immigrants were white; 15 percent were nonwhite. Today those percentages are reversed.[19] Over this period, the share of Central and South American immigrants climbed from 9 percent to 52 percent; of South and East Asian immigrants, from 5 percent to 26 percent; and of sub-Saharan immigrants from less than 1 percent to 4 percent.[20] Immigrants rose from 6 percent to 15 percent of the US population.[21]

This change in demographics has hatched a partisan ra-

---

*Prior to 2016, exit polls asked only if an individual was lesbian, gay, or bisexual. They did not ask if a voter was transgender until 2016.

cial divide. Recent immigrants are overwhelmingly black- and brown-skinned, Indian and Asian, and often of the Muslim, Buddhist, or Hindu religion. In the 2016 campaign, Democrats embraced a pro-immigration approach and sympathized with the discrimination claims of these new Americans. This positioning fit nicely into the party's emphasis on identity politics and its overwhelming share of minority voters. Donald Trump played on the fears of white middle- and lower-middle-class Americans that the influx of immigrants threatened their jobs and pay. He tapped into the feeling of many Republicans that, like minorities, white Christians were being discriminated against. Seventy-three percent of Republicans, but only 29 percent of Democrats, identify themselves as white and Christian.[22]

The racial, ethnic, and religious makeup of rural and urban residents, along with their cultural and economic differences, contribute to a political divide reminiscent of the north/south split during the last half of the nineteenth century.

A 2017 Kaiser Family Foundation survey found that 70 percent of white rural residents believe their values differ from those of urban residents. Most white rural Americans feel they are living in a separate and unequal society with different moral standards and fewer attractive opportunities. Rural Americans consider good jobs more difficult to find. They are likelier than city dwellers to believe that they will have to encourage their children to leave the area to find economic opportunity.[23] Perhaps this is why what so many white rural citizens once saw as the American Dream they now experience as a nightmare. Rural sections of the country are 78 percent white; urban areas are only 40 percent white.[24]

The economic and cultural disparity between rural and urban America helps explain the vast political party difference. In 2016, Trump won 62 percent of the vote in rural areas, almost twice

Hillary Clinton's 34 percent. In urban centers Clinton captured 60 percent of the vote, compared with Trump's 35 percent.[25] Clinton won 88 of the nation's 100 most populous counties by a margin of thirteen million votes. Trump won the rest of the country by ten million votes.[26] Colloquially put, Trump won 76 percent of counties with a Cracker Barrel Old Country Store, but only 22 percent of counties with a Whole Foods Market, a 54 percent gap, the widest rural/urban spread ever recorded for a successful presidential candidate.[27]

The Democratic decline in rural areas has been steady for a quarter of a century. Bill Clinton won almost half of the nation's 3,100 counties in his elections in 1992 and 1996. Barack Obama won 700 counties in 2008 and 2012. Hillary Clinton won only 472 in 2016.[28] Hillary Clinton didn't even hire a rural strategist for her campaign staff, as Obama had in his presidential campaigns. She did not dedicate resources to organizations in rural areas.[29]

THE PARTISANSHIP FAULT LINE

Partisanship is metastasizing throughout all branches of federal, state, and local governments and much of the news media. Animosity between the two main political parties as they tilt toward their left and right fringes is spreading like a consuming political weed devouring green grass.

That animosity is getting personal. In 1994, 16 percent of self-identified Democrats and 17 percent of self-identified Republicans surveyed by the Pew Research Center held a "very unfavorable" view of the other party. In 2016, 55 percent of Democrats and 58 percent of Republicans held "very unfavorable" views of the other party, a whopping more than threefold increase.[1] The editorial pages, and often much of the front and national news pages, of the *New York Times* are staunchly liberal. The *Wall Street Journal*'s editorial and most of its op-ed pages are resoundingly conservative.

Sixty-five percent of American adults believe that an individual's politics says a lot about the type of person he or she is.[2] This has led many to associate only with those who share their view. A 2015 study in the *American Journal of Political Science* found that partisan biases are now stronger than racial biases:

Unlike race, gender, and other social divides where group-related attitudes and behaviors are constrained by social norms there are no corresponding pressures to temper disapproval of political opponents. If anything, the rhetoric and actions of political leaders demonstrate that hostility directed at the opposition is acceptable, even appropriate.[3]

In 2010, half of Republicans and one-third of Democrats said they would be somewhat or very unhappy if their child married someone of the opposing political party. In 1960, a mere 4 percent of Democrats and 5 percent of Republicans expressed similar views.[4] In 2016, only 9 percent of couples reported having a spouse or live-in partner who was a member of the opposing political party.[5]

Partisanship not only infects the federal judicial nomination and confirmation process at every level. It also shows up in federal district, appellate, and Supreme Court decisions. It has produced campaigns so bitter and acrid for seats in the Senate and House of Representatives that elected members from different parties sometimes refuse to speak to one another. The Republican Senate leader Mitch McConnell announces his determination to make Obama a one-term president.[6] The Democratic Senate leader Chuck Schumer votes against Senator McConnell's wife for a cabinet position in the Trump administration. That may be the way Senate leaders have long thought and plotted, but they never would have admitted much less expressed it publicly. Gridlock jails one Congress after another.

Donald Trump has crudely tweeted, "If Hillary can't satisfy her husband, what makes her think she can satisfy America" and encouraged chants of "Lock Her Up" at his campaign rallies.[7] Hillary Clinton says, "Trump gives me the creeps," and, "You can put half of Trump supporters into what I call a basket of deplorables."[8] After the election, he keeps running crudely against her, and she announces her availability to lead "the resistance" against his presidency.

The most insidious damage of this politically brutish dialogue may be on the quality of individuals who are eager, even willing, to serve in public life, full or part time, as legislators, judges, or executive branch appointees. Public service harbors the risk of becoming involved in an ultimate fighting cage match.

Fear of a partisan attack based on some obscure past slip by a potential candidate for an executive post has engendered an elaborate clearance process. The president and White House personnel office delay sending a nominee to the Senate or naming individuals to the hundreds of high executive branch posts that do not require Senate confirmation until their lives have been meticulously vetted. More than 1,200 executive branch appointments require Senate approval, and nominating any individual can degenerate into a vicious proxy war.[9] Six months into Trump's presidency, several cabinet departments had no one requiring Senate confirmation in place except their cabinet officer.[10] Thanks to administration laxity and Senate partisanship, many departments and agencies are frozen in place. They are in the control of career bureaucrats who may have their own agendas or are reluctant to take any action lest it harm them with their new bosses. Even when presidents name White House aides, or cabinet officers appoint personal assistants to temporarily oversee an agency, new policies rarely get put in place, much less executed. The impact of presidential elections and the power of voters expressed through the ballot box to produce policy changes are thus undermined.

The confirmation rate of executive branch nominees has been consistent over the past few decades, in the 70 to 80 percent range. But the time it takes to get from vacancy to confirmation and the required paperwork have grown enormously and unacceptably: from an average of two months during the Kennedy administration to more than eight months during Obama's.[11] Administrations are taking longer to propose a nominee. Senate committee members spatter executive branch confirmation hearings with gotcha questions and efforts to elicit commitments on future policies. Even though Senator Ted Kennedy and I held similar public policy views, he questioned me for hours during my confirmation hearings as the nominee for secretary of health, education, and welfare in an incessant but unsuccessful effort to extract my commitment to take actions he wanted.

When positions go unfilled, agencies can be dangerously understaffed. In 2005, only a third of Federal Emergency Management Agency (FEMA) positions were filled when Hurricane Katrina ripped through New Orleans and Mississippi.[12] During the 2009 bank bailout, Treasury Secretary Timothy Geithner had no undersecretary or assistant secretary for financial markets, financial stability, or financial affairs.[13] Several months after his election, Donald Trump had only the secretaries of state and defense confirmed and in place in those critical departments.[14] When Hurricane Harvey hit Texas in August 2017, top federal emergency posts, including the National Hurricane Center directorship, were unfilled.[15]

Senators who disagree with the purpose or policy of an agency sometimes block the appointments of individuals to manage it. From 2010 through 2015, Republican senators blocked hearings for any candidates to fill the top positions on the Election Assistance Commission, an agency designed to make voting more efficient, because they considered it unnecessary.[16] A single senator can suspend a confirmation vote by placing a "hold" on the nominee.[17] They can do so to express opposition to some matter unrelated to the individual or agency involved in the proposed confirmation. In 2014, Cassandra Butts was nominated by Obama to be the US ambassador to the Bahamas. A hold was placed on her by Senator Ted Cruz because he opposed the Iran nuclear deal and by Senator Tom Cotton in order to pressure President Obama to punish those responsible for an unrelated Secret Service leak. Butts passed away in June 2016 while she was still awaiting her confirmation vote.[18]

Partisanship can motivate federal career workers to stymie presidents or senior officials whose policies they disapprove by leaking potentially embarrassing information. That is the little-understood backstory of the flow of leaks during the early months of the controversial Trump presidency. The press has every right to broadcast and publish news stories from such leaks. It's the bureaucrats doing the leaking who bear responsibility for hampering the president or the work of various executive agencies. After being fired by President Trump, FBI director James Comey admitted he leaked information about a meeting with Trump in order to use the press to push for a special counsel.[19] Comey got what he wanted from the press, and Trump is paying the price for his action. As this played out, I recalled that, when asked why he did not replace FBI director J. Edgar Hoover, who reportedly leaked adverse information about politicians he did not like, President Johnson snapped, "I'd rather have him inside the tent pissing out than outside the tent pissing in."

In May 2015, the *Washington Post* reported anonymously leaked information that President Trump had revealed classified material regarding a potential ISIS threat in a meeting with the Russian foreign minister and ambassador.[20] Later it was anonymously leaked to the *New York Times* that Israel was the source of the intelligence Trump revealed.[21] The leaks both inform adversaries of the intelligence channel between the two nations and discourages future intelligence sharing.

That same month, following the Manchester bombing in the United Kingdom, pictures of the explosive device and container as well as the name of the suspect that the British had shared with the United States were leaked to the *New York Times*.[22] UK prime minister Theresa May angrily suspended intelligence sharing with the United States over the ordeal. When asked if American safety depended on such information sharing, Richard Clarke, a former national coordinator for security, answered, "Absolutely. We need to know the techniques. . . . The kinds of weapons. . . . The people involved so that we can make sure it doesn't happen to us here."[23]

Democrats can cheer such leaks when used to undermine the Republican Trump administration, but in partisan politics, what's good for the Democratic goose is someday going to be good for the Republican gander. Moreover, and troubling, the powerful intelligence community is learning that it has the power to derail a presidential administration, a potentially dangerous situation for our damaged democracy.

In the mid-1960s while on the White House staff, I had my own experience with similar leaks. To combat an increasing heroin problem, we decided to consolidate scattered drug enforcement activities from the Treasury and Health, Education, and Welfare (HEW) Departments in the FBI at the Department of Justice. Attorney General Nick Katzenbach agreed. FBI Director J. Edgar Hoover opposed the move. He argued that the Treasury and HEW personnel were not as well educated or trained as his agents. He told me that many of them were corrupt. In a series of meetings and phone conversations, I pressed Hoover to go along with the move. His opposition was unyielding and eventually angry. Then Drew Pearson, the most-read and widely syndicated *Washington Post* columnist, wrote about corruption in drug enforcement at Treasury and HEW. After the third time, President Johnson asked one evening if I had seen the Pearson columns. I had. "That's Hoover," he said. "I know," I responded, "He's fighting like hell against taking Treasury and HEW agents into the FBI." Wryly smiling, LBJ responded, "You keep pushing on him and you'll read about yourself protecting corrupt drug enforcement people at Treasury and HEW. I suggest you move those folks just into Justice, but not part of the FBI. Otherwise you're going to end up in a pissing contest with Hoover. You've got more important things to do than that. And anyway most people don't win those pissing contests." That's how the Drug Enforcement Administration came to be an agency of the Justice Department separate from the FBI.

22

INCOME AND EDUCATION INEQUALITY FAULT LINES

One of American democracy's most attractive characteristics for the rest of the world's population has been that no hard-and-fast class lines lock an individual into certain economic and education categories. Immigrants in the past, and most Americans over the years, believed that study in school and hard work after that were steps all people could climb to secure a better life for themselves and their families. This right to be all that each human being has the talent to be has been the source of the survival and vitality of our freedom for more than two centuries.

That's why the fault lines in income and education inequality damage our democracy. They are so wide and deep that many, perhaps most, Americans at the lowest economic levels, and their children attending public schools in rural and urban ghettos of poverty, see virtually no opportunity to leap across them. These Americans' sense of being locked in a lower caste has the makings of a fire down below that threatens our democratic way of life.

It's not simply that the share of wealth owned by the top 1 percent of Americans is larger than the share owned by the bottom 90 percent. For three decades, the share of wealth held by America's top 10 percent has been growing while the share in the hands of the remaining 90 percent has been shrinking.[1]

In 1971, the 14 percent of Americans who were upper-class earned 29 percent of household income; the 61 percent who were middle-class earned about roughly 62 percent; and the 25 percent who were lower-class earned 10 percent. Just a generation later, in 2014, the 21 percent of Americans who were upper-class earned 49 percent of household income; the 50 percent who were middle-class earned 43 percent; the 29 percent who were lower-class earned 9 percent.[2]* This income and resulting wealth inequality has a serrated racial edge. In 2014, the median net worth for a white household was thirteen times higher than for a black household and eight times higher than for a Latino one.[3]

Even more troubling for the future—since education level offers a solid correlation to wealth and income potential—the education gap between the poor and the affluent in America has also grown. From 1970 to 2013, the percentage of adults in the highest income quartile who earned bachelor's degrees by age twenty-four rose from 40 percent to 77 percent. The percentage of those in the lowest income quartile who earned bachelor's degrees by that age rose only from 6 percent to 9 percent.[4] The so-called educational gap doubled in a single generation, the spread jumping from 34 to 68 percentage points.

In 2015, 72 percent of all students at the two hundred most selective universities† came from the top economic quartile while only 3 percent were from the bottom economic quartile, a 24-to-1 ratio.[5] A 2017 analysis found that thirty-eight of America's top colleges, including five from the Ivy League, had more students from families in the top 1 percent of income earners than from those in the bottom 60 percent.[6]

Unfortunately, racially based affirmative action policies at

---

*Numbers add up to 101 percent due to rounding.

†As ranked by *Barron's 2015 Guide to American Schools.*

universities have maintained roughly the same economic gap among African American students. In their 1998 book, Princeton and Harvard University presidents Bill Bowen and Derek Bok pointed out that at the nation's top twenty-eight universities, 86 percent of all black students were upper- or middle-class, as were 98 percent of all white students.[7] Later reports and a 2007 study in the *American Journal of Education* found that at elite universities, the largest segment of black undergraduates came from well-off African, West Indian, and mixed-race families.[8] A 2011 study determined that at the top twenty law schools, 89 percent of African American students and 63 percent of Hispanic students came from the top socioeconomic half of the population, as did more than 90 percent of Asian American and white students.[9]

This is not the affirmative action espoused by President Johnson in his 1965 Howard University speech.[10] He spoke of two runners, one training for months and the other locked in chains during that time. To place them at the same starting line, he said, was not a fair race. The idea was to jump-start an entire generation of lower-class blacks into the middle and upper classes by making up for the slavery and discrimination that had shackled them. At the nation's top-tier universities, that concept has been clouded. The beneficiaries of affirmative action are often upper-class minorities whose families have the resources to send their children to first-rate elementary and high schools and hire college entrance exam tutors.

The unpopularity of the term "affirmative action" and the Supreme Court decisions raising constitutional questions about it have morphed the concept into a quest for "diversity." Top-tier universities as well as corporations, law firms, and not-for-profits seek diversity in their ranks. Diversity now includes, in addition to African Americans, other minorities like Latinos, Asians, Indians, and American Indians, as well as women, the disabled, and members of the LGBTQ community. While the importance of diverse viewpoints is appreciated, each of these diversity subgroups contains an abundance of poor and near poor members. Unfortunately, they are not the ones likeliest to receive the benefits of diversity or affirmative action programs at universities today.

Martin Luther King Jr. understood this. He told his editor in 1964 that "many white workers whose economic condition is not too far removed from the economic condition of his black brother will find it difficult to accept a 'Negro Bill of Rights.'"[11] Bayard Rustin, one of King's intimates, drove home the point. He wrote in *The New Republic*, "Any preferential approach postulated on racial, ethnic, religious, or sexual lines will only disrupt a multicultural society and lead to a backlash." Rustin believed that special help could be provided if "predicated on class lines, precisely because all . . . groups have a depressed class who would benefit."[12]

Much of the economic disparity at the higher-education level reflects the deplorable condition of public elementary and secondary schools across America, especially in poor urban and rural areas. The US Department of Education has reported that less than half of high school seniors are prepared to go to college even though the US graduation rate is 83 percent.[13] The City University of New York has found that only 40 percent of the city's high school graduates are ready for *any* college-level courses.[14]

Here again, there is a cutting racial and ethnic edge: Census Bureau data indicate that among adults age twenty-five to sixty-four, the percentage with at least a four-year bachelor's degree is 54 for Asians, 33 for whites, 23 for blacks, and 16 for Hispanics.[15] Poverty plays a dominant role: half of black and Latino students, but only 8 percent of white students, attend public elementary and high schools where at least three-fourths of the students qualify for federal lunch programs for children from low-income families.[16] Students in these schools are less likely to have the high-quality teachers and facilities of public and private schools in affluent areas. The poor have also been smacked by the fact that from 2007 to 2015 funding for public colleges fell by 21 percent as tuition rose 28 percent.[17]

A healthy democratic society needs an educated electorate that can decipher bumper sticker and tweet politics crafted by the cleverest public relations professionals. Ignorance about history and fundamental facts and difficulty with basic reading and math open the doors of government for demagogic and incompetent leaders. This is particularly true in a world of social media and as-it-happens communications in which powerful executive branch leaders face a crippled Congress and politicized Supreme Court. The collapse of public elementary and secondary education is a leading candidate to be public enemy number one for our democratic way of life.

THE EDUCATED ELITE VERSUS
THE LESS-EDUCATED FAULT LINE

The 2016 presidential election exposed a growing fault line between the politically correct college-educated elites and members of the middle and lower-middle classes educated at or below the high school level. The voting gap in education was wider in that election than in any over the past thirty-six years, the period for which comparable exit poll data exists.

Normally, the spread between college graduates and non-college graduates in a presidential election is 1 or 2 percentage points. In the 2016 election, the spread was 17 percentage points.

Hillary Clinton won college graduates by 9 percentage points, 52 to 43 percent. Trump won noncollege graduates by 8 percentage points, 52 to 44 percent. White voters without a college degree supported Donald Trump over Hillary Clinton by a more than two-to-one ratio, 67 to 28 percent. Clinton bested Trump in voters with a postgraduate degree by 58 to 37 percent.[18]

Similar divides among the college and noncollege educated exist on matters such as building an immigration wall, free trade, race relations, a number of secular-versus-sacred issues regarding freedom of religion, and local church/state issues like putting a nativity scene or menorah on government property. Two-thirds of working-class whites believe discrimination against whites is as serious as discrimination against blacks.[19] Students from universities like Yale in Connecticut and Evergreen State College in Washington recklessly hurl the term "racist" at white professors, administrators, and speakers they dislike. They urge their dismissal or shout them down. Unfortunately, there are precious few university presidents with the stature and spine of Harvard's Derek Bok. In 1991, when some students hung Confederate flags in their windows, Bok expressed his disapproval of their conduct, but insisted that they be allowed their free expression, and urged "discourse, not destructive actions."[20] He pretty much got it.

The Brookings Institution in one study found an "increasing ideological distance between the Democratic Party's socioeconomic elites and the Republican Party's disinherited working class."[21] Less-educated citizens can see the educated elite as not understanding, or even caring, how limited their economic options are. That's why the poorest among them fear immigration as a threat to their economic security. Midwestern white- and blue-collar workers who attend church or temple each week feel mocked by the secular faculty and students who profess to be agnostics or atheists at elite colleges. They see the political correctness practiced in enclaves of higher education, Beverly Hills, and the Upper East and West Sides of Manhattan as condescending put-downs. That's why Clinton's calling them "deplorables" for supporting Trump was so costly to her campaign.

23

SINGLE-ISSUE FAULT LINES

Call it litmus-test politics, identity politics, secular-versus-sacred politics. An increasing number of voters, institutions, and thick-wallet contributors cast their ballots, spend their energies, and invest their dollars depending on a candidate's position on a single issue. Political candidates, especially those in tight races, are ready prey for these voters and the well-heeled donors with tunnel vision.

THE ABORTION FAULT LINE

A half-century ago, issues of decisive importance for a voter were usually broad-based—civil rights for African Americans and the Vietnam War. Today there are numerous single issues. They are narrower. They are of overriding importance to true believers on both sides. I was present at the creation of what has become for many voters the most searing and persistent litmus-test and secular-versus-sacred issue: the gloves-off battle over federal funding for abortion.

At the 1972 Democratic convention in Miami Beach I was counsel to the Democratic Party and its national committee. The party's nominee, George McGovern, and his campaign staff were committed to what was then called "my body, myself" abortion rights. Yet they engineered a decisive (1,573–1,101) defeat of the party plank supporting "a person's right to control reproduction" and calling for the legalization of abortion. Why? Because they, including campaign manager Gary Hart and the outspoken Mc-Governite actress Shirley MacLaine, feared the plank might cost McGovern the election.

The following year the Supreme Court decided that a woman's constitutional right to privacy included her right to have an abortion, at least during the early months of her pregnancy. By 1977, the year I became secretary of health, education, and welfare (HEW), Medicaid was funding 300,000 abortions a year.[1] On many mornings as I entered the HEW building, women would be protesting outside. The pro-lifers held roses and the pro-choicers held hangers, the ends of which had been dipped in red nail polish to symbolize back-alley abortions. Late that year, Congress passed the Hyde Amendment, which prohibited federal funding for abortions unless the life of the mother was at stake or in cases of rape or incest.* In slightly varying versions that provision has remained in place for more than forty years, surviving many Congresses, political campaigns, and legal challenges.[2]

For legions of party activists and voters, the issue became and has remained a political litmus test. Democratic presidential candidates and most party leaders must be aggressively pro-choice. Republican presidential candidates and most party leaders must be aggressively pro-life. At the 1992 Democratic convention, Bob Casey, then the governor of Pennsylvania, supported the

---

*The Hyde Amendment was named after Henry Hyde, then a Republican congressman from Illinois.

minority pro-life platform plank.[3] He was denied the opportunity even to speak from the floor.

During her presidential campaign, Hillary Clinton touted her determination to seek the repeal of the Hyde Amendment's limits on federal funding of abortions.[4] Donald Trump reversed his earlier pro-choice position and professed a staunch, unyielding pro-life stand.[5] In 2017, pro-choice groups like NARAL condemned Democratic National Committee chair Tom Perez and Senator Bernie Sanders for campaigning with Heath Mello. Why? Because Mello, the Democratic candidate for mayor of Omaha and a pro-life liberal, refused to toe the pro-choice party line. Sanders also drew the wrath of pro-choice Democrats for making clear that his major interest was a candidate's stand on economic issues.[6] Tom Steyer announced in August 2017 that his super PAC NextGen would support only Democratic candidates who were pro-choice.[7]

The depth of genuine feeling on both sides of this issue stems from an individual's conviction whether the fetus is a human life. That makes it a defining political issue: on one side for practicing Catholics, evangelicals, and Orthodox Jews; on the other for secular feminists and other Christians and Jews. For legions on both sides, a candidate's stand overrides his or her positions on economic issues like jobs and increasing the minimum wage, or protecting the environment and climate change. For many with money, whether to bankroll wannabe presidents, senators, and representatives is a function of a candidate's position on federal funding for abortion.

This single-issue fault line has persisted for half a century. It dominated the battle over confirming Neil Gorsuch as a Supreme Court justice and is likely to do so in confirmation proceedings for justices for some time. Future court nominees and politicians will face some budding secular-versus-sacred issues. These include the right of employers like Catholic hospitals to refuse to provide insurance coverage for family-planning services as an exercise of their religious freedom, or the obligation of public officials to perform same-sex marriages when such services conflict with their religious beliefs.

RIGHT TO DIE FAULT LINE

The next searing secular-versus-sacred clash with a high potential to become a litmus test for political candidates and Supreme Court justice nominees is whether individuals have a constitutional right to determine when and how they will die. This issue arises particularly with the terminally ill. A related dispute will be whether federal funding under Medicare and Medicaid should be available to pay for the services of physicians assisting a patient's suicide. The secular-versus-sacred issue here—Is it God's life or the individual's?—exposes a fault line so fundamental that, like the chasm on abortion, it is unlikely to be closed for decades.

GUN CONTROL FAULT LINE

Gun control has also become a single-issue fault line in recent years. Tragic mass killings, Wild West shooting deaths in some inner cities like Chicago, and irrational and terrorist incidents in several communities like Newtown, San Bernardino, and Las Vegas have brought gun violence into living rooms and on cell phones across America. Most Democrats position themselves for tight gun control. Most Republicans align themselves for individual Second Amendment gun rights as set forth in Justice

Antonin Scalia's 5–4 majority opinion in *District of Columbia v. Heller*.*

What has put compromise beyond reach here is the impact this issue has during primaries. Candidates must often embrace the party activist's hard line on the issue to survive such contests. Conservative Texas senator Ted Cruz described the situation during a 2016 Republican presidential debate, saying, "In any Republican primary, everyone is going to say they support the Second Amendment. Unless you are clinically insane, that's what you say in a primary."[8] Presidential candidate Donald Trump heard him. So did Florida governor Jeb Bush, a moderate Republican, who tweeted a picture of a personalized pistol with the caption "America."[9] On the Democratic left, not having a pristine gun-control voting record can be fatal. As one *Politico* article described it, even "a stray vote or two [on gun control] . . . could cause [Democratic candidates] trouble in a contested primary race."[10] Hillary Clinton repeatedly slammed her primary opponent Vermont senator Bernie Sanders on his 2005 Senate vote to shield gun vendors from civil liability.[11]

As always, the flow of money hardens these political stands. The National Rifle Association (NRA) spent $54 million during the 2016 election. They put millions more into federal lobbying and direct donations to congressional candidates and state party committees.[12] Former New York City mayor Michael Bloomberg has shoveled millions of dollars through his organizations to support candidates who have adopted his gun control position and has spent similar amounts to defeat candidates who have not. Bloomberg spent $3 million in 2012 to replace a sitting

---

*Justice Samuel Alito authored the subsequent 2010 opinion in *McDonald v. City of Chicago*, which held that the Second Amendment applied to the states. This was also a 5–4 decision, with the usual suspects on each side.

US representative, Joe Baca, a California Democrat, with Gloria Negrete McLeod, who supported his position on gun control.[13]

Many other single issues may determine an individual's vote. Some are personal, like race, religion, or ethnicity. Others involve public policy, like the environment, states' rights, federal spending, immigration, and school vouchers. All voters are entitled to cast their ballots for whatever reasons they wish in our free country. My point here is not to dispute that; rather, it is to indicate that some of these single-issue voters and contributors have created fault lines that help fragment our society as they influence our politics.

24

THE MILITARY/CIVILIAN FAULT LINE

An unfortunate unintended consequence of the all-volunteer force is its tendency to isolate those who serve in the military from mainstream American society. Since World War II and until 1972, when President Nixon and Henry Kissinger created the all-volunteer military (enabling them to continue and expand the war in Southeast Asia), a large segment of male Americans served at least for a couple of years in the army, navy, marine corps, or air force. We (I served for three years as an active duty naval reserve officer) experienced military life and gained a respect for its benefits, as well as for its difficulty and discipline. We developed a firsthand appreciation for the men and women who make their careers in the military service.

Currently, only about 0.4 percent of the population, or 1.4 million men and women, actively serve in the military, and only 7 percent of the population has ever served.[1] In the years following World War II, about 10 percent of the population was serving in the military, and many millions more men and women had been in the armed services during that war.[2] In the 1977–78 Congress, more than three out of four senators and representatives had served in the military; in the 2017–18 Congress, that number is less than one in five.[3]

Three-quarters of Americans born before 1955 have an immediate family member who has been or is in the military. That number falls to one-third for those born after 1980.[4] The wars in the Middle East, spanning almost a quarter of a century, are our longest as a nation. Yet only 0.75 percent of Americans have served in Iraq or Afghanistan, and many of those who have were sent back for several tours of combat duty.[5] A 2015 Harvard study found that 60 percent of eighteen- to twenty-nine-year-old Americans supported sending ground troops to the Middle East to defeat ISIS, but only 16 percent were willing to go themselves.[6] That reflects a prevailing attitude among that age group since the institution of an all-volunteer force.

Members of the all-volunteer military tend to live in their own social sphere. Almost 80 percent of active military men and women have a parent or sibling who is also in the military.[7] Half of all military personnel hail from five states: California, Florida, Georgia, Texas, and Virginia. Overall, the South provides a significantly higher percentage of personnel to the military than any other region of the country. Rural areas deliver many more recruits per capita than cities.[8] The all-volunteer enlisted military below the rank of non-commissioned officer (NCO) is composed of a disproportionate share of minorities, and the experience has benefited many of those men and women.[9]

Even after service members retire, we put them in their own separate and unequal health care and social service system, the troubled Veterans Health Administration. Sure, we try to take care of our veterans. We salute our active-duty soldiers, marines, sailors, and air force personnel. Civilian respect for the men and women who put themselves in harm's way to protect our freedom remains high.

Nevertheless, the opening fault line between civilian and military is troubling for our democracy. A number of Americans, particularly younger ones, sometimes tend to think of the military as "them," compared to "us." This sentiment will encourage our singularly powerful military to look at the rest of our people as "them," not "us," a different society, one the military may never be a part of. These unhealthy us-and-them attitudes would damage our democracy under any circumstances. But they are of notable concern when a president or a significant clique of congressional leaders promote themselves as outspoken supporters of a strong military and charge that their political opponents are not. Moreover, with an all-volunteer force from such a thin slice of our population, few Americans have any sense that the nation has been engaged in wars and other hostilities for the past three decades. This lack of realization and attention hurts, in some cases aggravates, those who risk their lives in these wars. This is especially so when, as senator and war hero John McCain has pointed out, these volunteers are disproportionately lower-income and minority Americans. As discussed in chapter 2, presidents are subject to relatively little blowback for ordering men and women volunteers into combat when the population at large is not subject to a military draft or in any way inconvenienced.

These fault lines present complicating backdrops of media, cultural, partisan, and bureaucratic scenery for the functioning of our government and its political systems on the federal, state, and local stages. They have significant and pervasive political implications. They can become pits filled with poisonous political snakes during campaigns for elective office. They fragment our nation and make compromise infernally difficult.

They influence who decides to run for public office—from president to city hall and county council—and who gets appointed to executive offices at every level of government. These fault lines also affect whether an individual even wants to pursue, full- or part-time, careers in public life, especially in the scalding litmus-test heat and partisan political smog of the nation's capital. Becoming a public servant exposes an individual to the power of social media to manufacture false news and take it viral. A potential appointee or candidate can face anonymous venomous insinuations or claims about what he or she, now in midlife, might have done in the backseat of a car in high school.

PART VII

WE THE PEOPLE

WE THE PEOPLE MUST ACT

We have a lot of work to do to repair our damaged democracy, so let's get started.

Job number one is to check the unremitting concentration and proliferation of power in the presidency and executive branch. This is not, as liberal Democrats might see it, a Donald Trump or a Richard Nixon problem. Nor is it, as Tea Party members and Republican leaders might see it, a hangover from the hundreds of Great Society domestic programs adopted in the 1960s. This is about the persistent aggrandizement of power by one president after another, regardless of party or conservative or liberal bent. It runs far deeper than Trump's coarse bullying, Nixon's criminality, Clinton's perjury, FDR's New Deal, LBJ's vast domestic agenda, and Obama's venting his frustration with the gridlocked legislative process by issuing executive orders to implement his policies.

Checking excesses in the exercise of presidential power requires us to be abandon knee-jerk or even benefit-of-the-doubt support for the actions of successful candidates we support. Examining whether a president has exceeded his or her constitutional powers is not a partisan exercise. In this era of searing political party division, we have been too willing to accept, even defend, trespasses on legislative and judicial constitutional property and invasions of state and local matters by presidents we support and to attack similar actions by those we oppose.

Democratic liberals complained about George W. Bush's bill-signing statements expressing his intent to ignore laws passed by Congress or his creation of military tribunals for terrorists incarcerated at Guantánamo Bay. Conservatives complained about Barack Obama's executive directives on immigration, campus sexual abuse, and family-planning health insurance coverage by Catholic hospitals. All of us must be willing to question the conduct of presidents, especially those we voted for, who push through the envelopes of power, when they do things that should and would be done by a Congress we consider inept, partisan, and uncooperative. Our vote is not a grant of presumptive constitutional propriety for every exercise of power by the successful presidential candidate we backed, even when he does something we heartily agree with and want to see done.

To corral presidential power, we must recognize that no branch or level of government is a political island. A nonfunctioning legislative branch offers irresistible temptations to the executive branch to overstep its constitutional boundaries. A court system with judicial robes donned by individuals blindly loyal to the party of the president who nominated them forfeits the respect of that president and the people. These are serious threats to our democracy. They leave the field wide open for a president to rule by edicts euphemistically called executive orders and clarifying regulations. They offer wiggle room for incumbents to cut corners to achieve their ends.

States, once considered institutional counterpoints to overreach by the central federal executive and legislative branches, come on bended knee to Washington for resources to fulfill their governmental responsibilities. They bow to mandates that accompany money. They kowtow to a president with the discretion to distribute a wide swatch of federal dollars who says (perhaps more discreetly), "Do it my way or no highway."

We need leaders, men and women, who see serving the good of all the people as their duty. They should regard public service as an honor that comes with a sacred obligation to bring out the best in our citizens and inspire them to work together for the common good. We want public servants to fight for what they believe and act with courage and commitment to fulfill their responsibilities. We need politicians and elected executives and legislators who respect their opponents as well as their supporters and honor the constitutional space of individuals and institutions.

How do we get leaders like that?

The key to having good leaders is having good citizens. The demands of the citizens motivate the leaders. It's from we the people, the men and women on the city street and rural road, that the leaders at the top come. So the first thing we should do is look in the mirror.

What do we see? Do we see a citizen who votes? Do we see a television viewer who looks only at the cable "news" channels he or she agrees with? Do we see someone who decides whom to vote for solely on the basis of his or her position on just one issue? Do we see someone who casts a ballot only for candidates who will protect her personal financial interests or share his racial bias? Do we see a person who seeks a candidate with the character to fall on his or her own sword, if that's what it takes, to do what's right? Or do we see someone dazzled by flashy candidates who lust for more—more attention, more publicity, more personal power, or those who cleverly demean opponents in campaigning against them? Do we see a voter who doesn't take the time to find out what a candidate plans to use power for or against? Or a voter who is charmed by a candidate who cannot stand the heat of fair and unfair public criticism, but insists on staying in the political kitchen? Do we see a person who looks for candidates who might make mistakes, even crash and burn, but who know that how a leader gets up is far more important than licking his or her personal wounds—or seeking someone else to blame?

It's up to us to find good leaders and encourage them to seek and take public office. How? Give them our encouragement and, if they run for office, our vote. Lyndon Johnson often told me that he regarded the Voting Rights Act as his most important achievement because it enhanced every individual's right to vote regardless of color, creed, sex, or station in life. The vote, he believed, was essential "for the dignity of man and the destiny of democracy."[1] That's my point here: every man and woman should cut through the cacophony of candidate cajoling and carping, and cast his or her vote carefully—the higher the office, the greater the care, but always regarding it as a quintessential act of their citizenship. Congress must rejuvenate the Voting Rights Act, and state legislatures must make it easier, not harder, for their residents to vote.

Were you dissatisfied with the Republican and Democratic presidential candidates in the 2016 election? Do you think that Hillary Clinton considered herself so entitled that she didn't offer any program or vision for America? Did you find Donald Trump an embarrassing egomaniac who you thought had no chance to win and didn't deserve any chance to win?

If your complaint is that they were selected by a minority of party members, it is well taken. But were you in the more than 70 percent of eligible voters who were no-shows in your party's primaries? The turnout for each of the major parties in the 2016 presidential primaries was less than 15 percent of eligible voters.[2] Democratic nominee Hillary Clinton was selected in the Democratic primaries by only 8 percent of eligible voters. In the Republican primaries, only 7 percent of eligible voters cast a ballot for Donald Trump to be their party's nominee.

In the 2016 presidential election, only 60 percent of eligible voters participated.[3] Donald Trump was elected president of the United States by 28 percent of the nation's eligible voters, thanks to a decisive lift from the Electoral College, which provided him a victory despite Hillary Clinton capturing 28.6 percent of the vote. (See Appendix B.)

Since 1960, turnout of eligible voters in presidential elections has ranged between 51 percent and 64 percent.[4] Usually, only 30 to 40 percent of eligible voters under thirty go to the polls.[5] For more than half a century, the candidate who captured between a quarter and a third of all eligible voters was elected president. Since 1988 the percentages of eligible voters who cast a ballot in presidential elections have ranged among whites, between 61 percent and 68 percent, and among Hispanics, between 44 percent and 50 percent.* The range among blacks has been between 53 percent and 60 percent, except for the Obama spikes in 2008 and 2012 of 65 percent and 66 percent.[6] In off-year elections for House members and a third of the Senate, voter turnout plummets. In virtually all state and local elections, the percentage of eligible voters casting ballots declines further.

Among those of the thirty-five most developed nations in the world, US citizens rank twenty-seventh in voter turnout for the top job. *Indeed, only 65 percent of our nation's voting-age population even bothers to register to vote, compared with more than 90 percent in Canada, the United Kingdom, and Sweden, and 99 percent in Japan.*[7]

---

*The first year for which such breakdowns are available is 1988.

We must vote.

But we must not only vote.

We must demand that our votes be restored to their full value.

Among the most severe damage to our democracy is the devaluation of the individual citizen's vote. To a significant extent, the low percentage of our voting-age population that participates in elections is due to what we've heard so many people shrug and say: "What does my vote matter? What difference can it make?"

The difference can be big—and even bigger—if we take action to restore each individual vote to its full value. During the Constitutional Convention in 1787, James Madison argued that the right to vote was so fundamental to our new democracy that the legislature should not be allowed to regulate it.[8] Alexander Hamilton wrote, "Voting at elections is one of the most important rights of the subject, and in a republic ought to stand foremost in the estimation of the law."[9] Two hundred years later, in signing the Voting Rights Act of 1965 that he had asked Congress to pass earlier that year, President Johnson called the vote "the mightiest weapon in the arsenal of democracy."[10]

IT'S THE SUPREME COURT, STUPID!

The two greatest forces devaluing the value and power of an individual citizen's vote in America are gerrymandering and money.

Some gerrymandering has been going on since the birth of the republic. But in recent years, armed with the power of technology to identify which likely voters live in which neighborhood and postal zone, gerrymandering has been recast from a powerful political wrench into a vise around the throat of our freedom.

In the decade of the 2010s, Republicans top the charts in gerrymandering. But a few decades ago, Democrats strengthened their grip on the House of Representatives and lengthened their time in the majority there because they were the gerrymander champions. The answer to this problem is not to set off a financial arms race in which each party's national committee amasses the campaign money to obtain majorities in state legislatures. That will only either allow the Democrats the power to gerrymander to create more congressional seats for themselves, or let the Republicans hold on to their current carefully crafted districts.

The solution ultimately rests with the Supreme Court. When Earl Warren looked back on his years as chief justice in the 1950s and 1960s, he counted as his most important cases the one man, one vote decisions, which required similar population sizes for legislative districts. Like the lopsided populations in congressional districts before those decisions, today's districts of comparable populations, gerrymandered into grotesquely snarled shapes to favor one party or another, water down the vote of individual citizens. In Indiana, where the statewide congressional vote splits 54 percent for Republicans and 40 percent for Democrats, Republicans hold 78 percent of the House seats, Democrats only 22 percent (7 to 2).[11] In Massachusetts, where the statewide congressional vote splits 60 percent for Democrats and 32 percent for Republicans, the Democrats hold all nine House seats.[12]

The Supreme Court has dipped its toes into these waters with respect to districts carved to congest (or empower) black voters in states like North Carolina. It's time for the justices to jump all the way in to preserve the rights of every voter in every state. The *Gill v. Whitford* litigation, about the constitutionality of partisan political gerrymandering of Wisconsin's congressional districts, is pending in the Supreme Court as this book goes to press.[13] The case provides an opportunity for Chief Justice John Roberts to lead the court to step up to the constitutional plate and say,

"This fixing of elections by devaluing the votes of some citizens through political gerrymander is constitutionally unacceptable." Even with such a decision, we'll need additional measures like independent redistricting commissions to curb politicians' ingenuity to draw district lines in a way that deflates the value of the individual's vote.

The Supreme Court in the *Citizens United* case, and its prequels and progeny, vested money with First Amendment rights. By this decision, the court gave the top 1 percent in income the power of dozens of votes for any single vote cast by the average American, and the top 0.1 percent the power of hundreds of votes.* It denied Congress the power to protect the inherent value of a citizen's vote.

Like all judges, Supreme Court justices see and hear the media, so we must make ourselves seen and heard on this issue. For the finest attorneys among us there's hardly a higher calling than preparing the factual case to the justices that unlimited political contributions from the rich have become inimical to the equal protection guaranteed by our Constitution.

Big money devalues our vote by limiting the candidates we have to choose from and influencing the actions of those elected to office. This is true not only for the presidency but also for the Senate and the House of Representatives. It pollutes the political waters for would-be governors, state legislators, mayors, and members of city councils and county commissions. The first question in the mind of prospective candidates has become not

---

*The income threshold for one percenters is about $400,000; for one-tenth of one percenters, about $1.9 million.

"How can I make my country/state/district/town a better place?" but rather, "How can I raise the money to run for office?"

The very rich have created their own gated political communities with campaign contributions for candidates and fees for lobbyists to guard their financial and single-issue interests. There is no better example than the ability of Wall Street hedge fund managers to protect their "carried interest" income from being subjected to the same tax rates all other Americans pay on their earnings.

The wealthiest Americans have made "government redistribution of income" dirty words in American politics. They have financed the election of candidates who echo that thinking. Yet government does exactly that every minute of every day with Medicaid for the needy, Social Security and health care for seniors, school lunches for poor children, safety of public roads and airlines, tax breaks for real estate and oil and gas moguls. George Soros bankrolls federal, state, and local candidates who support legalization of marijuana and his criminal justice perspective. Tom Steyer is a financial ventriloquist with millions of dollars for politicians who mouth his position on climate change. The Koch brothers have a basket of single issues they fund on the right, including unlimited contributions to political campaigns and the use of dark money.

Freeing political candidates and public officeholders from big donors is central to leveling the electoral playing field sufficiently to offer citizens the best candidates to select for their votes. Legislation to mandate prompt disclosure of a candidate's financial supporters and campaign donors above a certain threshold, say $499, could also help. In this era of high-tech communications, we can calculate and report almost anything anywhere instantly. We can certainly publish online for all to see such amounts contributed to a candidate or super PAC within forty-eight hours of the commitment or delivery. We can encourage candidates to voluntarily limit the maximum amounts they will accept from individual donors and publicly embarrass those who refuse to honor that limit.

In the long haul, public financing of campaigns is the surest way to stem the overwhelming power of big donors. To do that, first the Supreme Court must toss the *Citizens United* decision into the dustbin of bad decisions where they dumped *Plessy v. Ferguson*. Then Congress needs to enact legislation appropriating sufficiently large amounts for campaigns of candidates to forgo raising private money.

ESSENTIALITY OF EDUCATION

Voting means more than pulling a lever or checking a box. It involves informed and engaged political participation. We must have the capacity and take the time to know what we are voting about and whom we are voting for. We must watch carefully over those who win elections and all other public servants, and hold them to high standards. We must call them out when they step over the line or exercise power with more grasp than reach—especially when they are individuals we voted for or members of the political party we belong to.

Governing fairly and effectively in the media-is-the-message world of high-tech communications and shrewd political advertising Mad Men depends on the participation of an informed citizenry. Such citizens are the best assurance we have to select our finest public officials at the federal, state, and local level. Their attention is how we can hold public servants accountable to serve all our citizens with justice and compassion.

For the voter and the active political participant to function at the highest potential, she or he must have at least a basic education. Citizens who cannot read well or do standard math, or who know little about history, are being relegated to second-class status. The US Department of Education reports that 40 percent of twelfth-grade students have a "below basic" reading level and 48 percent have a "below basic" math level.[14] Of course, like any citizen eighteen years or older, they all have the right to vote. By gutting the quality of their education we are diminishing the power of their votes and exacerbating their vulnerability to demagogues and fake news. All of us, educated or not, carry our own prejudices and fallibilities into the voting booth. But education does help citizens understand issues that are critical not only to themselves, but also to their children, their freedom, and their opportunities. It can make individuals likelier to participate in the public square and more effective there.

Education inequality is sorely testing the social and political integrity of our nation. The denial of a basic education is perhaps the most insidious form of discrimination in our society today. It has the potential force of a wrecking ball, and it is aimed at our democracy.

CONGRESS, COURTS, AND MEDIA

More power accrues to the president as members of Congress spend the bulk of their time raising money for reelection and in partisan street fights with each other. Senators and House members are so preoccupied and distracted with those activities that they don't have time to use their constitutionally unique powers to appropriate—or not to appropriate—funds for the executive branch and to legislate thoughtfully. For decades, Congress has neglected to pass individual appropriations bills for each of the federal government's departments and agencies. They have let the executive branch be guided by a single, humongous, and incomprehensible appropriations bill riddled with arcane riders that pander to special interests. The consequence of this congressional neglect is to cede to the president much of its independent power to watch over the federal agencies and how they spend their funds.

Thanks to this congressional abdication of its appropriations power and its failure to legislate with precision, the president—through executive orders, regulations, memoranda, and directing cabinet and agency heads to issue clarifying interpretations—has become the nation's chief legislator. Presidents use signing statements to flaunt their own spin on laws they don't like or could not get Congress to pass quite the way they desired. Committees and congressional leaders fail to use their power over funding to check such presidential conduct. They normally don't even consider going to court for injunctive relief, because the courts are too overcrowded or deferential to the claimed expertise of the executive department.

As the Supreme Court and lower federal district and appellate courts have become more politicized, presidents have resorted to selecting almost exclusively judges who comport with their own political ideology. For the highest court, the dominant confirmation issue is not legal qualification, intellectual capacity, or integrity, it is the single issue of the moment; for example, how a nominee will vote on restrictions on a woman's right to abortion, or an individual's right to buy and carry guns under the Second Amendment, or maintaining the First Amendment status of political money, or affirmative action for minorities, or interpreting the First Amendment's protection of "free exercise" of religion. In a politicized or single-issue federal court system, lawyers know where to file suit to block a president's executive order or have a law declared unconstitutional.

The persistent partisanship that dominates the political parties has infected much of the media. The press has lost some of the go-for-it guts that marked the years of Punch Sulzberger and Katharine Graham. Mrs. Graham put her entire fortune, and her newspaper and broadcasting empire, on the line when the *Washington Post* single-handedly led to exposing Richard Nixon's unconstitutional grab for power. Political correctness, financial pressures to seek readers and viewers at the expense of informing citizens, "news" from left- and right-wing cable shows, anonymous social media charges, and the follow-the-pack mentality of many national and political reporters is more characteristic of much of today's journalistic endeavors. We should cherish the First Amendment and make it clear that we celebrate documented and courageous reporting even when it attacks the politicians we support and ideas we cherish.

There is no silver bullet, no single answer. There's plenty for every one of us to do. I don't pretend to have all, or even many of the answers. We the people—all of us—must track them down.

We must start by going to the polls and demanding the political changes required to give the votes we cast their full value. We must insist on lots more from our politicians: eliminate the starring role of big money in our political system, tone down the partisanship, stop pandering to single-issue special interests, and wrestle to the mat education and income inequality. We must reshape the disparate racial, religious, ethnic, and cultural fault lines that stress our democracy into a beautiful political mosaic cemented by trust and respect.

We must seek public leaders who understand that petty partisanship and an insistence on ideological conformity promote rigor mortis in government and freedom. Shaping government to promote social justice for all the people requires pragmatism and tenacity. Electing a candidate, passing a law, confirming a nominee for high office, writing a regulation, or issuing an executive order is more often the beginning than the end. Engaged citizens and good leaders are needed to turn these first steps into enduring journeys of compassionate and just public policies.

We can move beyond our political comfort zones. We can refuse to regard members of the other party as the enemy and to ridicule their different but legitimate public policy views. We can accept having our views challenged and we should not shrink from challenging views we disagree with—but do so vigorously, thoughtfully, without animosity and anger. We can stay informed by getting news from a variety of sources, rather than in never-the-twain-shall-meet reliance on only Fox News or MSNBC and CNN, only the *New York Times* or the *New York Post*, only the *Washington Post* or the *Wall Street Journal*.

We must use our personal power to elect and place in public office thoughtful and effective leaders. We must also enlist in a committed and tenacious effort to give them the tools they need to deploy public power for all the people. I have always believed that the government has an obligation to help the weakest in our society. It can help the needy stand on their own by providing education, housing, and health care that most of us receive from our parents. For those who cannot help themselves—largely the poor who are old and the seriously disabled—government should provide the economic and medical assistance that they require to live in human dignity. Over the years, I have come to appreciate the wisdom of Martin Luther King and Bayard Rustin mentioned in chapter 22. In a multicultural and multiracial society, social programs and special opportunities in education will be more widely accepted and generously funded when predicated on class lines, since every group harbors needy individuals and families who can benefit. This might also help diminish ethnic and racial tensions.

Whatever our color, ethnic heritage, or religious belief, we must reach out to each other. Racial discrimination continues to haunt the American attic despite the progress of the civil rights movement and the legislative prowess of President Johnson. The persistence of discrimination against African Americans and their growing importance in the Democratic Party is almost certain to ensure a place on the national ticket for an African American in the future, just as years ago the growing power of Irish, Italians, and Jews in New York City politics required party tickets for the top few offices to be distributed among them. But unless we deal with the deeper aspects of discrimination in educational opportunity and income distribution, we will surely face a full-court press for reparations for African Americans.

Latinos are a rapidly growing but disproportionately poor segment of our population. They are gaining places in our major political parties. A wave of immigration from Muslim and Asian countries rubs on the raw nerves of middle- and lower-middle-class white Americans struggling for jobs amid the technological revolution in communications and robotics. Our increasingly secular elites trespass on what many religious Jews, Christians, Muslims, and others consider core convictions with respect to health care laws, and on the beliefs of devout Roman Catholics, Evangelicals, and other Christians, perhaps the last permissible objects of ridicule in our society. These cultural anxieties may be a slow-burning fuse, but they have in them the stuff of dangerously divisive fireworks. They spawn fault lines that fragment our nation at a time when we should be walking together, clasping each other's arms.

Repairing the damage to our democracy and keeping it strong and vibrant is a demanding and endless trek, and this book suggests a few steps along that way. But our democracy will never be a magic kingdom. We must be prepared to live in a world of incessant, vexing, hypersonic, and revolutionary change.

In the great philosopher Saint Thomas More's *Utopia*, the chief narrator comes upon a state that is fulfilled. Like most ideal societies of philosophical literature, it is a static society. In the nation of Utopia, time in a sense has stopped. There are fifty-four identical city-states, "all spacious and magnificent, identical in language, traditions, customs and laws." Each city considers itself a tenant rather than a master of its land and resources. Diseases are curable and medical care is plentiful.

Not only is there full employment, but each individual performs the work for which he or she is best suited. Poverty is nonexistent and leisure hours are spent in productive and invigorating relaxation. All the inhabitants are motivated by the highest ideals; pride, ambition, and avarice are unknown. The old are respected and secure. The young are healthy and educated. The government is always wise, compassionate, and just. Complete harmony reigns supreme. There is no need for change. More's Utopia has passed beyond progress and change to perfection. The city of man has very nearly become the city of God.

That's not the world we inhabit. Rapid and traumatic change and human fallibility will be perpetual conditions. Political dissembling, partisan conflict, corruption, and journalistic bias will occur. As the Jesuit priests say, we are all sinners. Repairing our

214

damaged democracy to manage that change, handling the real world of human fallibility and ambition, improving the lives of our citizens, and keeping watch on our public servants requires, most of all, trust.

Trust is critical. Change is enormously difficult to master under any circumstances, but brutally so when we have lost trust in our institutions—our presidents, our legislators, our courts, our media, our political opponents, our fellow citizens of different ethnic, racial, and religious backgrounds. Trust is possible in our complex society only with strong, honest leadership, of high competence and compassion, that encourages citizens to shake hands, not form fists. Reliable, consistent policies that are fairly applied must also be seen as fairly applied.

Political fairness, like justice, must not only be delivered but also be perceived as having been delivered. That is not possible in a mightily partisan and single-issue political culture in which the size of the bankroll smothers the soundness of the policy and the locked gates of a gerrymander gut the value of votes.

We have lots to do, a long, hard journey ahead. So did Christopher Columbus, the Founding Fathers, Abraham Lincoln, Martin Luther King Jr., and Susan B. Anthony. They had successes and failures and so will we. But each of us has to get involved. This is no time to sit back and leave it to the other gal or guy, or to fear failure. It is a time for all of us to speak up and exhibit and demand of our leaders the courage to take some risks and persevere until we repair our damaged democracy. It would be a tragedy for our children if we let the damage persist, increase, fracture, and petrify our society. We will make mistakes, some colossal ones. We will take plenty of missteps, and we will trip and fall down along the way. So what. Wouldn't we the people rather make mistakes than have our children and grandchildren say that we didn't even try?

ACKNOWLEDGMENTS

A few colleagues and friends—Rick Cotton, Ervin Duggan, Jonathan Fanton, and Matthew Nimetz—read all or parts of a draft of this manuscript. Their insights and thoughtful suggestions have been most helpful.

James Bristow was my research assistant on this book. He is a highly intelligent young man, diligent about fairness and the facts, unyielding in his research and insistence on double-checking everything, and a pleasure to work with. He is an attorney with a deep interest in public policy at every level of government and his hobby is studying history. He is committed to social justice and has a great career in government and politics ahead of him.

Sue Brown, who in 1992 returned with me to New York from Washington, DC, to establish the National Center on Addiction and Substance Abuse at Columbia University (CASA), has once again made it easier for me to write a book. Tim Su, the talented IT support manager in our office, has made the mechanics of writing this book efficient and smooth, whether I was at my home in Westport, Connecticut, or traveling in some foreign country. JoAnn McCauley, my executive assistant, has kept my schedule going smoothly, as she has done for more than a quarter century. Janis Brandt has helped keep my life in order for almost twenty years.

Trish Todd, vice president and executive editor at Touchstone, has been a superb editor, a great sounding board, careful and caring, a delight to work with. It has once again been a pleasure to be with all the Simon & Schuster and Touchstone folks, especially Carolyn Reidy, president and CEO of Simon & Schuster; Susan Moldow, publisher and president of the Scribner Publishing Group; Cherlynne Li, who did a fabulous job designing the eye-catching cover; David Falk, associate publisher; Brian Belfiglio, director of publicity; Sydney Morris; Meredith Vilarello, Kelsey Manning, Kaitlin Olson, copy editor Douglas Johnson, and senior production editor Mark LaFlaur.

As always, my wife, Hilary, has been understanding, loving, and immensely supportive. Her endurance of my work habits over the thirty-five years we've been married has been saintly.

With appreciation to all, responsibility for what's written on these pages is mine alone.

Joseph A. Califano Jr.
February 2018

APPENDIX A: DEMOCRATIC CONGRESSIONAL CAMPAIGN COMMITTEE

2013–14 ELECTION CYCLE DUES & MONEY RAISED (FEBRUARY FINAL)

DCCC Fund-Raising Tables Legend

<u>DCCC</u>: Democratic Congressional Campaign Committee
<u>COH</u>: Cash on Hand
<u>Frontline</u>: Competitive congressional districts currently in Democratic control
<u>R2B</u>: Red to Blue; competitive congressional districts currently in Republican control
<u>Member Points</u>: Attendance at party fund-raisers

Frontline Members in italics.
Dues subject to increase based on committee assignments.
DCCC Raised Goals are subject to change over the course of the cycle.
Democratic Steering & Policy Committee Members have an increased Raised Goal of $250,000 this cycle.

MEMBER	COH 12/31/13	Dues Goal	Dues Received
LEADERSHIP			
Pelosi, Nancy	$439,206.96	$800,000.00	$800,000.00
Hoyer, Steny	$1,178,349.89	$800,000.00	$800,000.00
Clyburn, Jim	$1,165,085.41	$600,000.00	$600,000.00
Becerra, Xavier	$847,334.65	$450,000.00	$450,000.00
Crowley, Joe	$1,121,559.78	$450,000.00	$290,000.00
Israel, Steve	$1,041,294.95	$450,000.00	$450,000.00
Andrews, Robert	$567,375.25	$450,000.00	$250,000.00
DeLauro, Rosa	$100,459.93	$450,000.00	$376,000.00
DCCC NATIONAL CHAIRS			
Himes, Jim	$1,217,794.21	$300,000.00	$203,000.00
Polis, Jared	$206,408.22	$300,000.00	$200,300.00
CHIEF DEPUTY WHIPS			
Butterfield, G.K.	$260,787.75	$300,000.00	$75,000.00
DeGette, Diana	$62,373.19	$300,000.00	$45,000.00
Ellison, Keith	$163,624.66	$300,000.00	$133,000.00
Lewis, John	$220,874.06	$300,000.00	$125,000.00
Luján, Ben Ray	$515,875.03	$300,000.00	$157,500.00
Matheson, Jim	$743,117.00	$300,000.00	$55,000.00
Schakowsky, Jan	$333,661.25	$300,000.00	$193,200.00
Sewell, Terri	$652,070.47	$300,000.00	$60,000.00
Wasserman Schultz, Debbie	$530,155.01	$300,000.00	$115,000.00
Welch, Peter	$1,442,240.40	$300,000.00	$195,000.00
EXCLUSIVE COMMITTEE RANKING MEMBERS			
Levin, Sander	$350,580.47	$500,000.00	$317,000.00
Lowey, Nita	$556,355.52	$500,000.00	$315,000.00

DCCC Raised Goal	DCCC Raised	Frontline & R2B Contributions/ Raised	Member Points
$25,000,000.00	$31,134,250.93	$1,624,029.00	781
$2,500,000.00	$1,792,917.00	$1,475,700.00	709
$1,500,000.00	$1,445,648.00	$389,750.00	324
$1,000,000.00	$1,042,980.00	$92,750.00	70
$3,000,000.00	$1,038,300.00	$1,065,000.00	223
$10,000,000.00	$11,794,374.85	$1,213,597.17	448
$500,000.00	$502,800.00	$2,000.00	1
$500,000.00	$239,550.00		6
$3,000,000.00	$954,246.00	$247,975.00	34
$500,000.00	$630,386.50	$452,069.00	87
$500,000.00	$31,000.00		
$500,000.00	$80,064.33	$1,000.00	1
$500,000.00	$53,250.00		1
$500,000.00	$17,500.00	$3,000.00	10
$500,000.00	$264,760.00	$31,500.00	15
$500,000.00	$20,000.00	$2,500.00	3
$500,000.00	$271,680.00	$145,584.00	105
$500,000.00	$230,000.00	$8,000.00	21
$500,000.00	$32,500.00	$1,186,539.00	240
$500,000.00	$55,500.00	$20,000.00	11
$1,000,000.00	$374,900.00	$158,500.00	16
$1,000,000.00	$937,573.00	$151,000.00	28

APPENDIX A

MEMBER	COH 12/31/13	Dues Goal	Dues Received
Slaughter, Louise	$316,966.70	$500,000.00	$36,000.00
Waters, Maxine	$266,355.33	$500,000.00	$35,000.00
Waxman, Henry	$757,269.00	$500,000.00	$10,000.00
RANKING MEMBERS			
Brady, Robert	$671,201.80	$250,000.00	$0.00
Conyers, John	$116,310.05	$250,000.00	$86,000.00
Cummings, Eljah	$876,307.65	$250,000.00	$146,000.00
DeFazio, Peter	$391,132.76	$250,000.00	$32,500.00
Engel, Eliot	$244,609.29	$250,000.00	$125,000.00
Johnson, Eddie Bernice	$174,584.23	$250,000.00	$20,000.00
Maloney, Carolyn	$601,479.89	$250,000.00	$127,900.00
Michaud, Mike	$58,885.00	$250,000.00	$45,000.00
Miller, George	$379,540.00	$300,000.00	$135,000.00
Peterson, Collin	$357,686.97	$250,000.00	$0.00
Rahall, Nick	$839,880.26	$250,000.00	$32,400.00
Ruppersberger, Dutch	$924,303.02	$250,000.00	$187,502.00
Sánchez, Linda	$354,943.90	$250,000.00	$97,000.00
Smith, Adam	$444,814.12	$300,000.00	$200,000.00
Thompson, Bennie	$1,345,846.73	$250,000.00	$50,000.00
Van Hollen, Chris	$1,767,841.76	$300,000.00	$300,000.00
Velázquez, Nydia	$394,654.03	$250,000.00	$160,000.00
EXCLUSIVE SUBCOMMITTEE RANKING MEMBERS			
Bishop, Sanford	$305,044.73	$250,000.00	$10,000.00
Capuano, Mike	$531,556.81	$250,000.00	$20,000.00
Clay, Lacy	$218,793.09	$250,000.00	$0.00
Doggett, Lloyd	$2,844,414.15	$250,000.00	$125,000.00
Eshoo, Anna	$494,740.92	$250,000.00	$250,000.00

APPENDIX A

DCCC Raised Goal	DCCC Raised	Frontline & R2B Contributions/Raised	Member Points
$1,000,000.00	$107,500.00	$56,000.00	23
$1,000,000.00	$69,500.00		2
$1,000,000.00	$45,000.00	$4,000.00	3
$250,000.00	$0.00		
$250,000.00	$5,000.00	$250.00	5
$250,000.00	$38,500.00		
$250,000.00	$64,900.00	$12,510.00	5
$250,000.00	$78,364.00	$56,000.00	9
$250,000.00	$44,400.00		3
$250,000.00	$87,500.00	$126,250.00	72
$250,000.00	$45,000.00		
$500,000.00	$725,000.00	$207,250.00	35
$250,000.00	$23,000.00	$14,750.00	1
$250,000.00	$128,000.00	$16,000.00	17
$250,000.00	$276,900.00	$29,500.00	8
$250,000.00	$20,000.00	$19,100.00	10
$500,000.00	$329,300.00	$111,000.00	74
$250,000.00	$31,000.00	$1,000.00	5
$500,000.00	$280,300.00	$124,000.00	9
$250,000.00	$15,500.00	$57,000.00	6
$250,000.00	$20,000.00		
$250,000.00	$15,000.00	$1,000.00	
$250,000.00	$17,500.00		
$250,000.00	$31,500.00		7
$250,000.00	$857,426.67	$6,000.00	8

APPENDIX A

MEMBER	COH 12/31/13	Dues Goal	Dues Received
Farr, Sam	$166,666.32	$250,000.00	$75,000.00
Fattah, Chaka	$16,877.36	$250,000.00	$0.00
Green, Al	$240,896.00	$250,000.00	$10,000.00
Kaptur, Marcy	$252,095.86	$250,000.00	$60,500.00
McDermott, Jim	$79,333.91	$250,000.00	$20,000.00
Meeks, Gregory	$86,117.45	$250,000.00	$10,000.00
Moran, James	$710,036.00	$250,000.00	$25,000.00
Neal, Richard	$2,362,150.46	$300,000.00	$100,000.00
Pallone, Frank	$1,076,464.87	$250,000.00	$250,000.00
Pastor, Ed	$1,355,738.39	$250,000.00	$50,000.00
Price, David	$147,807.36	$250,000.00	$25,000.00
Rangel, Charles	$211,461.34	$250,000.00	$0.00
Rush, Bobby	$46,000.61	$250,000.00	$0.00
Serrano, José	$17,620.05	$250,000.00	$17,500.00
Tonko, Paul	$441,889.50	$250,000.00	$171,511.00
Visclosky, Pete	$275,716.06	$300,000.00	$147,727.19
WAYS & MEANS			
Blumenauer, Earl	$758,478.59	$200,000.00	$125,000.00
Davis, Danny	$328,378.12	$200,000.00	$45,000.00
Kind, Ron	$1,106,264.39	$200,000.00	$40,000.00
Larson, John	$339,920.58	$200,000.00	$135,000.00
Pascrell, Bill	$725,902.19	$200,000.00	$30,000.00
Schwartz, Allyson	$36,517.00	$300,000.00	$25,000.00
Thompson, Mike	$1,492,399.52	$200,000.00	$150,250.00
APPROPRIATIONS			
Cuellar, Henry	$1,001,535.67	$300,000.00	$325,000.00
Honda, Mike	$622,989.66	$200,000.00	$0.00
Lee, Barbara	$101,247.50	$200,000.00	$49,000.00

APPENDIX A

DCCC Raised Goal	DCCC Raised	Frontline & R2B Contributions/ Raised	Member Points
$250,000.00	$14,500.00	$17,500.00	2
$250,000.00	$7,500.00		
$250,000.00	$0.00		1
$250,000.00	$121,150.00	$27,000.00	26
$250,000.00	$27,500.00		5
$500,000.00	$166,800.00	$56,000.00	6
$250,000.00	$43,000.00		
$500,000.00	$365,900.00	$34,500.00	4
$250,000.00	$389,000.00	$81,000.00	19
$250,000.00	$64,864.00	$2,000.00	1
$250,000.00	$30,000.00	$2,000.00	
$250,000.00	$10,000.00	$56,000.00	7
$250,000.00	$6,000.00		1
$250,000.00	$30,000.00	$59,000.00	6
$250,000.00	$0.00	$61,000.00	8
$500,000.00	$282,727.26		15
$250,000.00	$50,900.00	$135,050.00	44
$250,000.00	$5,500.00		2
$250,000.00	$467,500.00	$92,000.00	2
$250,000.00	$261,425.00	$39,500.00	2
$250,000.00	$17,500.00	$1,000.00	5
$250,000.00	$216,200.00	$80,000.00	1
$250,000.00	$211,750.00	$415,850.00	102
$500,000.00	$228,253.50	$15,000.00	1
$250,000.00	$5,000.00	$5,000.00	3
$250,000.00	$105,800.0 0	$7,500.00	7

MEMBER	COH 12/31/13	Dues Goal	Dues Received
McCollum, Betty	$124,088.88	$200,000.00	$31,000.00
Owens, Bill	$547,488.00	$200,000.00	$2,500.00
Pingree, Chellie	$247,085.33	$300,000.00	$129,600.00
Quigley, Mike	$527,586.05	$200,000.00	$110,000.00
Roybal-Allard, Lucille	$66,550.49	$200,000.00	$20,000.00
Ryan, Tim	$278,893.78	$200,000.00	$20,000.00
Schiff, Adam	$2,043,183.10	$200,000.00	$116,538.00
ENERGY & COMMERCE			
Barrow, John	$1,231,376.44	$200,000.00	$0.00
Braley, Bruce	$2,323,351.00	$200,000.00	$0.00
Capps, Lois	$953,583.29	$200,000.00	$1,000.00
Castor, Kathy	$724,340.73	$200,000.00	$75,000.00
Christian-Christensen, Donna	$50,692.28	$200,000.00	$0.00
Dingell, John	$331,366.90	$200,000.00	$0.00
Doyle, Mike	$335,741.78	$200,000.00	$25,000.00
Green, Gene	$1,075,643.92	$200,000.00	$115,000.00
Matsui, Doris	$407,097.59	$200,000.00	$132,500.00
McNerney, Jerry	$305,856.81	$300,000.00	$17,500.00
Sarbanes, John	$907,909.77	$200,000.00	$130,000.00
Yarmuth, John	$656,751.94	$200,000.00	$100,000.00
RULES			
Hastings, Alcee	$372,255.38	$200,000.00	$30,000.00
McGovern, Jim	$526,961.91	$200,000.00	$25,000.00
FINANCIAL SERVICES			
Beatty, Joyce	$262,887.28	$200,000.00	$35,000.00
Carney, John	$725,023.48	$200,000.00	$175,000.00

DCCC Raised Goal	DCCC Raised	Frontline & R2B Contributions/ Raised	Member Points
$250,000.00	$110,090.00		
$250,000.00	$32,400.00	$15,400.00	3
$500,000.00	$290,487.00	$140,500.00	8
$250,000.00	$92,400.00	$9,000.00	10
$250,000.00	$5,000.00	$6,000.00	3
$250,000.00	$0.00	$0.00	
$250,000.00	$69,800.00	$1,000.00	5
$250,000.00	$58,500.00	$21,200.00	1
$250,000.00	$0.00		
$250,000.00	$2,500.00	$7,575.00	11
$250,000.00	$128,068.00	$94,000.00	44
$250,000.00	$500.00		
$250,000.00	$12,500.00		
$250,000.00	$15,000.00		
$250,000.00	$16,000.00	$6,500.00	2
$250,000.00	$569,350.00	$118,000.00	15
$500,000.00	$12,500.00	$185,000.00	53
$250,000.00	$38,000.00	$2,000.00	
$250,000.00	$15,500.00	$2,000.00	5
$250,000.00	$1,600.00	$1,500.00	2
$250,000.00	$37,400.00	$2,000.00	2
$250,000.00	$38,000.00	$1,000.00	5
$250,000.00	$110,500.00	$64,250.00	4

APPENDIX A

MEMBER	COH 12/31/13	Dues Goal	Dues Received
Cleaver, Emanuel	$92,349.93	$200,000.00	$20,000.00
Delaney, John	$158,679.00	$200,000.00	$60,000.00
Foster, Bill	$819,229.11	$200,000.00	$2,000.00
Heck, Denny	$623,918.16	$200,000.00	$35,000.00
Hinojosa, Ruben	$195,871.62	$200,000.00	$25,000.00
Kildee, Dan	$250,816.60	$300,000.00	$40,000.00
Lynch, Stephen	$73,282.00	$200,000.00	$0.00
McCarthy, Carolyn	$649,440.18	$200,000.00	$120,000.00
Moore, Gwen	$55,760.82	$300,000.00	$30,000.00
Murphy, Patrick	$1,760,092.67	$200,000.00	$2,000.00
Perlmutter, Ed	$621,630.37	$200,000.00	$25,000.00
Peters, Gary	$2,923,660.00	$300,000.00	$5,000.00
Scott, David	$55,463.59	$200,000.00	$53,000.00
Sherman, Brad	$89,070.13	$200,000.00	$15,000.00
Sinema, Kyrsten	$1,021,589.67	$200,000.00	$1,000.00
NONEXCLUSIVE SUBCOMMITTEE RANKING MEMBERS			
Barber, Ron	$939,229.75	$150,000.00	$500.00
Bass, Karen	$192,351.63	$150,000.00	$30,000.00
Bishop, Tim	$565,456.02	$150,000.00	$0.00
Bonamici, Suzanne	$415,977.78	$150,000.00	$66,750.00
Bordallo, Madeleine	$58,127.08	$150,000.00	$0.00
Brown, Corrine	$28,939.53	$150,000.00	$10,000.00
Brownley, Julia	$884,875.23	$150,000.00	$1,000.00
Cartwright, Matt	$470,970.74	$150,000.00	$20,000.00
Chu, Judy	$1,478,489.79	$150,000.00	$90,000.00
Clarke, Yvette	$116,697.22	$150,000.00	$10,000.00
Cohen, Steve	$888,020.49	$150,000.00	$65,000.00

APPENDIX A

DCCC Raised Goal	DCCC Raised	Frontline & R2B Contributions/ Raised	Member Points
$250,000.00	$1,000.00		
$250,000.00	$18,000.00	$2,000.00	4
$250,000.00	$27,000.00	$1,500.00	8
$250,000.00	$101,255.00	$1,000.00	
$250,000.00	$5,000.00		5
$500,000.00	$215,630.00	$22,000.00	14
$250,000.00	$37,500.00		
$250,000.00	$3,000.00	$56,000.00	6
$500,000.00	$157,480.00	$11,800.00	18
$250,000.00	$27,750.00	$4,218.00	7
$250,000.00	$107,119.80	$4,000.00	1
$500,000.00	$127,500.00	$80,000.00	5
$250,000.00	$20,500.00	$35,000.00	
$250,000.00	$94,700.00	$500.00	2
$250,000.00	$97,000.00		4
$100,000.00	$15,000.00		3
$250,000.00	$242,207.12	$18,800.00	2
$100,000.00	$87,400.00		1
$100,000.00	$112,400.00	$9,000.00	
$100,000.00	$0.00		
$100,000.00	$72,900.00		2
$100,000.00	$15,000.00		2
$100,000.00	$5,000.00		3
$100,000.00	$212,925.00	$29,000.00	3
$250,000.00	$30,000.00	$56,000.00	5
$100,000.00	$15,000.00		5

MEMBER	COH 12/31/13	Dues Goal	Dues Received
Connolly, Gerry	$1,467,632.04	$150,000.00	$25,000.00
Cooper, Jim	$902,977.34	$150,000.00	$0.00
Costa, Jim	$554,312.38	$150,000.00	$0.00
Courtney, Joe	$767,386.68	$150,000.00	$45,900.00
Davis, Susan	$226,869.52	$150,000.00	$40,000.00
Deutch, Ted	$622,340.86	$150,000.00	$85,928.58
Edwards, Donna	$54,300.85	$300,000.00	$15,000.00
Faleomavaega, Eni	$6,402.54	$150,000.00	$0.00
Fudge, Marcia	$409,209.49	$150,000.00	$50,000.00
Garamendi, John	$216,183.63	$150,000.00	$6,500.00
Grijalva, Raúl	$109,158.85	$150,000.00	$0.00
Hahn, Janice	$118,169.10	$150,000.00	$6,000.00
Hanabusa, Colleen	$771,459.00	$150,000.00	$0.00
Higgins, Brian	$642,194.86	$150,000.00	$50,000.00
Holt, Rush	$309,356.04	$150,000.00	$30,000.00
Holmes Norton, Eleanor	$270,716.38	$150,000.00	$104,620.00
Jackson Lee, Sheila	$269,782.77	$150,000.00	$12,600.00
Keating, Bill	$418,871.00	$150,000.00	$5,000.00
Kirkpatrick, Ann	$824,159.48	$150,000.00	$1,450.00
Langevin, Jim	$291,315.01	$150,000.00	$20,000.00
Larsen, Rick	$386,841.70	$150,000.00	$100,000.00
Lipinski, Dan	$979,964.44	$150,000.00	$2,000.00
Lofgren, Zoe	$848,819.27	$150,000.00	$45,000.90
Maffei, Dan	$903,194.02	$150,000.00	$500.00
McIntyre, Mike	$633,021.71	$150,000.00	$0.00
Meng, Grace	$276,713.02	$150,000.00	$20,000.00
Nadler, Jerry	$294,314.99	$150,000.00	$95,454.00
Napolitano, Grace	$270,716.38	$150,000.00	$25,000.00
Payne, Jr., Donald	$69,576.45	$150,000.00	$5,000.00
Richmond, Cedric	$378,477.01	$150,000.00	$30,000.00

DCCC Raised Goal	DCCC Raised	Frontline & R2B Contributions/ Raised	Member Points
$100,000.00	$127,500.00	$3,000.00	20
$100,000.00	$1,500.00		
$100,000.00	$0.00		2
$100,000.00	$25,000.00	$500.00	5
$250,000.00	$0.00		2
$100,000.00	$105,700.00	$26,000.00	7
$500,000.00	$86,350.00	$147,250.00	126
$100,000.00	$0.00		
$100,000.00	$500.00		1
$100,000.00	$5,500.00	$9,000.00	3
$100,000.00	$59,044.00		2
$100,000.00	$33,000.00	$16,500.00	9
$100,000.00	$15,000.00		
$100,000.00	$15,000.00	$71,000.00	16
$100,000.00	$144,700.00	$1,000.00	5
$100,000.00	$1,000.00		
$100,000.00	$0.00		6
$100,000.00	$0.00		
$100,000.00	$56,364.00		1
$100,000.00	$50,000.00	$1,000.00	5
$100,000.00	$240,000.00	$85,000.00	2
$100,000.00	$16,500.00	$17,000.00	2
$100,000.00	$42,400.00	$215,000.00	25
$100,000.00	$79,800.00		
$100,000.00	$20,500.00		1
$100,000.00	$0.00	$56,000.00	6
$100,000.00	$64,800.00	$60,000.00	11
$100,000.00	$0.00	$1,000.00	3
$100,000.00	$1,250.00		
$250,000.00	$70,000.00	$157,000.00	28

APPENDIX A

MEMBER	COH 12/31/13	Dues Goal	Dues Received
Sablan, Gregorio	$60,393.00	$150,000.00	$1,500.00
Sánchez, Loretta	$399,719.60	$150,000.00	$10,000.00
Schrader, Kurt	$1,001,828.42	$150,000.00	$60,000.00
Scott, Bobby	$200,621.23	$150,000.00	$7,500.00
Sires, Albio	$46,541.64	$150,000.00	$0.00
Speier, Jackie	$1,125,064.43	$150,000.00	$105,000.00
Swalwell, Eric	$823,362.24	$150,000.00	$2,000.00
Takano, Mark	$432,964.77	$300,000.00	$13,500.00
Tierney, John	$708,940.68	$150,000.00	$0.00
Titus, Dina	$151,528.23	$150,000.00	$10,000.00
Walz, Tim	$293,490.85	$300,000.00	$10,000.00
Wilson, Frederica	$151,204.76	$150,000.00	$5,000.00
MEMBERS			
Bera, Ami	$1,151,637.34	$300,000.00	$1,000.00
Bustos, Cheri	$826,065.98	$125,000.00	$2,000.00
Cardenas, Tony	$77,384.11	$125,000.00	$60,000.00
Carson, André	$512,545.53	$125,000.00	$25,000.00
Castro, Joaquin	$308,366.80	$125,000.00	$55,000.00
Cicilline, David	$404,328.04	$300,000.00	$50,000.00
Clark, Katherine	$136,548.33	$125,000.00	$0.00
DelBene, Suzan	$674,740.95	$125,000.00	$2,000.00
Duckworth, Tammy	$904,697.42	$125,000.00	$42,400.00
Enyart, Bill	$409,119.34	$125,000.00	$500.00
Esty, Elizabeth	$846,353.96	$125,000.00	$1,000.00
Frankel, Lois	$349,515.56	$300,000.00	$26,000.00
Gabbard, Tulsi	$814,072.29	$125,000.00	$17,500.00
Gallego, Pete	$532,348.01	$125,000.00	$1,000.00
Garcia, Joe	$1,341,739.57	$125,000.00	$250.00
Grayson, Alan	$287,217.67	$125,000.00	$9,000.00

APPENDIX A

DCCC Raised Goal	DCCC Raised	Frontline & R2B Contributions/ Raised	Member Points
$100,000.00	$0.00		
$100,000.00	$5,000.00	$23,700.00	8
$100,000.00	$82,500.00	$22,000.00	1
$100,000.00	$15,000.00		
$100,000.00	$0.00		
$250,000.00	$36,000.00	$18,000.00	5
$100,000.00	$53,000.00		2
$500,000.00	$64,250.00	$7,620.00	26
$100,000.00	$1,000.00		
$100,000.00	$25,500.00	$6,000.00	5
$500,000.00	$27,900.00	$91,500.00	85
$100,000.00	$1,000.00		2
$500,000.00	$65,000.00		6
$75,000.00	$27,500.00	$10,400.00	14
$75,000.00	$26,200.00	$35,00.00	12
$75,000.00	$0.00		
$75,000.00	$121,000.00	$17,577.00	18
$500,000.00	$168,900.00		
$75,000.00	$15,500.00		
$75,000.00	$81,000.00	$30,750.00	
$250,000.00	$64,500.00	$30,225.00	21
$75,000.00	$66,000.00		
$75,000.00	$0.00		
$500,000.00	$680,537.00	$150,642.00	85
$75,000.00	$45,000.00	$1000.00	
$75,000.00	$32,400.00		
$75,000.00	$1,250.00	$12,850.00	18
$75,000.00	$1,500.00	$13,998.00	10

APPENDIX A

MEMBER	COH 12/31/13	Dues Goal	Dues Received
Gutiérrez, Luis	$228,009.64	$125,000.00	$0.00
Horsford Steven	$167,941.58	$125,000.00	$2,000.00
Huffman, Jared	$315,464.25	$125,000.00	$85,000.00
Jeffries, Hakeem	$369,272.92	$125,000.00	$25,000.00
Johnson, Hank	$85,296.56	$125,000.00	$10,000.00
Kelly, Robin	$136,067.28	$125,000.00	$19,000.00
Kennedy, Joe	$912,225.57	$125,000.00	$125,000.00
Kilmer, Derek	$981,058.56	$125,000.00	$50,000.00
Kuster, Annie	$1,069,513.93	$125,000.00	$1,000.00
Loebsack, Dave	$425,115.89	$125,000.00	$2,500.00
Lowenthal, Alan	$316,148.64	$125,000.00	$24,000.00
Lujan Grisham, Michelle	$681,834.34	$125,000.00	$17,000.00
Maloney, Sean Patrick	$1,144,636.37	$125,000.00	$1,000.00
McLeod, Gloria	$102,205.17	$125,000.00	$5,000.00
Nolan, Rick	$298,061.72	$125,000.00	$5,000.00
O'Rourke, Beto	$286,287.06	$125,000.00	$6,000.00
Peters, Scott	$1,147,137.27	$125,000.00	$1,000.00
Pierluisi, Pedro	$382.00	$125,000.00	$0.00
Pocan, Mark	$225,251.35	$300,000.00	$50,000.00
Ruiz, Raul	$1,198,007.67	$125,000.00	$250.00
Schneider, Brad	$1,001,739.23	$125,000.00	$4,000.00
Shea-Porter, Carol	$357,389.15	$125,000.00	$1,000.00
Tsongas, Niki	$336,266.79	$125,000.00	$35,000.00
Vargas, Juan	$73,496.04	$125,000.00	$17,000.00
Veasey, Marc	$527,483.49	$125,000.00	$1,000.00
Vela, Filemón	$115,256.37	$125,000.00	$25,000.00

DCCC Raised Goal	DCCC Raised	Frontline & R2B Contributions/ Raised	Member Points
$75,000.00	$0.00		1
$75,000.00	$56,000.00	$1125.00	6
$75,000.00	$165,450.00	$7,000.00	4
$75,000.00	$26,500.00	$58,000.00	8
$75,000.00	$500.00		9
$75,000.00	$14,000.00	$1,750.00	3
$75,000.00	$278,500.00	$16,891.00	30
$75,000.00	$331,780.00	$6,000.00	2
$75,000.00	$17,000.00		7
$75,000.00	$10,000.00		1
$75,000.00	$5,000.00	$4,000.00	9
$75,000.00	$135,750.00[t	4	
$75,000.00	$105,650.00		2
$75,000.00	$0.00		2
$75,000.00	$30,000.00		
$75,000.00	$500.00	$23,000.00	19
$75,000.00	$73,100.00	$3,750.00	1
$75,000.00	$87,102.00		
$500,000.00	$563,333.30	$1,000.00	12
$75,000.00	$95,800.00		1
$75,000.00	$43,750.00		1
$75,000.00	$0.00		
$250,000.00	$62,800.00	[n5	
$75,000.00	$164,380.49	$14,500.00	7
$75,000.00	$171,350.00		9
$75,000.00	$0.00	$43,600.00	4

APPENDIX B: THE ELECTORAL COLLEGE

Article II, section 1, clause 2, and the Twelfth Amendment to the US Constitution mandate that the candidate who receives a majority of Electoral College votes shall be president of the United States.

In the Electoral College, each state has one elector for each congressional district and each senator. There are 435 congressional districts and 100 senators. The District of Columbia has three votes, bringing the total number of electors to 538 and a majority to 270. The number of congressional districts for each state is determined after each decennial census in order to reflect population changes. California is the state with most electoral votes, at 55; some states, including Delaware and Wyoming, have the lowest number, three.

On five occasions, including the 2016 election, the candidate who won the most popular votes failed to receive a majority of votes in the Electoral College and did not become president.

In 1824, Andrew Jackson received more votes (41.4 percent) than any of the four major candidates, but none secured a majority of Electoral College votes. Pursuant to the Twelfth Amendment to the Constitution, the election was then decided by the US House of Representatives, which elected John Quincy Adams president. In 1876, Samuel Tilden won the most popular votes, but Rutherford B. Hayes won a majority of Electoral College votes and became president. In 1888, Grover Cleveland received the most popular votes, but Benjamin Harrison won a majority of Electoral College votes and became president. In 2000, Al Gore won the popular vote but lost in the Electoral College to George W. Bush. In the most recent election, Donald Trump received three million fewer votes than Hillary Clinton but still managed to win the Electoral College.

Each state determines how to cast its Electoral College votes. All but two states award all their electoral votes to the presidential candidate who receives the most popular votes in their state. Nebraska and Maine give two votes to the candidate who wins the most popular votes statewide. They award their remaining electoral votes to the candidate who wins the popular vote in each congressional district.

Eliminating the Electoral College and awarding the presidency to the popular vote winner requires amending the Constitution. Either two-thirds of the state legislatures must call for a constitutional convention, or two-thirds of both the House of Representatives and Senate must vote to propose such an amendment.* After an amendment is proposed, three-fourths of the states must ratify the amendment.

A decade ago, a National Popular Vote Interstate Compact was proposed. States that agree to this compact would award their electoral votes to the candidate receiving the largest share of the national popular vote. Only when states whose cumulative votes constitute a majority of the Electoral College agree would this compact become effective. To date, just decidedly Demo-

---

*None of the Constitution's twenty-seven amendments were proposed through a constitutional convention.

cratic states like California and New York, as well as Washington, DC, which hold 165 electoral votes, have signed on. Neither a constitutional amendment eliminating the Electoral College nor a compact of the sort described would deal with the fundamental problems damaging our democracy that are set forth in this book.

NOTES

INTRODUCTION

1. Lyndon Johnson, "Remarks at the University of Michigan," University of Michigan, Ann Arbor, Michigan, May 22, 1964.

CHAPTER 1: ENHANCING POTUS POWER

1. Lord Acton stated, "Power tends to corrupt, and absolute power corrupts absolutely." Acton to Bishop Mandell Creighton, April 5, 1887, in *Historical Essays and Studies*, eds. J. N. Figgis and R. V. Laurence (London: Macmillan, 1907); Daniel Webster, "A Speech Delivered in the Senate of the United States, on the 7th of May, 1834, on the Subject of the President's Protest against the Resolution of the Senate on the 28th of May," in *The Great Speeches and Orations of Daniel Webster, with an Essay on Daniel Webster as a Master of English Style* (Boston: Little, Brown, 1879), 385.

2. Lyndon Johnson, "Remarks in Memorial Hall," Akron University, Akron, Ohio, October 21, 1964.

3. Ronald Reagan, "Presidential Debate in Cleveland, Ohio," October 28, 1980.

4. "Lyndon B. Johnson: Foreign Affairs," Miller Center of Public Affairs,

University of Virginia, accessed February 2, 2016, https://millercenter
.org/president/lbjohnson/foreign-affairs; "Institutional History: NSC
and CIA," Understanding the Iran-Contra Affairs, ed. Ross Cheit,
Brown University, https://www.brown.edu/Research/Understanding
_the_Iran_Contra_Affair/about.php.

5. "GOP Town Hall Event with Voters in South Carolina," CNN, February 18, 2016.

6. Gerhard Peters and John T. Woolley, "Trump in Action: Comparing the
Pace of President Trump's Executive Orders & Memoranda to Other
Recent Presidents: An American Presidency Project Analysis," The
American Presidency Project, April 30, 2017, http://www.presidency
.ucsb.edu/trump_in_action_020217.php; Presidential Executive Order
13769, "Protecting the Nation from Foreign Terrorist Entry into the
United States," January 27, 2017; Presidential Executive Order 13795,
"Implementing an America-First Offshore Energy Strategy," April 28,
2017; Presidential Executive Order 13789, "Promoting Free Speech
and Religious Liberty," May 4, 2017.

7. Military Authorization Act of 1965, Pub. L. 89-188, enacted September 16, 1965, section 611(a). See also Joseph A. Califano Jr., *The Triumph and Tragedy of Lyndon Johnson: The White House Years* (New York:
Touchstone, 2015), 86–89.

8. Ronald Reagan, "Statement on Signing the Safe Drinking Water Act
Amendments of 1986," June 19, 1986. See Gerhard Peters and John T.
Woolley, The American Presidency Project, http://www.presidency.
ucsb.edu/ws/?pid=37485.

9. Charlie Savage, "Barack Obama's Q&A," *Boston Globe*, December 20,
2007, http://archive.boston.com/news/politics/2008/specials/Candidate
QA/ObamaQA/.

10. Barack Obama, "Campaign Event at West High School," Billings,
Montana, May 19, 2008.

11. Barack Obama, "Signing Statement for H.R. 644," February 24,
2016; Barack Obama, "Statement by the President on H.R. 4310,"
January 3, 2013.

12. Donald Trump, "Statement by President Donald J. Trump on the
Signing of H.R. 3364," August 2, 2017.

13. Interview with Darrell Issa on *America's Newsroom*, Fox News Network,

February 23, 2016, http://video.foxnews.com/v/4769856603001/?#sp=show-clips.

14. Barack Obama, "Remarks by the President at Univision Town Hall," Bell Multicultural High School, Washington, DC, March 28, 2011.

15. Jeh Johnson, "Exercising Prosecutorial Discretion with Respect to Individuals Who Came to the United States as Children and with Respect to Certain Individuals Who Are the Parents of U.S. Citizens or Permanent Residents," memorandum, November 20, 2014, http://www.dhs .gov/sites/default/files/publications/14_1120_memo_deferred_action .pdf, 3–4; "Fact Sheet: Immigration Accountability Executive Actions," The White House, Office of Press Secretary, November 21, 2014, https://obamawhitehouse.archives.gov/the-press-office/2014/11/20 /fact-sheet-immigration-accountability-executive-action; *Texas v. United States*, no. 15-40238 (5th Cir., November 25, 2015); *US v. Texas*, 136 S.Ct. 2271 (2016), Docket no. 15-674 (judgment affirmed by equally divided court).

16. Daniel Henninger, "Obama's Limitless Government." *Wall Street Journal*, October 1, 2014, www.wsj.com/articles/dan-henninger-obamas -limitless-government-1412203893.

17. "Trump's New Travel Ban Is as Arbitrary and Senseless as the First," Editorial Board, *Washington Post*, March 6, 2017, www.washingtonpost. com/opinions/trumps-new-travel-ban-is-as-arbitrary-and-senseless-as -the-first/2017/03/06/9480c860-ff84-11e6-8f41-ca6cd597e4ca_story .html?utm_term=.673739f862d5; "A Government on the Edge and in the Dark," Editorial Board, *New York Times*, February 1, 2017, A26.

CHAPTER 2: POTUS THE COMMANDER IN CHIEF

1. James Madison to Thomas Jefferson, April 2, 1798, in *The Founders' Constitution*, eds. Philip B. Kurland and Ralph Lerner, vol. 3, article 1, section 8, clause 11, document 8, University of Chicago Press, http:// press-pubs.uchicago.edu/founders/documents/a1_8_11s8.html.

2. "Principal Wars in Which the United States Participated—U.S. Military Personnel Serving and Casualties," US Department of Defense, Office of the Secretary of Defense, Defense Casualty Analysis System, https://www.dmdc.osd.mil/dcas/pages/report_principal_wars.xhtml;

"Factsheet: America's Wars (May 2017)," US Department of Veterans Affairs, Office of Public Affairs; "VA Benefits Activity, Veterans Deployed to the Global War on Terror," VBA Office of Performance Analysis and Integrity, December 2014, www.oprm.va.gov/docs/foia /GWOT_Rpt-Jun_2014_Final_Rerun_NoEDU.doc, 3.

3. Harry S. Truman, "The President's News Conference," June 29, 1950, available at the American Presidency Project, www.presidency.ucsb. edu/ws/?pid=13544. Additionally, Truman stated in a news conference on June 29, 1950, that "we are not at war" and again referred to the action as a "police action" in a news conference on July 13, 1950. See also Louis Fisher, "The Korean War: On What Legal Basis Did Truman Act?," *The American Journal of International Law* 89, no. 21 (1995); and William G. Howell, and Jon C. Pevehouse, *While Dangers Gather: Congressional Checks on Presidential War Powers* (Princeton, NJ: Princeton University Press, 2007), 3. For Korean and Vietnam War casualty numbers, see above, note 2).

4. Truman relied on the UN Security Council resolutions as approval for the actions, something both George H. W. Bush and Clinton also did.

5. "Desert Shield and Desert Storm: A Chronology and Troop List for the 1990–1991 Persian Gulf Crisis," United States War College, Strategic Studies Institute, March 25, 1991, 41.

6. George H. W. Bush, "The President's News Conference on the Persian Gulf Crisis," January 9, 1991, available online at the American Presidency Project, www.presidency.ucsb.edu/ws/?pid=19202.

7. George H. W. Bush, "Statement on Signing the Resolution Authorizing the Use of Military Force Against Iraq," January 14, 1991, available online at the American Presidency Project, www.presidency.ucsb.edu /ws/?pid=19217.

8. George H. W. Bush, "Remarks at the Texas State Republican Convention in Dallas, Texas," June 20, 1992, available online at the American Presidency Project, www.presidency.ucsb.edu/ws/?pid=21125.

9. William J. Clinton, "The President's News Conference," August 3, 1994, available online at the American Presidency Project, www.presidency.ucsb.edu/ws/?pid=48940.

10. Alison Mitchell, "Deadlocked House Denies Support for Air Campaign," *New York Times*, April 29, 1999, www.nytimes.com/1999/04/29

/world/crisis-balkans-capitol-hill-deadlocked-house-denies-support-for-air-campaign.html.

11. George W. Bush, "Statement on Signing the Authorization for Use of Military Force Against Iraq Resolution of 2002," October 16, 2002, available online at the American Presidency Project, www.presidency.ucsb.edu/ws/?pid=64386.

12. Savage, "Barack Obama's Q&A."

13. "Chart: How the U.S. Troop Levels in Afghanistan Have Changed Under Obama," NPR, July 6, 2016, www.npr.org/2016/07/06/484979294/chart-how-the-u-s-troop-levels-in-afghanistan-have-changed-under-obama; Lawrence Kapp, Heidi Peters, and Moshe Schwartz, "Department of Defense Contractor and Troop Levels in Iraq and Afghanistan: 2007–2017," CRS Report R44116 (Washington, DC: Congressional Research Service, April 28, 2017), 4–5.

14. "U.S. Military Casualties—Operation Enduring Freedom (OEF) Casualty Summary by Month and Service (Updated September 12, 2017)," US Department of Defense, Defense Casualty Analyst System, www.dmdc.osd.mil/dcas/pages/report_oef_month.xhtml.

15. "Press Briefing by Press Secretary Sean Spicer, 3/10/2017, #21," March 10, 2017, The White House, Office of Press Secretary, www.whitehouse.gov/the-press-office/2017/03/10/press-briefing-press-secretary-sean-spicer-3102017-21; "Statement by Secretary of Defense Jim Mattis on Afghanistan Troop Levels," US Department of Defense, Press Operations, News Release number NR-226-17, June 14, 2017.

16. "Factsheet: America's Wars (May 2017)"; "VA Benefits Activity."

17. Linda J. Bilmes, "The Financial Legacy of Iraq and Afghanistan: How Wartime Spending Decisions Will Constrain Future National Security Budgets," HKS Faculty Research Working Paper Series RWP13-006, March 2013. Bilmes puts total medical, disability, and related costs at $836.1 billion. This was based only on casualties up to mid-2013.

18. Donald J. Trump (@realDonaldTrump), "What will we get for bombing Syria besides more debt and a possible long term conflict? Obama needs Congressional approval," Twitter, August 29, 2013, 3:14 p.m.

19. "Press Briefing by Secretary of State Rex Tillerson and National Security Advisor General H. R. McMaster," April 6, 2017.

20. Caroline Krass, Memorandum Opinion for the Attorney General, "Au-

thority to Use Force in Libya," *Office of Legal Counsel Opinions* 35, April 1, 2011, www.justice.gov/file/18376/download; "Basis for Using Force," Press Guidance, The White House, Office of Press Secretary, April 8, 2017. Accessible via: www.justsecurity.org/39803/apparent -administration-justifications-legality-strikes-syria/; Also, both Presidents Obama and Trump referenced "humanitarian catastrophe" and international security in their letters to Congress as justifications for military operations. "Letter from the President [Obama] regarding the commencement of operations in Libya," March 21, 2011, The White House, Office of Press Secretary; "Text of a Letter from the President to the Speaker of the House of Representatives and the President Pro Tempore of the Senate," April 8, 2017, The White House, Office of Press Secretary.

21. Selective Training and Service Act of 1940, Pub. L. 76-783, 54 Stat. 885, enacted September 16, 1940, amended August 1941 and December 19, 1941. Repealed by the Act of March 31, 1947, Pub. L. 80-26, 61 Stat. 31, enacted March 31, 1947; Selective Service Act of 1948, Pub. L. 80-759, 62 Stat. 604, enacted June 24, 1948; "Background of Selective Service" Selective Service System, 2017, www.sss .gov/About/History-And-Records/Background-Of-Selective-Service. See also Kristy N. Kamarck, "The Selective Service System and Draft Registration: Issues for Congress," CRS Report R44452 (Washington, DC: Congressional Research Service, April 11, 2015); Califano Jr., *Triumph and Tragedy of Lyndon Johnson*, 193–202.

22. "New Draft Policy to Cut Graduate School Enrollment," in *CQ Almanac 1968*, 24th ed., 15-783-15-786 (Washington, DC: Congressional Quarterly, 1969), http://library.cqpress.com/cqalmanac/cqal 68-1282246. See also Lyndon B. Johnson: "Special Message to the Congress on Selective Service," March 6, 1967. The lottery, though authorized under President Johnson, was not undertaken until Richard Nixon was president. "The Vietnam Lotteries," Selected Service System, www.sss.gov/About/History-And-Records/lotter1.

23. "Nixon Conversation with Henry Kissinger following Nixon's Speech on the Situation in Vietnam on April 7, 1971," Conversation number 1–21, Richard Nixon Presidential Library and Museum, www.nixonli brary.gov/virtuallibrary/tapeexcerpts/1-21-draft.mp3.

24. Henry Kissinger, *Ending the Vietnam War: A History of America's Involvement in and Extrication from the Vietnam War* (New York: Simon & Schuster, 2003), 296.

25. Interview with Charles Rangel on *Face the Nation*, CBS, November 19, 2006.

26. "2015 Demographics Report: Profile of the Military Community," US Department of Defense, http://download.militaryonesource. mil/12038/MOS/Reports/2015-Demographics-Report.pdf, 24–25; *Population Representation in the Military Services: 2015*, "Table B-10: Non-Prior Service (NPS) Active Component Enlisted Accessions, FY15: by Service, Gender, Race, and Ethnicity with Civilian Comparison Group," US Department of Defense, Office of the Under Secretary of Defense, Personnel and Readiness, 2016.

27. 50 U.S.C. 1541(a): "It is the purpose of this chapter to fulfill the intent of the framers of the Constitution of the United States and insure that the collective judgment of both the Congress and the President will apply to the introduction of United States Armed Forces into hostilities, or into situations where imminent involvement in hostilities is clearly indicated by the circumstances, and to the continued use of such forces in hostilities or in such situations."

28. Barbara Salazar Torreon, "Instances of Use of United States Armed Forces Abroad, 1798–2016," CRS Report 42738 (Washington, DC: Congressional Research Service, September 13, 2012).

29. "Remarks by the President in a Press Conference," The White House, Office of Press Secretary, November 5, 2014, https://obamawhite house.archives.gov/the-press-office/2014/11/05/remarks-president -press-conference.

CHAPTER 3: POTUS THE LEGISLATOR

1. The first Congress established the first administrative agency to take care of pension claims of Revolutionary War veterans. Act of September 29, 1789, 1 Stat. 95 (1st Congress, 1st Session).

2. Donald Barry and Harry Whitcomb, *The Legal Foundations of Public Administration*, 3rd ed. (Lanham, MD: Rowman & Littlefield 2005), 24.

3. *Final Report of the Attorney General's Committee on Administrative Procedure* (Washington, DC: US Government Printing Office, 1941), 8.

4. James Madison, "The Particular Structure of the New Government and the Distribution of Power among Its Different Parts," *Federalist*, no. 47 (1788). Retrieved from The Avalon Project, Yale Law School, http://avalon.law.yale.edu/18th_century/fed47.asp.

5. Stanton Glantz, "The White House Told FDA That Black Lives Don't Matter," University of California-San Francisco Center for Tobacco Control and Research and Education, June 6, 2016, https://tobacco .ucsf.edu/white-house-told-fda-black-lives-don%E2%80%99t-mat ter; "Deeming Tobacco Products to Be Subject to the Federal Food, Drug, and Cosmetic Act, as Amended by the Family Smoking Prevention and Tobacco Control Act; Restrictions on the Sale and Distribution of Tobacco Products and Required Warning Statements for Tobacco Products," Final Rule Redline Changes, Department of Health and Human Services, Food and Drug Administration, 21 CFR Parts 1100, 1140, and 1143, Docket No. FDA-2014-N-0189, https:// www.regulations.gov/document?D=FDA-2014-N-0189-83193.

6. Connor Raso, "Agency Avoidance of Rulemaking Procedures," *Administrative Law Review* 67, no. 1 (2015): 101–67.

7. Peter H. Schuck, "A Bathroom of One's Own?," *New York Times*, May 18, 2016. Referenced in his book *Why Government Fails* (Princeton, NJ: Princeton University Press, 2014).

8. Administrative Procedure Act, 5 U.S.C. 553(b)(3)(A) (1966).

9. Directive number 357, US Department of Labor, Office of Federal Contract Compliance Programs, February 28, 2013; Catherine E. Lhamon and Vanita Gupta, "Dear Colleague Letter on Transgender Students," May 13, 2016, Washington, DC, Office for Civil Rights, US Department of Education and Civil Rights Division, US Department of Justice, https://www2.ed.gov/about/offices/list/ocr/letters/col league-201605-title-ix-transgender.pdf; Russlyn Ali, "Dear Colleague Letter: Sexual Violence," April 4, 2011, Washington, DC, Office of Civil Rights, US Department of Education, https://www2.ed.gov /about/offices/list/ocr/letters/colleague-201104.pdf.

10. *State of Texas v. US*, Civil Action No. 7:16-cv-00054-O (Northern Dis-

trict of Texas, 2016) (ordering preliminary injunction of transgender bathroom directive).

11. Sandra Battle and T. E. Wheeler II "Dear Colleague Letter," February 22, 2017, Washington, DC, Office for Civil Rights, US Department of Education, Civil Rights Division, US Department of Justice, https:// www2.ed.gov/about/offices/list/ocr/letters/colleague-201702-title-ix .docx.

12. "Enacted Legislation (114th Congress): January 1, 2016–December 31, 2016." GovTrack, accessed June 1, 2017, www.govtrack.us/con gress/bills/browse?congress=114&status=28,29,32,33; "Thousands of Pages and Rules in the Federal Register," Competitive Enterprise Institute, May 31, 2017, https://cei.org/10KC/Chapter-2.

13. Brian R. Dirck, *The Executive Branch of Federal Government: People, Process, and Politics* (Santa Barbara, CA: ABC-CLIO, 2007), 102.

14. Presidential Executive Order No. 9066, "Authorizing the Secretary of War to Prescribe Military Areas," February 19, 1942.

15. Presidential Executive Order No. 10340, "Directing the Secretary of Commerce to Take Possession of and Operate the Plants and Facilities of Certain Steel Companies," April 8, 1952. See also *Youngstown Sheet & Tube Co. v. Sawyer*, 343 US 579 (1952).

16. Presidential Executive Order 10730, "Providing Assistance for the Removal of an Obstruction of Justice Within the State of Arkansas," September 23, 1957.

17. Linda Greenhouse, "Justices Say E.P.A. Has Power to Act on Harmful Gases," *New York Times*, April 3, 2007, www.nytimes.com/2007/04/03 /washington/03scotus.html.

18. Fair Housing Act, 42 U.S.C. 3601, Pub. L. 90-284, 82 Stat. 81, enacted April 11, 1968.

CHAPTER 4: THE FOUR PILLARS OF POTUS POWER

1. Jack Valenti, "The White House Experience," *Washington Post Magazine*, March 4, 1984, 12–14. Lear had previously been Washington's personal secretary.

2. Valenti, "White House Experience," 12–14.

3. Valenti, "White House Experience," 12–14. (Referring to: An Act making Appropriations for Certain Civil Expenses of the Government for the Year ending the thirtieth of June, eighteen hundred fifty-eight, 11 Stat. 221, 228, enacted March 3, 1857.)

4. Shirley Anne Warshaw, *Guide to the White House Staff* (Thousand Oaks, CA: CQ Press, 2013), 2.

5. Warshaw, *Guide to the White House Staff*, 35.

6. Warshaw, *Guide to the White House Staff*, 36. Warshaw does mention that President Benjamin Harrison's private secretary handled some speechwriting duties. Cortelyou later held the offices of secretary of labor and commerce, postmaster general, and secretary of the treasury.

7. Valenti, "White House Experience," 13. The two advisers were Representatives Bascom Slemp and Everett Sanders.

8. Valenti, "White House Experience," 12–14.

9. Different scholars include different offices in their White House staff count, and the size of White House staff offices fluctuates. Executive branch expert Stephen Robertson writes, "The problem of how to count the White House Office staff is a factor in any discussion of its growth. No universally accepted figures exist on the precise size of the White House staff, and published estimates vary considerably depending on who is counting and how." "Executive Office of the President," in *Guide to the Presidency and Executive Branch*, ed. Michael Nelson, 5th ed. (Thousand Oaks, CA: CQ Press, 2013), 1123. For the purposes of this book, "White House staff" refers to policy or political staff and includes detailees, interns, and any sort of attaché as well as presidential policy offices such as the National Security Council. "43 Top Aides Served President Johnson Since 1963," in *CQ Almanac 1968*, 24th ed., 17-921-17-922 (Washington, DC: Congressional Quarterly, 1969), http://library.cqpress.com/cqalmanac/cqal68-1282543.

10. National Security Act of 1947, 50 U.S.C. 15 401; P.L. 80-253; 61 stat. 495, enacted July 26, 1947.

11. Richard A. Best Jr., "The National Security Council: An Organizational Assessment," CRS Report RL30840 (Washington, DC: Congressional Research Service, December 28, 2011), 7–23.

12. Shawn Brimley et al., "Enabling Decision: Shaping the National Security Council for the Next President," Center for a New American

Security, June 2015, www.cnas.org/sites/default/files/publications-pdf/CNAS%20Report_NSC%20Reform_Final.pdf, p. 2.

13. Ivo H. Daalder and I. M. Destler, *In the Shadow of the Oval Office: Profiles of the National Security Advisers and the Presidents They Served—From JFK to George W. Bush* (New York: Simon & Schuster, 2009), 12–56.

14. Brimley et al., "Enabling Decision," 2–4.

15. Robert Gates, *Duty: Memoirs of a Secretary at War* (New York: Alfred A. Knopf, 2014), 587.

16. Brimley et al., "Enabling Decision," 2; Karen DeYoung, "Rice Favors 'Mean but Lean' National Security Council," *Washington Post*, January 17, 2017, www.washingtonpost.com/world/national-security/rice-favors-mean-but-lean-national-security-council/2017/01/16/6244aa3c-dc49-11e6-ad42-f3375f271c9c_story.html?utm_term=.690e9985a3fc.

17. Nick Glass, "Kerry Passes Clinton's State Dept. Total of Miles Traveled Abroad," *Politico*, December 7, 2015, www.politico.com/story/2015/12/john-kerry-miles-traveled-secretary-state-216493.

18. Gates, *Duty*, 301.

19. Colum Lynch, "The Libya Debate: How Fair Is Obama's New Claim That the U.S. Led from the Front?," *Foreign Policy*, October 23, 2012, http://foreignpolicy.com/2012/10/23/the-libya-debate-how-fair-is-obamas-new-claim-that-the-u-s-led-from-the-front.

20. Amy B. Zegart, *Flawed by Design: The Evolution of the CIA, JCS, and NSC* (Stanford, CA: Stanford University Press, 1999), 76.

21. DeYoung, Karen, "How the Obama White House Runs Foreign Policy," *Washington Post*, August 4, 2015, www.washingtonpost.com/world/national-security/how-the-obama-white-house-runs-foreign-policy/2015/08/04/2befb960-2fd7-11e5-8353-1215475949f4_story.html?utm_term=.faf5bcc79041.

22. Gates, *Duty*, p. 587. During the Obama administration, the NSC was briefly named the National Security Staff (NSS). The name was changed back to the National Security Council in 2014.

23. "Report of the Congressional Committees Investigating the Iran Contra Affair with Supplemental, Minority, and Additional Views," S. Rept. No. 100-216, H. Rept. No. 100-433 (Washington, DC: US Government Printing Office, December 17, 1987). See also Theodore

Draper, *A Very Thin Line: The Iran-Contra Affair* (New York: Hill and Wang, 1991), 17–27, 51.

24. Ron Suskind, *The Price of Loyalty* (New York: Simon & Schuster, 2004), 70–76.

25. "U.S. Ambassador to the United Nations Susan Rice," *ABC This Week,* September 16, 2012; "Libyan Pres. Magariaf, Amb. Rice and Sen. McCain," *Face the Nation,* CBS, September 16, 2012; "Interview with Benjamin Netanyahu; Interview with Susan Rice; Interview with Nancy Pelosi; Interview with Rudy Giuliani," *State of the Union,* CNN, September 16, 2012; "Amb. Susan Rice, Rep. Mike Rogers Discuss Violence Against Americans in the Middle East," *Fox News Sunday,* September 16, 2012.

26. David Samuels, "The Storyteller and the President," *New York Times Magazine,* May 8, 2016, MM44.

27. Eli Rake and Josh Rogin, "Military Hates White House 'Microman-agement' of ISIS War," *Daily Beast,* October 31, 2014, www.thedaily beast.com/military-hates-white-house-micromanagement-of-isis-war.

28. National Defense Authorization Act of 2017, Pub. L. No. 114-328, enacted December 23, 2016.

29. Joseph A. Califano Jr., *Governing America: An Insider's Report from the White House and the Cabinet* (New York: Simon & Schuster, 1981), 27.

30. Michael Nelson, ed., *Guide to the Executive Branch,* 5th ed. (Thousand Oaks, CA: CQ Press, 2013), 1188.

31. James P. Pfiffner, *The Modern Presidency,* 6th ed. (Boston: Wadsworth Cengage Learning, 2010), 108. See also Robert Pear, "Ending Its Secrecy, White House Lists Health-Care Panel," *New York Times,* March 27, 1993, www.nytimes.com/1993/03/27/us/ending-its-se crecy-white-house-lists-health-care-panel.html. Pfiffner and Pear put the total task force at over five hundred employees. Pear points out that most of these people were already government employees and that about one hundred were temporary employees or consultants hired solely for the health care legislation.

32. This figure includes individuals whose work focused substantially on domestic policy, such as those in the AIDS Policy Office, the Faith-Based Development Office, the Social Innovation Office, the White House Rural Council, the Office of Native American Affairs, and the

Office of Urban Affairs, as well as policy teams for health, education, environment, justice and regulatory affairs, immigration, and finance. Others included in the count were those employed in the Office of Public Engagement (formerly the Office of Public Liaison), the Office of Intergovernmental Affairs, the Office of Political Affairs, the National Economic Council Staff, as well as interns assigned to these offices. Since the White House staff listings include only employees on the official payroll, other sources were consulted, including statements by White House staff, news articles, other White House documents, and academic estimates. For the White House staff list used, see "2014 Annual Report to Congress on White House Staff," The White House, Office of Press Secretary, https://obamawhitehouse.archives.gov/brief ing-room/disclosures/annual-records/2014.

33. Presidential Executive Order 13507, "Establishing the White House Office of Health Reform," April 8, 2009.

34. Noelle Straub, "Sen. Byrd Questions Obama's Use of Policy Czars," *New York Times*, January 25, 2009, www.nytimes.com/gwire/2009/02 /25/25greenwire-byrd-questions-obamas-use-of-policy-czars-9865.html.

35. Manu Raju, "Democrats Join GOP Czar Wars," *Politico*, September 17, 2009, www.politico.com/story/2009/09/democrats-join-gop-czar -wars-027265.

36. As of mid-July 2017, Trump had still yet to name a nominee for two-thirds of key positions requiring Senate approval. See "Political Appointee Tracker," Partnership for Public Service, retrieved July 17, 2017, https://ourpublicservice.org/issues/presidential-transition/political -appointee-tracker.php. See also Tal Kopan, "At 200-Day Mark, Trump Nominations Still Lag," CNN, August 7, 2017, www.cnn .com/2017/08/07/politics/trump-200-days-nominations/index.html.

37. John Jay to George Washington, August 8, 1793, in *The Founders' Constitution*, eds. Philip B. Kurland and Ralph Lerner, vol. 4 (Chicago: University of Chicago Press, 1987), 258. Accessible via www.acslaw .org/files/2004%20programs_OLC%20principles_white%20paper .pdf. For an overview of the events surrounding the 1793 request, see William R. Casto, "The Early Supreme Court Justices' Most Significant Opinion," *Ohio Northern University Law Review* 29 (2002): 173.

38. Independent Offices Appropriation Act of 1933, Pub. L. No. 73-78,

16(a), 48 Stat. 283, 307 (June 16, 1933). This created an assistant solicitor general (within the Department of Justice) to assist the solicitor general in the performance of his duties. The new office was tasked by Attorney General Homer Cummings with providing legal counsel to the president as well as other executive branch agencies. Attorney General Order No. 23,507 (December 30, 1933).

39. "The White House Counsel," The White House Transition Project, report 2017–29, 2017, http://whitehousetransitionproject.org/wp-content/uploads/2016/03/WHTP2017-29-Counsel.pdf, 56–57.

40. "White House Counsel," 56–57.

41. "White House Counsel," 56–57. See also "White House Staff, Alphabetical List (1981–1989)," Ronald Reagan Presidential Library Archives, https://reaganlibrary.archives.gov/archives/reference/whitehousestaff alpha.htm.

42. "White House Counsel," 56–57. Lloyd Cutler states that the counsel could have had as many as fifty attorneys at one point.

43. "White House Counsel's Office George W. Bush 2008," White House Transition Project, Individual Office Organizational Charts, Office of the Counsel, 2015, http://whitehousetransitionproject.org/transition -resources-2/office-briefs/.

44. "White House Counsel," 56. (The White House Transition Project stated that Obama's White House counsel topped out at thirty-five attorneys. Other sources put the high-water mark at forty-one). See David Lat, "Making the White House Counsel's Office Great Again," AbovetheLaw.com, March 7, 2017, http://abovethelaw.com/2017/03 /making-the-white-house-counsels-office-great-again/.

45. "President Donald J. Trump Announces Key Additions to the Office of the White House Counsel," Press Release, The White House, Office of Press Secretary, March 7, 2017.

46. Bruce Ackerman, "Legal Acrobatics, Illegal War," *New York Times*, June 20, 2011, www.nytimes.com/2011/06/21/opinion/21Ackerman .html/; Andrew Cohen, "The Torture Memos, 10 Years Later," *The Atlantic*, February 6, 2012, www.theatlantic.com/national/archive/2012 /02/the-torture-memos-10-years-later/252439/.

47. Charlie Savage, "Departing White House Counsel Held Powerful Sway," *New York Times*, April 7, 2014, A14.

48. Ackerman, "Legal Acrobatics."

49. Ackerman, "Legal Acrobatics."

50. Matt Appuzzo and Emmarie Huetteman, "Sally Yates Tells Senators She Warned Trump About Michael Flynn," *New York Times*, May 8, 2017, www.nytimes.com/2017/05/08/us/politics/michael-flynn-sally -yates-hearing.html.

51. Martha Joynt Kumar, *Managing the President's Message: The White House Communications Operation* (Baltimore, MD: Johns Hopkins University Press, 2010), loc. 397, Kindle.

52. Kumar, *Managing the President's Message,* loc. 6325, Kindle.

53. Kumar, *Managing the President's Message*, loc. 548–49, Kindle.

54. Julie Hirschfeld Davis, "Injecting Personality into @POTUS," *New York Times*, November 9, 2015, A15.

55. Reported numbers for Donald Trump's communications department put it at around forty staff members, a bit lower than the official totals of fifty-two and sixty-nine for George W. Bush and Barack Obama. The true number of staffers, interns, and others working on communications is likely higher by several magnitudes, as it was with previous administrations.

56. Kumar, *Managing the President's Message*, loc. 3414–15, Kindle.

57. Sam Stein, "Here's the Full Transcript of Obama's Interview with Huff-Post," *Huffington Post*, March 21, 2015, www.huffingtonpost.com /2015/03/21/obama-huffpost-interview-transcript_n_6905450.html ?1426972456.

58. Martha Joynt Kumar, "Presidential Interchanges with Reporters: Six Observations," *The White House Transition Project*, report 2017–40, http://whitehousetransitionproject.org/wp-content/uploads/2017/01 /WHTP2017-40-Presidential-Interchanges-with-Reporters.pdf. (Numbers valid through September 30, 2016.)

59. Bill Plante, "Reliable Sources," CNN, February 24, 2013.

60. Kumar, *Managing the President's Message*, loc. 4873–4874, Kindle.

61. Hadas Gold and Sarah Wheaton, "Is the White House Press Corps Becoming Obsolete?," *Politico Magazine*, April 25, 2015, www.politico .com/story/2015/04/is-the-white-house-press-corps-becoming-obso lete-117330.

62. See "Watch Trump Ignore Several Questions on Russia," CNN, Feb-

ruary 15, 2017, www.cnn.com/videos/politics/2017/02/15/president-trump-ignores-media-questions-about-russian-contacts-orig-aa.cnn. See also Susan Milligan, "The President and the Press," *Columbia Journalism Review*, March/April 2015, www.cjr.org/analysis/the_president_and_the_press.php.

63. Julie Hirschfeld Davis and Michael D. Shear, "Trump, on YouTube, Pledges to Create Jobs," *New York Times*, November 21, 2016, https://www.nytimes.com/2016/11/21/us/politics/donald-trump-presidency.html.

64. David M. Jackson, "Trump Promises to Keep Tweeting, Accuses Media of Trying to Convince Him Otherwise," *USA Today*, June 6, 2017, www.usatoday.com/story/news/politics/onpolitics/2017/06/06/donald-trump-twitter-qatar-travel-ban-supreme-court/102542850/.

65. "Executive Branch Civilian Employment Since 1940," *Historical Federal Workforce Tables; Federal Employee Reports; Data, Analysis, and Documentation*, Office of Personnel and Management, www.opm.gov/policy-data-oversight/data-analysis-documentation/federal-employment-reports/historical-tables/executive-branch-civilian-employment-since-1940/.

66. Gates, *Duty*, 586–87.

67. Jamie Gorelick, "Defense Reform in the 21st Century; Panel 1: Guiding Principles for Reform," Center for Strategic and International Studies, Washington, DC, March 14, 2016.

68. Madison, "The Particular Structure."

CHAPTER 5: THE GRIP OF THE GERRYMANDER

1. "Elbridge Gerry, 5th Vice President," United States Senate Historical Office, accessed July 20, 2017, www.senate.gov/artandhistory/history/common/generic/VP_Elbridge_Gerry.htm.

2. Thomas Rogers Hunter, "The First Gerrymander? Patrick Henry, James Madison, James Monroe, and Virginia's 1788 Congressional Districting," *Early American Studies* 9, no. 3 (Fall 2011): 781–83. (Citing William C. Rives, *History of the Life and Times of James Madison*, vol. 2 [Boston: Little, Brown, 1859–68], 653–55.)

3. John Nowakowski, "Dubious Democracy 2016: Data by District,

115th House," FairVote, February, 23 2017, https://fairvote.app.box.com/v/DubiousDemocracy2016.

4. "Election Returns—Representative in Congress," Pennsylvania Department of State, accessed September 13, 2017, www.electionreturns.pa.gov/General/OfficeResults?OfficeID=11&ElectionID=54&ElectionType=G&IsActive=0.

5. "11/08/2016 Official General Election Results—Statewide," North Carolina State Board of Elections, accessed July 9, 2017, http://er.ncsbe.gov/?election_dt=11/08/2016&county_id=0&office=FED&contest=0.

6. "Election Center—2016 Presidential Election," Connecticut Secretary of State, accessed July 1, 2017, http://ctemspublic.pcctg.net/#/home.

7. "Official 2016 Presidential General Election Results for Representative in Congress," Maryland State Board of Elections, accessed July 8, 2017, www.elections.state.md.us/elections/2016/results/general/gen_results_2016_4_008X.html.

8. *Fletcher v. Lamone*, 831 F. Supp. 887, 903 (2011).

9. See "2012 REDMAP Summary Report," The Redistricting Majority Project, January 4, 2013, www.redistrictingmajorityproject.com/?p=646.

10. Patrick Marley, "Reince Priebus Backs Electoral Vote Change, but It's State's Decision," *Milwaukee-Wisconsin Journal Sentinel*, January 13, 2013, http://archive.jsonline.com/news/statepolitics/reince-priebus-backs-electoral-vote-change-but-its-states-decision-fp8bqc3-186720481.html/.

11. Edward-Issac Dovere, "Obama, Holder to Lead Post-Trump Redistricting Campaign," *Politico*, October 17, 2016, www.politico.com/story/2016/10/obama-holder-redistricting-gerrymandering-229868.

12. Nowakowski, "Dubious Democracy."

13. "State Health Facts—Demographics and the Economy—Population Distribution by Race/Ethnicity, 2015," Henry J. Kaiser Family Foundation, www.kff.org/other/state-indicator/distribution-by-raceethnicity/?currentTimeframe=0&sortModel=%7B%22colId%22:%22Location%22,%2 2sort%22:%22asc%22%7D.

14. *Cooper v. Harris*, Docket No. 15-1262, 581 U.S. (2017). The last white Democratic congressman in the Deep South, John Barrow of Georgia, lost reelection in 2014.

15. Michael Grunwald, "Immigrant Son," *Time*, February 7, 2013, http://swampland.time.com/2013/02/07/immigrant-son/3/.

16. "Final Vote Results from Roll Call 396, On Passage of the Bill (H.R. 3590 as Amended)," United States Senate, December 24, 2009, www.senate.gov/legislative/LIS/roll_call_lists/roll_call_vote_cfm.cfm?congress=111&session=1&vote=00396.

17. *Gill v. Whitford*, Docket No. 16-1161, 2017 (cert. granted).

18. Eric Ostermeier, "Senate Will Have Historic Number of Ex-US Reps in 114th Congress," *Smart Politics*, University of Minnesota Libraries, December 4, 2014, http://editions.lib.umn.edu/smartpolitics/2014/12/04/senate-will-have-historic-numb/.

19. James Madison, *Federalist* no. 62, "The Senate" (1787).

20. "Senate Roll Call Vote No. 242," *Congressional Record*, November 21, 2013, daily edition, S8417. Sixty votes are required to break filibusters, which are still permitted to block votes on legislation. Permitting filibusters with respect to legislation is a bow to the idea that they are part of the more deliberative role of the Senate. Senate Roll Call Vote no. 109, 115th Congress, 1st Session, April 6, 2017; Pub L. 112–166, enacted August 10, 2012, and Sen. Res 116 (112th Congress), passed June 29, 2011 (reinterpreting Senate Rule XXII); Matt Flegenheimer, "Senate Republicans Deploy 'Nuclear Option' to Clear Path for Gorsuch," *New York Times*, April 6, 2017, www.nytimes.com/2017/04/06/us/politics/neil-gorsuch-supreme-court-senate.html.

21. Lee Hamilton, "Why Holding the Majority Matters," Indiana University Center of Representative Government, August 28, 2008, http://corg.indiana.edu/why-holding-the-majority-matters.

CHAPTER 6: PAY-TO-PLAY CONGRESS

1. "Committees," United States House of Representatives, accessed July 23, 2017, https://www.house.gov/committees/; "Committees," United States Senate, accessed July 23, 2017, www.senate.gov/committees/committees_home.htm.

2. Norman Ornstein et al., *Vital Statistics on Congress* (Washington, DC: Brookings Institution, January 7, 2017), "Table 4-4: Committee Assignments for Representatives, 84th–113th Congresses, 1955–2014"

and "Table 4-5: Committee Assignments for Senators, 84th–113th Congresses, 1955–2014."

3. Craig Volden and Alan Wiseman, "How Term Limits for Committee Chairs Make Congress Less Effective," *Washington Post*, January 4, 2017, www.washingtonpost.com/news/monkey-cage/wp/2017/01/04 /how-term-limits-for-committee-chairs-make-congress-less-effective /?utm_term=.c05fd0e78b5c.

4. James A. Thurber, "What's Wrong with Congress and What Should Be Done About It?," in *Can Government Be Repaired?: Lessons from America*, eds. Iwan Morgan and Philip Davies (London: University of London/Institute for the Study of the Americas Press, 2012).

5. "2013–2014 Election Cycle Due & Money Raised (February Final)," Democratic Congressional Campaign Committee; see Appendix A; Mike DeBonis, "Nancy Pelosi's Fundraising Breaks $25 Million for 2017," *Washington Post*, July 31, 2017, https://www.washingtonpost .com/news/powerpost/wp/2017/07/31/nancy-pelosis-fundraising -breaks-25-million-for-2017/?utm_term=.51a38be13f9e.

6. Lauren French, "After Clash, More Black Lawmakers Paying 'Dues' to Party," *Politico*, November 17, 2015, www.politico.com/story/2015/11 /democrats-seek-to-repair-campaign-rift-with-black-caucus-215705.

7. Ken Buck, *Drain the Swamp* (Washington, DC: Regnery, 2017), 74.

8. "Team Ryan—Summary," Center for Responsive Politics, accessed May 5, 2017, www.opensecrets.org/jfc/summary.php?id=C00545947; "Rep. Paul Ryan—Expenditures (2013–2014)," Center for Responsive Politics, accessed May 5, 2017, www.opensecrets.org/politicians /expend.php?cid=N00004357&cycle=2014.

9. Lee Drutman, "Ways and Means, Financial Services, and Energy and Commerce Are Top House Fundraising Committees," Sunlight Foundation, April 2, 2012, https://sunlightfoundation.com/2012/04/02 /housecommittees/.

10. Niv Sultan, "Defense Sector Contributions Locked in on Committee Members," Center for Responsive Politics, March 2, 2017, https:// www.opensecrets.org/news/2017/03/defense-sector-contributions/.

11. Alexander Cohen, "Meet the Defense Industry's Favorite Committee," *Politico*, July 15, 2015, www.politico.com/magazine/story/2015/07 /defense-industry-money-congress-120134.

12. Ryan Grim and Sabrina Siddiqui, "Call Time for Congress Shows How Fundraising Dominates Bleak Work Life," *Huffington Post*, January 8, 2013, www.huffingtonpost.com/2013/01/08/call-time-congressional-fundraising_n_2427291.html.

13. Grim and Siddiqui, "Call Time for Congress."

14. Mark Barabak, "Iowa's Harkin Says Fundraising, Lack of Relationships Hurt Senate," *Los Angeles Times*, June 23, 2014, www.latimes.com/nation/politics/politicsnow/la-pn-iowa-tom-harkin-on-40-years-in-the-senate-20140623-story.html. Senator Tom Harkin is quoted as stating, "Schlepping from here to New York to L.A. to Chicago to New Orleans to Miami to, my God, I don't know where. Ten thousand here, 20,000 there, 15,000 there. Boy. I don't miss that."

15. "Counter Methodology," Issue One, accessed January 10, 2017, www.issueone.org/counter-methodology/.

CHAPTER 7: CONGRESSIONAL CHAOS

1. See "Past Days in Session of the U.S. Congress," Congress.gov, accessed October 20, 2017, www.congress.gov/past-days-in-session. From 2001 to 2016, the House averaged 139 days in session and the Senate averaged 162 days in session.

2. See Dana Milbank, "Congress Should Work Five Days a Week," *Chicago Tribune*, November 6, 2015, www.chicagotribune.com/news/opinion/commentary/ct-congress-paul-ryan-newt-gingrich-perspec-1109-20151106-story.html.

3. Milbank, "Congress Should Work."

4. Joshua Green, "The Pampered World of Congressional Air Travel," *Bloomberg Businessweek*, April 30, 2013, www.bloomberg.com/news/articles/2013-04-30/the-pampered-world-of-congressional-air-travel.

5. Lisa Desjardins, "CNN Analysis: Congress in D.C. Far Less than It Used to Be," CNN, August 1, 2013, www.cnn.com/2013/08/01/politics/congress-work-time/index.html.

6. Ornstein et al., *Vital Statistics*, "Table 6-1. House Workload, 80th–113th Congresses (1947–2014)."

7. Lee Hamilton, "Members of Congress Need to Spend More Time on Capitol Hill," Indiana University Center on Representative Govern-

ment, November 25, 2015, http://corg.indiana.edu/members-con
gress-need-spend-more-time-capitol-hill.

8. Carl Hulse, "Rep. Israel of New York Won't Seek Re-Election," *New York Times*, January 6, 2015, A15.

9. See "2013–2014 Election Cycle," Democratic Congressional Campaign Committee.

10. Trevor Potter, "Our Money-in-Politics Problem: Building a Campaign Finance System for the People," College of Charleston, November 1, 2016. A transcription of this speech is available at the website of the Campaign Legal Center: www.campaignlegalcenter.org/sites/default /files/Trevor%20Charleston%20Speech%20for%20Publication.pdf. Andy Kroll, "Retiring GOP Congressman: Fundraising Is 'The Main Business' of Congress," *Mother Jones*, August 8, 2013, www.mother jones.com/politics/2013/08/retiring-rodney-alexander-congressman -fundraising-congress/.

11. Barabak, "Iowa's Harkin Says."

12. "Interview with Presidential Candidate Donald Trump; Interview with Vermont Senator Bernie Sanders; Interview with Florida Senator Marco Rubio; State of the Cartoonion: Republicans' 'Super Heroic' Lineup," CNN, October 25, 2015.

13. "Steyer, Thomas: Donor Detail" (based on May 2016 FEC data), Center for Responsive Politics, accessed July 8, 2017, www.opensecrets .org/outsidespending/donor_detail.php?cycle=2016&id=U0000003 652&type=I&super=N&name=Steyer%2C+Thomas. See also Jason Plautz, "Tom Steyer Spent $74 Million on the Election. He Didn't Get Much to Show for It," *The Atlantic*, November 5, 2014, www.the atlantic.com/politics/archive/2014/11/tom-steyer-spent-74-million -on-the-election-he-didnt-get-much-to-show-for-it/452727.

14. Ornstein et al., *Vital Statistics*, "Table 6-4: Congressional Workload, 80th–113th Congresses (1947–2014)."

15. "Cloture Motions," US Senate, accessed August 1, 2017, www.senate .gov/pagelayout/reference/cloture_motions/clotureCounts.htm.

16. Ornstein et al., *Vital Statistics*, "Table 5-1: Congressional Staff, 1979– 2015."

17. Ornstein et al., "Table 5-8: Staffs of Congressional Support Agencies, FY1946–FY2015."

18. Lee Drutman and Steven Teles, "Why Congress Relies on Lobbyists Instead of Thinking for Itself," *The Atlantic*, March 10, 2015, www .theatlantic.com/politics/archive/2015/03/when-congress-cant-think -for-itself-it-turns-to-lobbyists/387295/.

19. "Lobbying Database," Center for Responsive Politics, accessed August 1, 2017, www.opensecrets.org/lobby/. The so-called Honest Leadership and Government Act, passed in 2007, requires individuals to register as lobbyists only if at least 20 percent of their time is spent lobbying. There were 14,000 registered lobbyists the year before the act took effect in 2007; thanks to this loophole, only 11,500 were registered in 2015.

20. Ornstein et al., *Vital Statistics*, "Table 5-10. Legislative Branch Appropriations, by Category, Fiscal Years 1984–2016 (In Thousands of Dollars)"; "Lobbying Database," Center for Responsive Politics.

21. Ernest F. Hollings and Kirk Victor, *Making Government Work* (Columbia, SC: University of South Carolina Press, 2008), 328.

22. Ornstein et al., *Vital Statistics*, "Table 5-1."

23. Matt Viser, "Lawmaker Finds New Realities in Return to Congress," *Boston Globe*, May 28, 2013, www.bostonglobe.com/news /nation/2013/05/27/representative-returns-house-after-three-decades -and-finds-eroded-traditions/U49Txz7dENOLu1crHD6pN/story .html. In this interview with the *Boston Globe*, Representative Rick Nolan, who had a three-decade break between stints in Congress, lamented how the influence of committees on legislation had waned.

CHAPTER 8: CUTTING OFF ITS NOSE TO SPITE ITS FACE

1. United States Constitution, Article I, section 7, clause 1.

2. James Saturno and Jessica Tollestrup, "Omnibus Appropriations Acts: Overview of Recent Practices," CRS Report RL32473 (Washington, DC: Congressional Research Service, January 14, 2017), 2. See also Consolidated Appropriations Act of 2017, Pub. Law 115-31, Sec. 537, enacted May 5, 2017.

3. Consolidated and Further Continuing Appropriations Act, 2015, Pub. L. 113-235, Sec. 630(d), 128 Stat. 2146, enacted December 16, 2014. See also Steven Mufson and Tom Hamburger, "Jamie Dimon

Himself Called to Urge Support for the Derivatives Rule in the Spending Bill," *Washington Post*, December 11, 2014, www.washingtonpost .com/news/wonk/wp/2014/12/11/the-item-that-is-blowing-up-the -budget-deal/?utm_term=.5ba31cfec25c.

4. Consolidated Appropriations Act, 2016, Pub. L. 114-113, 129 Stat. 2897, Sec. 101 (a)–(b), enacted December 18, 2015.

5. Consolidated Appropriations Act of 2017, Pub. L. 115-31, Sec. 537, enacted May 5, 2017.

6. The omnibus acts for fiscal years 2015 and 2016 were both passed the week before Christmas recess.

7. Dan Clark, "Yes, New York Has More Corrupt Officials than Any Other State," *PolitiFact New York*, September 19, 2016, http://www .politifact.com/new-york/statements/2016/sep/19/elaine-phillips /new-york-has-been-most-corrupt-state-decades/.

8. Kelsey Snell and Karoun Dermirjian "Congress Passes Budget Deal and Heads Home for the Year," *Washington Post*, December 18, 2015, www.washingtonpost.com/news/powerpost/wp/2015/12/18/house -to-vote-on-spending-bill-that-would-avert-shutdown/?utm_term=.4 4b2a263f70b.

9. Everett Burgess and Seung Min Kim, "Senate Republicans Fear 'Train Wreck' in September," *Politico*, June 5, 2017, www.politico.com /story/2017/06/05/senate-republicans-shutdown-debt-default-239083.

10. Burgess and Kim, "Senate Republicans Fear."

11. "The Federal Budget in 2016: An Infographic," Congressional Budget Office, February 8, 2017, www.cbo.gov/publication/52408.

12. Harry Reid, "Senate Democratic Legislative Agenda," press conference, November 16, 2016. Accessible via C-SPAN at www.c-span.org /video/?418605-101/senate-harry-reid-speaks-reporters-capitol-hill.

13. Scott Wong, "Senate Dems Give In on Earmark Ban," *Politico*, February 1, 2011, www.politico.com/story/2011/02/senate-dems-give-in-on -earmark-ban-048623.

14. Russell Berman, "Republicans Get Ready to Welcome Back Earmarks," *The Atlantic*, November 25, 2016, www.theatlantic.com/politics/ar chive/2016/11/republicans-earmarks-congress/508328.

15. Robert A. Caro, *The Passage of Power* (New York: Alfred A. Knopf, 2012), loc. 13857–58, Kindle. Senator Hayden actually abstained during the

vote for cloture. President Johnson and he had agreed that Hayden could abstain unless his vote was absolutely needed. It ended up that Johnson had more the sixty-seven votes by the time the floor vote came around.

16. Califano, *Triumph and Tragedy*, xxviii.

17. Keith Laing, "Durbin: Earmark Ban Preventing Federal Transportation Bills," *The Hill*, October 10, 2014, http://thehill.com/policy/transportation/219545-durbin-earmark-ban-created-a-situation-where-you-cant-get.

18. Rachael Bade and Ben Weyl, "Ryan Halts GOP Push to Restore Earmarks," *Politico*, November 16, 2016, www.politico.com/story/2016/11/gop-lift-earmark-ban-231500.

19. Carl Hulse, "Democrats Perfect Art of Delay While Republicans Fume over Trump Nominees," *New York Times*, July 17, 2017, www.nytimes.com/2017/07/17/us/politics/senate-democrats-art-of-delay-trump-nominees.html.

20. Glen Krutz and Jeffrey Peake, *Treaty Politics and the Rise of Executive Agreements: International Commitments in a System of Shared Powers* (Ann Arbor: University of Michigan Press, 2009), 2, 78; Adam Taylor, "The Slow Death of the Nuclear Deal with North Korea," *Washington Post*, January 6, 2016, www.washingtonpost.com/news/worldviews/wp/2016/01/06/the-slow-death-of-the-nuclear-deal-with-north-korea/?utm_term=.27d2b1aea866; Tonya Somanader, "President Obama: The United States Formally Enters the Paris Agreement," WhiteHouse.gov (blog), September 3, 2016, www.whitehouse.gov/blog/2016/09/03/president-obama-united-states-formally-enters-paris-agreement.

21. Michael John Garcia, "International Law and Agreements: Their Effect upon U.S. Law," CRS Report RL32528 (Washington, DC: Congressional Research Service, February 18, 2015), 4–5; "Treaties and Other International Agreements: The Role of the United States Senate," A Study Prepared for the Committee on Foreign Relations, United States Senate (Washington, DC: Congressional Research Service, January 2001), 39.

22. Kenneth Katzman and Paul K. Kerr, "Iran Nuclear Agreement," CRS Report R43333 (Washington, DC: Congressional Research Service, April 21, 2017), 30.

23. Deb Reichmann, "High-Stakes Lobbying on Iran Deal; Pressure for Congress," Associated Press, July 19, 2015; "The Complete Transcript of Netanyahu's Address to Congress," *Washington Post*, March 3, 2015, www.washingtonpost.com/news/post-politics/wp/2015/03/03/full -text-netanyahus-address-to-congress/?utm_term=.f62e01730759.

24. Karoun Demirjian, "Senate Rejects Attempt to Derail Iran Deal in Victory for Obama," *Washington Post*, September 10, 2015, https://www .washingtonpost.com/news/powerpost/wp/2015/09/10/senate-set-to -vote-on-iran-nuclear-deal/?utm_term=.983e3c928c1a. The next day, frustrated House Republicans held a vote on a resolution of approval, which forced 162 Democrats to cast a record vote in support of the Iranian deal (with 25 Democrats and all Republicans voting against it).

CHAPTER 9: WHERE WAR IS NOT WAR

1. Jennifer Elsea and Matthew Weed, "Declarations of War and Authorizations for the Use of Military Force: Historical Background and Legal Implications," CRS Report RL31133 (Washington, DC: Congressional Research Service, April 18, 2014), 1–3. There was no declaration of war for the American Civil War because the Confederate States of America were never recognized as a sovereign nation.

2. "Principal Wars in Which the United States Participated—U.S. Military Personnel Serving and Casualties," US Department of Defense, Office of the Secretary of Defense, Defense Casualty Analysis System, www.dmdc.osd.mil/dcas/pages/report_principal_wars.xhtml. See also "America's Wars," fact sheet, US Department of Veterans Affairs, Office of Public Affairs.

3. War Powers Resolution (1973), 50 U.S.C. 1544 (b).

4. Elsea and Weed, "Declarations of War."

5. Michael John Garcia, "War Powers Litigation Initiated by Members of Congress Since the Enactment of the War Powers Resolution," CRS Report RL30352 (Washington, DC: Congressional Research Service, February 17, 2012), 1.

6. "Clinton: My Vote for the Iraq War Was 'My Mistake,' " NBC News, September 7, 2016, www.nbcnews.com/video/clinton-my-vote-for -the-iraq-war-was-my-mistake-760014915605.

7. Authorization for Use of Military Force Against Terrorists, Pub. L. 107-40, 15 Stat. 224, enacted September 18, 2001; Authorization for Use of Military Force Against Iraq Resolution of 2002, Pub. L. 107-243, 116 Stat. 1498, enacted October 16, 2002.

8. Russell Berman, "The War Against ISIS Will Go Undeclared," *The Atlantic*, April 15, 2015, www.theatlantic.com/politics/archive/2015/04/the-war-against-isis-will-go-undeclared/390618/.

9. Mark Warner, "Statements on Introduced Senate Bills and Joint Resolutions," January 16, 2014, accessible via http://web1.millercenter.org/commissions/warpowers/2014_0116_CongressionalRecord-KaineMcCain.pdf.

10. Tim Kaine, "In the Fight Against the Islamic State, Congress Hides from Its Constitutional Duty," *Washington Post*, August 7, 2015, www.washingtonpost.com/opinions/in-the-fight-against-the-islamic-state-congress-hides-from-its-constitutional-duty/2015/08/07/c87a126c-3ad6-11e5-9c2d-ed991d848c48_story.html?utm_term=.f0e4a25 4d6da.

11. See Scott Beauchamp, "Why Clinton's Iraq Apology Still Isn't Enough," *The Atlantic*, September 8, 2016, www.theatlantic.com/international/archive/2016/09/clinton-iraq-bush-war-hussein-wmd-senate/499160/.

CHAPTER 10: POLITICAL LABOR PAINS

1. Robert M. Casale, "Revisiting One of the Law's Great Fallacies: *Marbury v. Madison*," *Connecticut Bar Journal* 89, no. 1 (March 2015): 62, 67–71.

2. *Marbury v. Madison*, 5 U.S. 137 (1803).

3. Tenth Circuit Act, 12 Stat. 794, enacted March 3, 1863; Judicial Circuits Act of 1866, 14 Stat. 209, enacted July 23, 1866.

4. The Judiciary Act of 1869, 16 Stat. 44, enacted April 10, 1869.

5. Sidney Ratner, "Was the Supreme Court Packed by President Grant?," *Political Science Quarterly* 50, no. 3 (September 1935): 343–58.

6. *Knox v. Lee*, 79 U.S. 457 (1871); consolidated with *Parker v. Davis* (same citation) in the opinion.

7. Alan Gevinson, "Court Packing Controversies," Teaching History, http://teachinghistory.org/history-content/ask-a-historian/19442.

8. Melvin Urofsky, *Louis D. Brandeis: A Life* (New York: Schocken, 2009), 439–40.

9. David Dalin, *Jewish Justices of the Supreme Court: From Brandeis to Kagan* (Waltham, MA: Brandeis University Press, 2017), 46.

10. *US v. Butler*, 297 U.S. 1, 78 (1936) (striking down the Agricultural Adjustment Act); *ALA Schechter Poultry Corp. v. United States*, 295 U.S. 495 (1935) (holding the National Recovery Administration to be unconstitutional); *Louisville Joint Stock Land Bank v. Radford*, 295 U.S. 555 (1935) (holding the 1934 Farm Bankruptcy Act to be an unconstitutional taking under the Fifth Amendment).

11. *US v. Butler*, 297 U.S. 1, 78 (1936).

12. Marian Cecilia McKenna, *Franklin Roosevelt and the Great Constitutional War: The Court-Packing Crisis of 1937* (New York: Fordham University Press, 2002), 183.

13. William E Leuchtenburg, *The Supreme Court Reborn: The Constitutional Revolution in the Age of Roosevelt* (New York: Oxford University Press, 1995), 124.

14. Franklin Roosevelt, "Fireside Chat 9: On Court-Packing," March 9, 1937.

15. *West Coast Hotel Co. v. Parrish*, 300 U.S. 379 (1937).

16. *Brown v. Board of Education*, 347 U.S. 483 (1954); *Loving v. Virginia*, 388 U.S. 1 (1967).

17. *Miranda v. Arizona*, 384 U.S. 436 (1966).

18. *Engel v. Vitale*, 370 U.S. 421 (1962); *Abington School District v. Schempp*, 374 U.S. 203 (1963).

19. *New York Times Co. v. Sullivan*, 376 U.S. 254 (1964).

20. Eisenhower is reported on PBS.org to have used this language when referring to his nomination of Justice Warren. Other scholars and historians have supported this report while some have refuted it. In Kim Eisler's biography of Justice William Brennan (*A Justice for All* [New York: Simon & Schuster, 1993]) she reports that Eisenhower referred to his appointments of Brennan and Warren as "mistakes," which she states was present in Justice Harold Burton's personal diary.

21. J. Douglas Smith, *On Democracy's Doorstep: The Inside Story of How the Supreme Court Brought "One Person, One Vote" to the United States* (New York: Hill & Wang, 2014), 78–79.

22. *Reynolds v. Sims*, 377 U.S. 533 (1964). (In this decision, the US Supreme Court held that in states with bicameral legislatures, one person, one vote applies to both chambers. It was in this case that Chief Justice Warren stated, "People, not land or trees or pastures, vote."); *Wesberry v. Sanders*, 376 U.S. 1 (1964) (applied one person, one vote to US congressional districts).

23. Earl Warren, *The Memoirs of Earl Warren* (Garden City, NY: Doubleday, 1977), 306.

24. Jack Balkin, "*Roe v. Wade*: An Engine of Controversy," in *What Roe v. Wade Should Have Said: The Nation's Top Legal Experts Rewrite America's Most Controversial Decision*, ed. Jack Balkin (New York: New York University Press, 2005), 3.

25. Donald Trump, speech given at campaign rally in Cedar Rapids, Iowa, July 28, 2016; Hillary Clinton, "Remarks on the Supreme Court and What's at Stake in the 2016 Election," University of Wisconsin-Madison, July 17, 2017.

26. Senate Roll Call Vote no. 109, April 6, 2017. See also Valerie Heitshusen, "Senate Proceedings Establishing Majority Cloture for Supreme Court Nominations: In Brief," CRS Report R44819 (Washington, DC: Congressional Research Service, April 14, 2017).

27. *Congressional Record*, daily edition, vol. 159, November 21, 2013, S8416–S8418; Valerie Heitshusen, "Majority Cloture for Nominations: Implications and the 'Nuclear' Proceedings of November 21, 2013," CRS Report R43331 (Washington, DC: Congressional Research Service, December 16, 2013).

28. Bridget Bowman and Niels Lesniewski, "Senate GOP Deploys 'Nuclear Option' for Supreme Court," *Roll Call*, April 6, 2017, www.rollcall.com/news/politics/senate-gop-deploys-nuclear-option-supreme-court.

29. See Neil Gorsuch, *The Future of Assisted Suicide and Euthanasia* (Princeton, NJ: Princeton University Press, 2006).

30. John Boehner, interviewed by Brit Hume, *On the Record*, Fox News Network, October 12, 2016.

31. Donald Trump, speech given at campaign rally in Cedar Rapids, Iowa, July 28, 2016.

32. Clinton, "Remarks on the Supreme Court."

33. Robert Gebelhoff, "A Popular Vote for the Supreme Court? We're Already There," *Washington Post*, November 21, 2016, www.wash ingtonpost.com/news/in-theory/wp/2016/11/21/a-popular-vote-for -the-supreme-court-were-already-there/?utm_term=.ebec5929efd 3.

CHAPTER 11: PARTISAN POLITICAL POLARIZATION

1. Adam Liptak, "Ginsburg Has a Few Words About Trump," *New York Times*, July 11, 2016, A1; Joan Biskupic, "Justice Ruth Bader Ginsburg Calls Trump a 'Faker,' He Says She Should Resign," CNN, July 13, 2016, www.cnn.com/2016/07/12/politics/justice-ruth-bader-ginsburg -donald-trump-faker/index.html.

2. "On reflection, my recent remarks in response to press inquiries were ill-advised and I regret making them," Ginsburg said in a statement. "Judges should avoid commenting on a candidate for public office. In the future I will be more circumspect." Ariane de Vogue, "Ruth Bader Ginsburg: 'I Regret Making' Donald Trump Remarks," CNN, July 14, 2016, www.cnn.com/2016/07/14/politics/ruth-bader-ginsburg-i-regret -making-donald-trump-remarks/index.html.

3. Linda Hirshman, "RBG Is Hardly the First Supreme Court Justice to Mess with Presidential Politics," *Politico*, July 13, 2016, www.politico .com/magazine/story/2016/07/ruth-bader-ginsburg-donald-trump -supreme-court-politics-history-214044.

4. Richard K. Neumann Jr., "Conflicts of Interest in *Bush v. Gore*: Did Some Justices Vote Illegally?," *Georgetown Journal of Legal Ethics* 16 (2003): 375.

5. Elspeth Reeve, "Just How Bad Was *Bush v. Gore*?," *The Atlantic*, November 29, 2010, www.theatlantic.com/politics/archive/2010/11/just -how-bad-was-bush-v-gore/343247/.

6. Liptak, "Ginsburg Has a Few."

7. Chris W. Cox, "Justice Ginsburg Reminds Us What Is at Stake in November," National Rifle Association Institute for Legislative Action,

February 13, 2012, http://www.nraila.org/news-issues/articles/2012/justice-ginsburg-reminds-us-what-isat-stake-in-november.aspx.

8. *Republican Party of Minn. v. White*, 536 U.S. 765, 778 (2002).

9. "Scalia: Abortion, Death Penalty 'Easy' Cases," Associated Press, republished by CBS News, October 5, 2012, www.cbsnews.com/news/scalia-abortion-death-penalty-easy-cases.

10. Robert Barnes, "Scalia: 'You Either Believe in a Democracy or You Don't," *Washington Post*, November 17, 2015, https://www.washingtonpost.com/news/post-nation/wp/2015/11/17/scalia-you-either-believe-in-a-democracy-or-you-dont/?utm_term=.dc4f785fdd8c.

11. Richard L. Hasen, "Celebrity Justice: Supreme Court Edition," *Green Bag*, 2nd sec., 19, no. 2 (Winter 2016): 157, 170–71.

12. Hasen, "Celebrity Justice," 158.

13. Meredith Heagney, "Justice Ruth Bader Ginsburg Offers Critique of *Roe v. Wade* During Law School Visit," University of Chicago School of Law, Office of Communications, May 15, 2013.

14. Todd Ruger, "Alito Defends 'Citizens' in Speech to Federalist Society," *New Jersey Law Journal*, November 16, 2012, www.njlawjournal.com/id=1202578770445/Alito-Defends-Citizens-in-Speech-to-Federalist-Society?slreturn=20170709122255.

15. Liptak, "Ginsburg Has a Few."

16. Ruger, "Alito Defends 'Citizens.' "

17. Robert Barnes et al., "Justice Thomas Lashes Out in Memoir," *Washington Post*, September 29, 2007, www.washingtonpost.com/wp-dyn/content/article/2007/09/28/AR2007092801634.html.

18. Greg Stohr, "Sotomayor's Book Advances from Knopf Surpass $3 Million," *Bloomberg*, June 7, 2013, www.bloomberg.com/news/articles/2013-06-07/sotomayor-s-book-advances-from-knopf-surpass-3-million.

19. Eric Lipton, "Scalia Took Dozens of Trips Funded by Private Sponsors," *New York Times*, February 26, 2017, www.nytimes.com/2016/02/27/us/politics/scalia-led-court-in-taking-trips-funded-by-private-sponsors.html.

20. *Cheney v. United States District Court*, 542 U.S. 367 (2004).

21. "Sanders Supreme Court Litmus Test: I Will Nominate Justices Who

Would Overturn *Citizens United*," press release, BernieSanders.com, May 10, 2015.

22. Melissa Murray, "The Future of the Supreme Court: Part 1," *Tavis Smiley*, PBS, February 25, 2016.

23. Lawrence Baum and Neal Devins, "Split Definitive: How Party Polarization Turned the Supreme Court into a Partisan Court," *Supreme Court Review*, 2016: 311–16.

24. Khedar S. Bhatia, "Stat Pack for October Term 2016," *SCOTUSBlog*, June 18, 2017, www.scotusblog.com/wp-content/uploads/2017/06/SB _Stat_Pack_2017.06.28.pdf, pp. 18–21.

25. *National Federation of Independent Business v. Sebelius*, 567 U.S. 519 (2012).

26. Jeffrey Rosen, "The Supreme Court Has a Legitimacy Crisis, but Not for the Reason You Think," *New Republic*, June 11, 2012, https://new republic.com/article/103987/the-supreme-court-has-legitimacy-crisis -not-the-reason-you-think.

27. "Negative Views of Supreme Court at Record High, Driven by Republican Dissatisfaction," Pew Research Center, July 29, 2015.

28. Ramesh Ponnuru, "Judging Gonzales," *National Review*, February 11, 2003, www.nationalreview.com/article/205885/judging-gonzales-ram esh-ponnuru.

29. Richard Posner et al., "Revisiting the Ideology Rankings of Supreme Court Justices," *Journal of Legal Studies* 44 (January 2015): S304, table 1b.

30. "Brownsville Division," United States District & Bankruptcy Court, Southern District of Texas, accessed September 1, 2017, http://www .txs.uscourts.gov/offices/brownsville-division. Judge Jose Rolando Olvera Jr. was confirmed in August 2015. The case was filed in February 2015, when only two judges served in the division. Garrett Epps, "Will the U.S. Supreme Court Tell Obama to 'Take Care'?," *The Atlantic*, January 21, 2016, www.theatlantic.com/politics/archive/2016/01 /supreme-court-united-states-texas/425031.

31. *Texas v. US*, 86 F. Supp. 3d 591 (S.D. Texas 2015).

32. *Washington v. Trump*, no. 2:17-cv-00141, 2017 WL 462040 (W.D. Wash. 2017); *Hawaii v. Trump*, no. 1:17-cv-000502017, WL 1167383 (D Haw. 2017).

33. *City and County of San Francisco*, No. 17-cv-00485-WHO (N.D. Cal. 2017).

34. "Heller Meets with Judge Elissa Cadish," press release, Dean Heller, US Senator for Nevada, April 23, 2012, www.heller.senate.gov /public/index.cfm/2012/4/heller-meets-with-judge-elissa-cadish. See also Steve Tetreault, "Heller Meets Nominee Cadish, Won't Budge," *Las Vegas Review-Journal*, April 20, 2012, www.reviewjournal.com /crime/courts/heller-meets-nominee-cadish-wont-budge.

35. Aaron Blake, "Did Dianne Feinstein Accuse a Judicial Nominee of Being Too Christian?," *Washington Post*, September 7, 2017, www .washingtonpost.com/news/the-fix/wp/2017/09/07/did-a-demo cratic-senator-just-accuse-a-judicial-nominee-of-being-too-christian /?utm_term=.a8337efa9051.

36. Sheldon Goldman, "Tracking Obstruction and Delay in U.S. Senate Confirmations of Judges to the Federal Courts," Scholars Strategy Network, July 2013, www.scholarsstrategynetwork.org/brief/track ing-obstruction-and-delay-us-senate-confirmations-judges-federal -courts.

37. "Judgeship Appointments by President," United States Courts, accessed August 1, 2017, www.uscourts.gov/judges-judgeships/autho rized-judgeships/judgeship-appointments-president.

38. "Judicial Emergencies," United States Courts, accessed June 1, 2017, www.uscourts.gov/judges-judgeships/judicial-vacancies/judicial-emer gencies.

39. Amy B. Wang, "Trump Lashes Out at 'So-Called Judge' Who Temporarily Blocked Travel Ban," *Washington Post*, February 4, 2017, www .washingtonpost.com/news/the-fix/wp/2017/02/04/trump-lashes -out-at-federal-judge-who-temporarily-blocked-travel-ban/?utm _term=.e1f5960d7232.

CHAPTER 12: MONEY MAKES THE RULES

1. "Fiscal 50: State Trends and Analyses," Pew Charitable Trusts, July 28, 2016, www.pewtrusts.org/en/research-and-analysis/analy sis/2016/07/28/federal-funds-supply-308-cents-of-each-state-reve nue-dollar.

2. Robert Levinson et al., "Impact of Defense Spending: A State by State Analysis," Bloomberg Government, November 17, 2011.
3. Thomas L. Hungerford, "U.S. Federal Government Revenues: 1790 to the Present," CRS Report RL 33665 (Washington, DC: Congressional Research Service, April 11, 2016), 3.
4. R. L. Worsnop, "Federal-State Revenue Sharing," *Editorial Research Reports 1964*, vol. 2 (Washington, DC: CQ Press), http://library.cqpress.com/cqresearcher/cqresrre1964122300.
5. An Act to Promote the Education of the Blind, Pub. L. 45-186, Sec. 3, enacted March 3, 1879.
6. Agricultural College Act of 1890, 26 Stat. 417, Sec. 1, enacted August 30, 1890.
7. Robert J. Dilger, "Federal Grants to State and Local Governments: A Historical Perspective on Contemporary Issues," CRS Report R40638 (Washington, DC: Congressional Research Service, June 22, 2017), 16.

CHAPTER 13: THE GAME CHANGERS

1. Revenue Act of 1913, 38 Stat. 114, enacted October 3, 1913.
2. Smith-Hughes National Vocational Education Act of 1917, 39 Stat. 929, enacted February 20, 1917.
3. Advisory Commission on Intergovernmental Relations, "Periodic Congressional Reassessment of Federal Grants-in-Aid to State and Local Governments," A-8 (Washington, DC: US Government Printing Office, June 1961), 7.
4. Dilger, "Federal Grants," 16.
5. "Categorical Grants: Their Role and Design," A-52 (Washington, DC: US Advisory Commission on Intergovernmental Relations, 1978), 18–19, www.library.unt.edu/gpo/acir/Reports/policy/a-52.pdf.
6. Social Security Act of 1935, Title IV, Pub. L. 74-271, 49 Stat. 620, enacted August 14, 1935.
7. "A Brief History of the AFDC Program," in *Aid to Families with Dependent Children: The Baseline* (Washington, DC: United States Department of Health and Human Services, Office of the Assistant Secretary for Planning and Evaluation, June 1998), 4.

8. Liz Schott et al., "How States Use Federal and State Funds Under the TANF Block Grant," Center on Budget and Policy Priorities, October 15, 2015, www.cbpp.org/sites/default/files/atoms/files/4-8-15tanf _0.pdf.

9. "Periodic Congressional Reassessment," 46.

10. "Periodic Congressional Reassessment," 18.

11. Servicemen's Readjustment Act of 1944, Pub. L. 78-346, 58 Stat. 284, enacted June 22, 1944.

12. Federal-Aid Highway Act of 1956, Pub. L. 84-627, 70 Stat. 374, enacted June 29, 1956.

13. National Defense Education Act, Pub. L. 85-864, 752 Stat. 1580, enacted September 2, 1958.

14. Jennifer Hoschschild and Nathan Scovronick, "School Desegregation and the American Dream," in *The End of Desegregation?*, eds. Stephen J. Caldas and Carl L. Bankston III (New York: Nova Science Publishers, 2003), 28.

15. Preston Reynolds, "The Federal Government's Use of Title VI and Medicare to Racially Integrate Hospitals in the United States, 1963 Through 1967," *American Journal of Public Health* 87, no. 11 (November 1997): 1856.

16. Reynolds, "Federal Government's Use of Title VI," 1853 (citing J. M. Quigley, "Hospitals and Civil Rights Act of 1964," *Journal of the National Medical Association* [1965]: 455–59).

17. Reynolds, "Federal Government's Use of Title VI," 1853.

18. Irving Bernstein, *Guns or Butter: The Presidency of Lyndon Johnson* (New York: Oxford University Press, 1996), 231.

19. Hoschschild and Scovronick, "School Desegregation," 28.

20. Wholesome Meat Act, Pub. L. 90-201, 81 Stat. 584, enacted December 15, 1967; National Traffic and Motor Vehicle Safety Act, Pub. L. 89-563, enacted September 9, 1966; Fair Packaging and Labeling Act, Pub. L. 89-755, 80 Stat. 1296, enacted November 3, 1966; Truth in Lending Act, Pub. L. 90-321, 82 Stat. 146, enacted May 29, 1968; Motor Vehicle Air Pollution Control Act, Pub. L. 89-272, enacted October 20, 1965; Water Quality Act, Pub. L. 89-234, enacted November 10, 1965; Fire Research and Safety Act, Pub. L. 90-259, 82 Stat. 34, enacted March 1, 1968.

21. "Table 12.2: Total Outlays for Grants to State and Local Governments by Function and Fund Group: 1940–2022," *Historical Tables*, The White House, Office of Management and Budget, www.whitehouse.gov/omb/budget/Historicals.

22. Dilger, "Federal Grants," 7; Housing and Community Development Act of 1974, Pub. L. 93-383, 88 Stat. 633, enacted August 22, 1974; Education for All Handicapped Children Act, Pub. L. 94-142, enacted November 30, 1975.

23. Steven Maguire, "General Revenue Sharing: Background and Analysis," CRS Report RL31936 (Washington, DC: Congressional Research Service, January 9, 2009), 2.

24. Maguire, "General Revenue Sharing," 15.

25. Telecommunications Act of 1996, Pub. L. 104-104, 110 Stat. 56, Sec. 153, enacted February 8, 1996; Balanced Budget Act of 1997, Title IV, Subtitle J, Pub. L. 105-33, 111 Stat. 251, enacted August 5, 1997.

26. The budget of the Department of Education increased 64 percent from 2001 to 2008. "Education Budget by Major Program: 1980–2015," Department of Education, September 15, 2015, https://www2.ed.gov/about/overview/budget/history/edhistory.pdf.

27. "Table 12.1: Summary Comparison of Total Outlays for Grants to State and Local Governments: 1940–2022," *Historical Tables*, The White House, Office of Management and Budget, www.whitehouse.gov/omb/budget/Historicals.

28. "Fact Sheet: Medicaid Makes Up Nearly Two-Thirds of Federal Grants to States," Pew Charitable Trusts, September 2015.

29. Dilger, "Federal Grants," 9–10.

30. Dilger, "Federal Grants," 7.

31. *Gannon v. Kansas*, no. 133,267 (Supreme Court for the State of Kansas, 2016); *Abbeville County School Districts v. South Carolina*, Appellate Case no. 2007-065159 (Supreme Court for the State of South Carolina, 2014).

32. "Funding Challenges in Highway and Transit: A Federal-State-Local Analysis," Pew Charitable Trusts, February 24, 2015, www.pewtrusts.org/en/research-and-analysis/analysis/2015/02/24/funding-challenges-in-highway-and-transit-a-federal-state-local-analysis.

33. "State Balanced Budget Provisions," National Conference of State

Legislatures, accessed August 14, 2017, www.ncsl.org/research/fiscal
-policy/state-balanced-budget-requirements-provisions-and.aspx.

34. Edward Glaeser, "When States Become Dependent on Federal Aid," *New York Times*, February 23, 2010, https://economix.blogs.nytimes.com/2010/02/23/when-states-become-dependent-on-federal-aid/.

35. "2017 Budget Overview," City of Chicago, Office of Budget and Management, 31.

36. Binyamin Appelbaum and Julie Hirschfeld Davis, "Obama Unveils Stricter Rules Against Segregation in Housing," *New York Times*, July 8, 2015, www.nytimes.com/2015/07/09/us/hud-issuing-new-rules-to-fight-segregation.html.

37. National Minimum Drinking Age Act of 1984, Pub. L. 98-363, 98 Stat. 435, enacted July 17, 1984.

38. Presidential Executive Order 13768, "Enhancing Public Safety in the Interior of the United States," January 25, 2017.

39. Patricia Mazzei, "Miami-Dade Mayor Orders Jails to Comply with Trump Crackdown on 'Sanctuary' Counties," *Miami Herald*, January 26, 2017, www.miamiherald.com/news/local/community/miami-dade/article128984759.html.

40. David Eggert and Jeff Karoub, "After Trump Threats, Michigan Capital Rescinds Calling Itself 'Sanctuary City,' " *Chicago Tribune*, April 13, 2017, www.chicagotribune.com/news/nationworld/midwest/ct-lansing-michigan-sanctuary-city-20170412-story.html.

41. "2017 COPS Hiring Program Application Guide" (Washington, DC: United States Department of Justice, Office of Community Oriented Policing Services), 2.

42. "Testimony in Front of House Appropriations Subcommittee on Labor, Health and Human Services, Education, and Related Agencies Regarding Fiscal Year 2018 Education Budget," C-SPAN, May 24, 2017, www.c-span.org/video/?428714-1/education-secretary-betsy-devos-pressed-accountability-charter-schools.

CHAPTER 14: PRESIDENTIAL PREEMPTION AND PREROGATIVES

1. Catherine M. Sharkey, "Preemption by Preamble: Federal Agencies and the Federalization of Tort Law," *DePaul Law Review* 56 (2007): 227.

2. Frank R. Lautenberg Chemical Safety for the 21st Century Act, Pub. L. 114-182, Sec. 13, enacted June 22, 2016.

3. Stuart Caplan, Brian Harns, and Emily Prince, "Trump Administration Considers Preemption of State Renewable Policies," *Renewable Energy Insights*, May 24, 2017, www.renewableinsights.com/2017/05/trump-administration-considers-preemption-state-renewable-policies/.

4. "Defense Spending by State—Fiscal Year 2015" (Washington, DC: US Department of Defense, Office of Economic Adjustment, 2015), 3.

5. Joshua Levy, *The Economic Impact of the Military on North Carolina* (Raleigh, NC: North Carolina Department of Commerce and North Carolina Military Affairs Commission, Labor and Economic Analysis Division, 2015), 1.

6. Kay Schlozman et al., "Organizations and the Democratic Representation of Interests: What Does It Mean When Those Organizations Have No Members?," *Perspectives on Politics* 13, no. 4 (December 2015): 1017–29.

7. "Lobbying Database: Civil Service/Public Officials," Center for Responsive Politics, accessed July 1, 2017, www.opensecrets.org/lobby/indusclient.php?id=W03&year=2016.

CHAPTER 15: DAY OF POLITICAL INFAMY

1. Jack Beatty, *Age of Betrayal: The Triumph of Money in America, 1865–1900* (New York: Vintage, 2007), 367.

2. The Federal Election Campaign Act of 1971, Pub. L. 92-225, 86 Stat. 3, enacted February 7, 1972.

3. *Buckley v. Valeo*, 424 US 1 (1976).

4. "Cost of Election," Center for Responsive Politics, accessed August 2, 2017, www.opensecrets.org/overview/cost.php.

5. "2016 Presidential Race," Center for Responsive Politics, accessed August 2, 2017, www.opensecrets.org/pres16.

6. "States' Proposed and Enacted Budgets," National Association of State Budget Officers, accessed August 1, 2017, www.nasbo.org/mainsite/resources/proposed-enacted-budgets; "NCI Budget and Appropriations," National Cancer Institute, May 11, 2017, www.cancer.gov/about-nci/budget.

7. Derek Thompson, "Why There Are So Many Rich Counties Concentrated Around Washington, DC," *The Atlantic*, December 18, 2013, www.theatlantic.com/business/archive/2013/12/why-there-are-so-many-rich-counties-concentrated-around-washington-dc/282481/.

CHAPTER 16: THE MONEY GAME

1. Adam Bonica et al., "Why Hasn't Democracy Slowed Rising Inequality?," *Journal of Economic Perspectives* 27, no. 3 (Summer 2013): 111.
2. Libby Watson, "How Political Megadonors Can Give Almost $500,000 with a Single Check," Sunlight Foundation, June 1, 2016, https://sunlightfoundation.com/2016/06/01/how-political-megadonors-can-give-almost-500000-with-a-single-check.
3. "Contribution Limits for 2017–2018 Federal Elections," Federal Elections Commission, https://transition.fec.gov/info/contriblimits chart1718.pdf.
4. "Contribution Limits for 2017–2018 Federal Elections." Note that the 2015–16 individual to national party committee contribution maximum stood at $33,400. With adjustment for inflation, this was increased to $33,900 for the 2017–18 cycle.
5. Watson, "How Political Megadonors."
6. "Contribute Today," Team Ryan website, accessed August 1, 2017, https://secure.speakerryan.com/contribute-today/?source=SpeakerRyanHero.
7. Jake Sherman, "Bulk of Ryan's Fundraising Haul in $50k-Plus Chunks," *Politico*, April 13, 2016, www.politico.com/story/2016/04/paul-ryan-fundraising-analysis-221920.
8. Roger Simon, "The GOP and Willie Horton: Together Again," *Politico,* May 19, 2015, www.politico.com/story/2015/05/jeb-bush-willie-horton-118061.
9. Bipartisan Campaign Reform Act of 2002, Pub. L. 107-155, 116 Stat. 82, Sec. 101–214, enacted March 27, 2002.
10. *Citizens United v. Federal Election Commission,* 558 U.S. 310, 339–45 (2010).
11. *Citizens United v. Federal Election Commission,* at 348 (citing *Buckley,*

424 U.S. 47). The majority also relied on the *Buckley* opinion's concern with preventing quid pro quo corruption, something that the court in *Citizens United* felt was avoided by the "independent" nature of outside groups.

12. See *SpeechNow.org v. Federal Election Commission*, 599 F. 3d 686 (CADC 2010) (en banc); FEC Advisory Opinion 2010–09 (Club for Growth); FEC Advisory Opinion 2010–11 (Commonsense Ten) (this is what truly created super PACs, removing the last restrictions on from whom such organizations may seek donations); *Carey v. FEC*, 791 F. Supp. 2d 121 (D. D.C. 2011).

13. "2010 Outside Spending, by Super PAC," Center for Responsive Politics, accessed August 20, 2017, www.opensecrets.org/outsidespending/summ.php?cycle=2010&chrt=V&disp=O&type=S.

14. "2012 Outside Spending, by Super PAC," Center for Responsive Politics, accessed August 27, 2017, www.opensecrets.org/outsidespending/summ.php?cycle=2012&chrt=V&disp=O&type=S.

15. "2016 Outside Spending, by Super PAC," Center for Responsive Politics, accessed August 20, 2017, www.opensecrets.org/outsidespending/summ.php?cycle=2016&chrt=V&disp=O&type=S.

16. "2016 Top Donors to Outside Spending Groups," Center for Responsive Politics, Accessed March 15, 2017, www.opensecrets.org/outsidespending/summ.php?cycle=2016&disp=D&type=V&superonly=S.

17. Nicholas Confessore, "Jeb Bush Outstrips Rivals in Fund-Raising as 'Super PACs' Swell Candidates' Coffers," *New York Times*, July 9, 2015, www.nytimes.com/2015/07/10/us/politics/jeb-bush-races-past-rivals-in-fund-raising-aided-by-super-pac-cash.html.

18. Nick Corasaniti, "Carly Fiorina's 'Super PAC' Aids Her Campaign, in Plain Sight," *New York Times*, September 30, 2015, www.nytimes.com/2015/10/01/us/politics/as-carly-fiorina-surges-so-does-the-work-of-her-super-pac.html.

19. Phillip Bump, "Republicans, Twitter and the Brave New World of Campaign/Outside Group Coordination," *Washington Post*, November 17, 2014, www.washingtonpost.com/news/the-fix/wp/2014/11/17/republicans-twitter-and-the-brave-new-world-of-campaignoutside-group-coordination/?u tm_term=.f596ba6c0833.

20. "Dark Money Basics," Center for Responsive Politics, accessed August 29, 2017, www.opensecrets.org/dark-money/basics?range=tot #outside-spending.

21. "Dark Money Basics."

22. *McCutcheon v. Federal Elections Commission*, 134 S. Ct. 1434, 1459–60.

23. Hamden Azhar, "This Year's Top Presidential Campaigns Spent Over $1B—Here's Where It All Went," *Forbes*, November 4, 2016, www .forbes.com/sites/realspin/2016/11/04/this-years-top-presidential -campaigns-spent-over-1b-heres-where-it-all-went/#318a5aafa3a9. This figure includes spending by all Democratic and Republican primary contenders.

24. "Expenditures Breakdown, Hillary Clinton, 2016 Cycle," Center for Responsive Politics, accessed August 1, 2017, https://www.open secrets.org/pres16/expenditures?id=n00000019; "Expenditures Breakdown, Donald Trump, 2016 Cycle," Center for Responsive Politics, accessed August 1, 2017, https://www.opensecrets.org/pres16 /expenditures?id=N00023864.

25. Chris Good, "Breakdown: How Campaigns Spend Their Millions," ABC News, July 25, 2012, http://abcnews.go.com/blogs/poli tics/2012/07/breakdown-how-campaigns-spend-their-millions. Note: this breakdown is based on campaign spending numbers for June 2012.

26. Katherine Seelye, "About $2.6 Billion Spent on Political Ads in 2008," *New York Times*, December 2, 2008, https://thecaucus.blogs.nytimes .com/2008/12/02/about-26-billion-spent-on-political-ads-in-2008/; "The Financial Analysis: What Happened to Political Advertising in 2016 (and Forever)," Borrell Associates, executive summary, 2017.

27. Erika Franklin Fowler and Travis N. Ridout, "Negative, Angry, and Ubiquitous: Political Advertising in 2012," *The Forum* 10, no. 4 (2012): 51–61.

28. "Donald Trump, Expenditures Breakdown"; "Hillary Clinton, Expenditures Breakdown"; Azhar, "This Year's Top Presidential Campaigns."

29. *America Goes to the Polls 2016: A Report on Voter Turnout in the 2016 Election* (Cambridge, MA: Nonprofit Vote and the US Elections Project, 2017), 12.

30. Andrea Levien and Robert Richie, "How the 2012 Presidential Elec-

tion Has Strengthened the Movement for the National Popular Vote Plan," *Presidential Studies Quarterly* 43, no. 2 (June 2013): 353–76.

31. "Obama 2009 Inauguration Donors," Center for Responsive Politics, accessed August 5, 2017, www.opensecrets.org/obama/inaug_2009 .php.

32. "Fundraising Rules Change for 2013 Presidential Inauguration Ceremonies," *PBS NewsHour*, January 14, 2013, www.pbs.org/newshour /bb/politics-jan-june13-inauguration_01-14/.

33. Theodore Schleifer, "Trump Shatters Fundraising Record with $107 Million for Inauguration," CNN, April 19, 2017, www.cnn.com/2017 /04/18/politics/donald-trump-fundraising-record-inauguration/index .html.

34. Timothy Dwyer, "Inaugural Donors Add $3.3 Million in 6 Days," *Washington Post*, December 24, 2004, B2.

35. Sebastian Payne, "President Obama Has Held 393 Fundraisers in His Six Years in Office," *Washington Post*, July 16, 2014, www.washington post.com/news/the-fix/wp/2014/07/16/president-obama-has-held -393-fundraisers-in-his-six-years-in-office/?utm_term=.9 f21254fbc99.

36. Brendan Doherty, *The Rise of the President's Permanent Campaign* (Lawrence, KS: University Press of Kansas, 2012), 69–72.

37. "Table 3-1, Cost of Winning a House or Senate Seat, 1986–2016," The Campaign Finance Institute, 2016, www.cfinst.org/pdf/vital/Vital Stats_t1.pdf.

38. Soo Rin Kim, "The Price of Winning Just Got Higher, Especially in the Senate," Center for Responsive Politics, November 9, 2016, www .opensecrets.org/news/2016/11/the-price-of-winning-just-got-higher -especially-in-the-senate.

39. "Most Expensive Races, 2016," Center for Responsive Politics, accessed August 9, 2017, www.opensecrets.org/overview/topraces.php ?cycle=2016&display=allcandsout.

40. "Most Expensive Races, 2016."

41. Alicia Parlapiano and Rachel Shorey, "The Most Expensive House Election: Where the Money Came From," *New York Times*, June 21, 2017, A16. In this case, "large individual contributions" are defined as individual donations over $200, the amount that triggers donor location reporting requirements.

42. Parlapiano and Shorey, "Most Expensive House Election."
43. Trevor Potter, "Follow the Money: Courts, Corruption, and the Future of American Elections," presented to the 16th Annual Goldstone Forum at the University of Pennsylvania, April 21, 2016.

CHAPTER 17: MONEY OPENS DOORS AND EARS

1. John McCain, "Statement upon the Introduction of the Bipartisan Campaign Finance Act of 1999," *Congressional Record—Senate* 145, pt. 18 (October 14–25, 1999): 25411–12.
2. *Federal Election Commission v. Wisconsin Right to Life, Inc.*, 551 U.S. 449, 520 (2007)(Dissent).
3. "D.C. Personal Giving Memberships," National Republican Senatorial Committee—PAC Program, 2017. See also Rebecca Savransky, "Report: GOP Lawmakers Selling Access to Top Staffers," *The Hill*, April 20, 2017, http://thehill.com/homenews/house/329697-report -republicans-selling-access-to-congressional-staffers.
4. Nicholas Confessore and Steve Eder, "In Hacked D.N.C. Emails, a Glimpse of How Big Money Works," *New York Times*, July 25, 2016, www.nytimes.com/2016/07/26/us/politics/dnc-wikileaks-emails-fun draising.html.
5. "Top Individual Contributors: All Federal Contributions," Center for Responsive Politics, accessed August, 1, 2017, www.opensecrets .org/overview/topindivs.php; Fredreka Schouten, "Charles Koch Says His Network Offers 'Vision' for a Divided Nation," *USA Today*, November 10, 2017, https://www.usatoday.com/story/news/politics/elections /2016/2016/11/10/charles-koch-say-his-network-offers-better-vision -angry-n ation/93608404/; Tim Alberta and Eliana Johnson, "Exclusive: In Koch World 'Realignment,' Less National Politics," *National Review*, May 16, 2016, http://www.nationalreview.com/article/435418 /koch-brothers-scale- back-campaign-spending-nr-exclusive.
6. "Election 2016: Iowa Caucus Results," *New York Times*, February 1, 2016, www.nytimes.com/elections/2016/results/primaries/iowa.
7. Julie Bykowicz, "Cash-Rich Super PACs Prolong Flagging Presidential Campaigns," *San Diego Union-Tribune*, January 5, 2016, www.sandi

egouniontribune.com/sdut-cash-rich-super-pacs-prolong-flagging
-2016jan05-story.html.

8. Nicholas Confessore, " 'Super PAC' for Gingrich to Get $5 Million Infusion," *New York Times*, January 23, 2012, www.nytimes.com/2012/1/24
/us/politics/super-pac-for-gingrich-to-get-5-million-infusion.html.

9. Noah Bierman and Lisa Mascaro, "Forget Voters: Presidential Rivals Battle to Win Over Billionaires," *Los Angeles Times*, June 9, 2015,
www.latimes.com/nation/politics/la-na-battle-for-the-billionaires
-20150609-story.html. See also Fenit Nirappil and Gregory S. Schneider,
"Perriello's Va. Governor Bid Boosted by Several Big Donors, Including
George Soros," *Washington Post*, April 18, 2017, www.washingtonpost
.com/local/virginia-politics/northam-has-financial-edge-in-virginia
-governors-race-gillespie-leads-gop-field/2017/04/18/a44452f0-23a4
-11e7-a1b3-faff0034e2de_story.html?utm_term=.27675f40f 380.

10. Lee Drutman, *The Business of America Is Lobbying: How Corporations
Became Politicized and Politics Became More Corporate* (New York: Oxford University Press, 2015), 9–10, 34.

11. Thomas Donohue to Roy E. Marden (Philip Morris), January 5, 1998,
available at the University of San Francisco Industry Documents Library, document ID pqmv0031.

12. "Top Spenders (All Years: 1998–2017)," Center for Responsive Politics,
accessed August 31, 2017, www.opensecrets.org/lobby/top.php?show
Year=a&indexType=s.

13. "Tobacco's Powerful Ally Inside the Chamber of Commerce," *New York
Times*, October 9, 2015, www.nytimes.com/interactive/2015/09/18
/business/international/documents-chamber-commerce-tobacco-ties
.html.

14. Alyssa Katz, *The Influence Machine: The U.S. Chamber of Commerce
and the Corporate Capture of American Life* (New York: Spiegel & Grau,
2015), 120–27.

15. Evan Mackinder, "Pro-Environment Groups Outmatched, Outspent
in Battle over Climate Change Legislation," Center for Responsive
Politics, August 23, 2010, www.opensecrets.org/news/2010/08/pro
-environment-groups-were-outmatc.

16. Rebecca Lefton and Noreen Neilsen, "Interactive: Big Polluters' Big

Ad Spending," Center for American Progress, October 27, 2010, www
.americanprogressaction.org/issues/green/news/2010/10/27/8530
/interactive-big-polluters-big-ad-spending/.

17. "Oil & Gas: Money to Congress," Center for Responsive Politics, accessed September 13, 2017, www.opensecrets.org/industries/summary
.php?cycle=2016&ind=E01.

18. Marian Lavelle, "Partisan Divide in Congress Wider than Ever on Environmental Issues, Group Says," *Inside Climate News*, February 23, 2017, https://insideclimatenews.org/news/23022017/congress-environ mental-climate-change-league-conservation-voters.

19. "Republicans, Clean Energy, and Climate Change," survey conducted by Echelon Insights, North Star Opinion Research, and Public Opinion Strategies, on behalf of Clear Path, August 24–27, 2015.

20. "Tobacco: Lobbying," Center for Responsive Politics, accessed September 1, 2017, www.opensecrets.org/industries/lobbying.php?cycle =2016&ind=A02.

CHAPTER 18: STATES, JUDGES, AND THINK TANKS IN THE POLITICAL MONEY MIX

1. Javier Panzar, "GOP Assemblyman Scott Wilk Wins State Senate Seat," *Los Angeles Times*, November 9, 2016, www.latimes.com/nation /politics/trailguide/la-na-election-aftermath-updates-trail-gop-assem blyman-scott-wilk-wins-state-1478714087-htmlstory.html.

2. Rick Pearson, "Ken Griffin Gives Gov. Bruce Rauner's Campaign Record $20 Million," *Chicago Tribune*, May 17, 2017, www.chicago tribune.com/news/local/politics/ct-bruce-rauner-ken-griffin-20-mil lion-met-20170517-story.html; Natahsa Korecki, "Billionaire Ken Griffin Pours $2M. into Illinois GOP Account," *Politico*, October 7, 2016, www.politico.com/states/illinois/story/2016/10/billionaire-ken -griffin-pours-2m-into-gop-account-106201.

3. Zuisha Elinson and Joe Palazzolo, "Billionaire Soros Funds Local Prosecutor Races," *Wall Street Journal*, November 3, 2016, www.wsj.com /articles/billionaire-soros-funds-local-prosecutor-races-1478194109.

4. Chris Brennan, "$1.45 Million Soros Investment in Philly DA's Race Draws Heat for Krasner," *Philadelphia Inquirer*, May 5, 2017, www

.philly.com/philly/news/politics/Soros-145-million-investment-in
-DAs-race-draws-heat-for-Krasner.html.

5. Paul Blumenthal, "Your State and Local Elections Are Now a Super
PAC Playground," *Huffington Post*, October 31, 2015, www.huff
ingtonpost.com/entry/2015-elections-super-pac_us_5633d165e4b0
c66bae5c7bbb.

6. Shandra Martinez, "Betsy DeVos Details $5.3M in Political Dona-
tions over Past 5 Years," *Michigan Live*, January 13, 2017, www.mlive
.com/news/grand-rapids/index.ssf/2017/01/betsy_devos_53m_politi
cal_dona.html.

7. Kate Vinton, "Billionaire Mike Bloomberg's $18 Million Helped Soda
Tax Measures Win in San Francisco, Oakland," *Forbes*, November 6,
2017, https://www.forbes.com/sites/katevinton/2016/11/09/michael
-bloomberg-scores-with-18-million-on-measures-taxing-soda-in-san
-francisco-oakland-this-election/#1c56f1cb102d.

8. Christopher Ingraham, "A Casino Magnate Is Spending Millions to Fight
Legal Marijuana in Three States," *Washington Post*, October 26, 2016,
www.washingtonpost.com/news/wonk/wp/2016/10/26/a-casino
-magnate-is-spending-millions-to-fight-legal-marijuana-in-three-states
/?utm_term=.cb8583419af4.

9. Nathan Vardi, "Sheldon Adelson Says He Is 'Willing to Spend Whatever It Takes' to Stop Online Gambling," *Forbes*, November 22, 2013,
www.forbes.com/sites/nathanvardi/2013/11/22/sheldon-adelson
-says-he-is-willing-to-spend-whatever-it-takes-to-stop-online-gam
bling/#235 754f24034.

10. Patrick McGreevy, "Ex-Facebook President Sean Parker Donates Another $1.25 Million to Pot Legalization Campaign," *Los Angeles Times*,
July 30, 2016, www.latimes.com/politics/lapol-sac-essential-politics-up
dates-ex-facebook-president-sean-parker-1467917815-htmlstory.html.

11. Eric Lichtblau, "Cato Institute and Koch Brothers Reach Agreement,"
New York Times, June 25, 2012, https://thecaucus.blogs.nytimes
.com/2012/06/25/cato-institute-and-koch-brothers-reach-agreement;
"Staff—George Soros—Founder/Chairman," Open Society Foundations, www.opensocietyfoundations.org/people/george-soros.

12. "Spending by Outside Groups in Judicial Races Hits Record High,
Secret Money Dominates," Brennan Center for Justice, November 15,

2016, www.brennancenter.org/press-release/spending-outside-groups -judicial-races-hits-record-high-secret-money-dominates.

13. *Bill Moyers Journal*, PBS, February 19, 2010.

14. "Spending by Outside Groups."

15. Pound's speech can be found in "The Causes of Popular Dissatisfaction with the Administration of Justice," *Baylor Law Review* 8, no. 1 (1956): 23.

16. Mark Godsey, *Blind Injustice: A Former Prosecutor Exposes the Psychology and Politics of Wrongful Convictions* (Oakland: University of California Press, 2017), 68.

17. *Republican Party of Minnesota v. White*, 536 U.S. 765 (2002) (O'Connor, concurring).

18. *Caperton v. A. T. Massey Coal Co.*, 556 U.S. 868 (2009).

19. Kristina Cooke and Dan Levine, "In States with Elected High Court Judges, a Harder Line on Capital Punishment," Reuters, September 22, 2015, www.reuters.com/investigates/special-report/usa-deathpenalty -judges/.

20. See comments by Senators Grassley and Feinstein at the Senate Judiciary Committee vote on the confirmation of Supreme Court nominee Neil Gorsuch, April 3, 2017. See also Daniel Bush and Geoffrey Lou Guray, "Conservative Group Launches Ad Blitz Pressuring Senate Dems to Back Neil Gorsuch," PBS, March 31, 2017, www.pbs.org /newshour/updates/conservative-group-launches-ad-blitz-pressuring -senate-dems-back-neil-gorsuch/.

CHAPTER 19: THE MEDIA FAULT LINE

1. Brooks Boliek, "FCC Finally Kills Off Fairness Doctrine," *Politico*, August 22, 2011.

2. Amy Mitchell et al., "Political Polarization & Media Habits," Pew Research Center, October 21, 2014, http://www.journalism.org/2014 /10/21/political-polarization-media-habits/.

3. Thomas E. Patterson, *News Coverage of Trump's First 100 Days* (Cambridge, MA: Harvard Kennedy School–Shorenstein Center on Media, Politics and Public Policy, May 2017), 10.

4. Patterson, *News Coverage*, 8. The seven outlets are NBC, CBS, CNN,

Fox News, the *New York Times*, the *Washington Post*, and the *Wall Street Journal*.

5. "Trump's War on Journalism," editorial, *Los Angeles Times*, April 5, 2017, www.latimes.com/projects/la-ed-trumps-war-on-journalism; Kyle Pope, "Trump Is at War with the Press and It's Time for the Press to Stop Helping Him," *Washington Post*, July 27, 2017, www.washingtonpost .com/news/democracy-post/wp/2017/07/27/trump-is-at-war-with-the -press-and-its-time-for-the-press-to-stop-helping-him/?utmterm=.6eb 35fbebf29.

6. Michael Barthel and Amy Mitchell, "Americans' Attitudes About the News Media Deeply Divided Along Partisan Lines," Pew Research Center, May 20, 2017, 3.

7. Louis Jacobson, "Donald Trump Wrong That Murder Rate Is Highest in 47 Years," *PolitiFact*, February 8, 2017, www.politifact.com /truth-o-meter/statements/2017/feb/08/donald-trump/donald-trump -wrong-murder-rate-highest-47-years; Lauren Carroll, "Donald Trump Wrongly Blames Barack Obama for Former Guantanamo Detainees Returning to Terrorism," *PolitiFact*, March 7, 2017, www.politifact .com/truth-o-meter/statements/2017/mar/07/donald-trump/donald -trump-wrongly-blames-barack-obama-former-gu.

8. "Obama: 'If You Like Your Health Care Plan, You'll Be Able to Keep Your Health Care Plan," *PolitiFact*, www.politifact.com/obama-like -health-care-keep/.

9. Peggy Noonan, "Peggy Noonan's Commencement Speech—128th Annual Commencement Remarks," Upper Church, Basilica of the National Shrine of the Immaculate Conception, May 13, 2017, https://www .catholic.edu/speeches-and-homilies/2017/commencement-2017.html.

10. "Employment Trends in Newspaper Publishing and Other Media, 1990–2016," US Department of Labor, Bureau of Labor Statistics, June 2, 2016.

11. Bob Schieffer, "Veteran Newsman Bob Schieffer as He Steps Down from 'Face the Nation,'" *Diane Rehm*, NPR, May 26, 2015.

12. David Simon, "Testimony in Hearing on the Future of Journalism and Newspapers" held by the Senate Commerce, Science and Transportation Subcommittee on Communications, May 9, 2009.

13. Tucker Doherty and Jack Shafer, "The Media Bubble Is Worse than You

Think," *Politico*, May/June 2017, http://www.politico.com/magazine /story/2017/04/25/media-bubble-real-journalism-jobs-east-coast -215048.

14. Patterson, *News Coverage*, 16.

CHAPTER 20: RACIAL AND CULTURAL
POLITICAL PARTY FAULT LINES

1. Data taken from "US Presidential Election Center," Gallup, www.gallup .com/poll/154559/US-Presidential-Election-Center.aspx, and "Election Polls—Votes by Groups," Gallup, www.gallup.com/poll/9454/election -polls-vote-groups-19601964.aspx. Also used were 2016 exit polls from the *New York Times* and CNN. (Hereinafter "Exit Polls Data.")

2. Leah Wright Riguer, *The Loneliness of the Black Republican: Pragmatic Politics and the Pursuit of Power* (Princeton, NJ: Princeton University Press, 2015), 52.

3. Wright Riguer, *Loneliness*, 133, 194. See also "Exit Polls Data."

4. William H. Frey, "Minority Turnout Determined the 2012 Election," Brookings Institution, May 10, 2013, www.brookings.edu/research /minority-turnout-determined-the-2012-election.

5. Kendall Breitman, "Axelrod: Romney '12 Concession Call 'Irritated' Obama," *Politico*, February 4, 2017, http://www.politico .com/story/2015/02/david-axelrod-mitt-romney-obama-2012-elec tions-114896.

6. Thomas Wood, "Racism Motivated Trump Voters More than Authoritarianism," *Washington Post*, April 17, 2017, www.washingtonpost .com/news/monkey-cage/wp/2017/04/17/racism-motivated-trump -voters-more-than-authoritarianism-or-income-inequality/?utm_term =.240a4380a84a.

7. Conversation between Lyndon Johnson and Nick Katzenbach, July 25, 1964, conversation WH6407-14-4337, 4338, 4339, Presidential Records Digital Collection, Miller Center for Presidential Studies.

8. Mark K. Updegrove, "When LBJ and Goldwater Agreed to Keep Race Out of the Campaign," *Politico*, August 28, 2016, www.politico.com /magazine/story/2016/08/goldwater-lbj-racism-campaign-trump-big otry-214191.

9. "The Parties on the Eve of the 2016 Election: Two Coalitions, Moving Farther Apart," Pew Research Center, September 13, 2016.

10. Philip Bump, "The Two Conventions Don't Look Like Each Other, but They Look Like Each Party's Voters," *Washington Post*, July 27, 2016, www.washingtonpost.com/news/the-fix/wp/2016/07/27/the-two-conventions-dont-look-like-each-other-but-they-look-like-each-par tys-voters/?utm_term=.45ac55b224ee.

11. Suzzane Gamboa, "GOP: At Least 133 Latino Delegates at Republican Convention," NBC News, July 21, 2016, www.nbcnews.com /storyline/2016-conventions/gop-least-133-latino-delegates-republi can-convention-n614376.

12. "Member Data—Demographics," US House of Representatives Press Gallery, accessed June 1, 2017, https://pressgallery.house.gov/member -data/demographics.

13. See chairperson and ranking members in "Committees," United States House of Representatives, accessed June 1, 2017, www.house.gov /committees.

14. "Election 2016—Exit Polls: National President," CNN, http://edition .cnn.com/election/results/exit-polls.

15. "America's Choice 2012 Election Center—President: Full Results," CNN, www.cnn.com/election/2012/results/race/president.

16. "Election 2016—Exit Polls."

17. Immigration Act of 1924, Pub. L. 68-139, 43 Stat. 153, enacted May 26, 1924.

18. Immigration and Nationality Act of 1965, Pub. L. 89-236, 79 Stat. 911, enacted October 3, 1965.

19. "America's Foreign Born in the Last 50 Years," United State Census Bureau, 2010.

20. "America's Foreign Born"; Gustavo Lopez and Jynnah Radford, "Statistical Portrait of the Foreign-Born Population in the United States: Table 3, Population, by Nativity, Race and Ethnicity: 2015," Pew Research Center, May 2, 3017. See also "Modern Immigration Wave Brings 59 Million to U.S., Driving Population Growth and Change Through 2065," Pew Research Center, September 28, 2015, 66.

21. "Modern Immigration Wave," 65.

22. Daniel Cox and Robert P. Jones, *America's Changing Religious Identity:*

Findings from the 2016 American Values Atlas (Washington, DC: Public Religion Research Institute, September 6, 2017), 9.

23. "Survey of Rural America," Washington Post–Kaiser Family Foundation, June 2017, http://apps.washingtonpost.com/g/page/national /washington-post-kaiser-family-foundation-rural-and-small-town -america-poll/2217/.

24. William H. Frey, *Melting Pot Cities and Suburbs: Racial and Ethnic Change in Metro America in the 2000s* (Washington, DC: Brookings Institution Metropolitan Policy Program, May 2011), 3. Urban population numbers taken from the study's figures for "primary cities." William H. Frey, "Census Shows Nonmetropolitan America Is Whiter, Getting Older, and Losing Population," The Aroma (blog), Brookings Institute Metropolitan Policy Program, June 27, 2017. Rural population numbers taken from the study's figures for "non-metropolitan areas."

25. Danielle Kurtzleben, "Rural Voters Played a Big Part in Helping Trump Defeat Clinton," NPR, November 14, 2016, www.npr .org/2016/11/14/501737150/rural-voters-played-a-big-part-in-help ing-trump-defeat-clinton.

26. David A. Graham, "Red State, Blue City," *The Atlantic*, March 2017.

27. "The Herbal Tea Party," *The Economist*, January 26, 2017, www.econ omist.com/news/united-states/21715732-scolding-trump-voters-will -not-carry-democrats-back-power-rise-herbal-tea.

28. Ronald Brownstein, "How the Election Revealed the Divide Between City and Country," *The Atlantic*, November 17, 2016, www.the atlantic.com/politics/archive/2016/11/clinton-trump-city-country -divide/507902/.

29. Helena Bottemiller Evich, "Revenge of the Rural Voter," *Politico*, November 13, 2016, www.politico.com/story/2016/11/hillary-clinton -rural-voters-trump-231266.

CHAPTER 21: THE PARTISANSHIP FAULT LINE

1. "Partisanship and Political Animosity in 2016," Pew Research Center, June 26, 2016, www.people-press.org/2016/06/22/partisanship-and -political-animosity-in-2016, "1. Feelings About Partisans and the Parties."

2. "Partisanship and Political Animosity in 2016," "3. Partisan Environments, Views of Political Conversations and Disagreements."

3. Shanto Iyengar and Sean J. Westwood, "Fear and Loathing Across Party Lines: New Evidence on Group Polarization," *American Journal of Political Science* 59, no. 3 (July 2015): 690.

4. Thomas B. Edsall, "How Did Politics Get So Personal?" *New York Times*, January 28, 2015, https://www.nytimes.com/2015/01/28/opinion/how-did-politics-get-so-personal.html.

5. "Partisanship and Political Animosity in 2016," "3. Partisan Environments, Views of Political Conversations and Disagreements."

6. Glenn Kessler, "When Did McConnell Say He Wanted to Make Obama a 'One-Term President'?," Fact-Checker, *Washington Post*, September 25, 2012, www.washingtonpost.com/blogs/fact-checker/post/when-did-mcconnell-say-he-wanted-to-make-obama-a-one-term-president/2012/09/24/79fd5cd8-0696-11e2-afff-d6c7f20a83bf_blog.html?utm_term=.5e066f546c28.

7. Catherine Thompson, "Trump Lets His Followers Know 'Hillary Clinton Can't Satisfy Her Husband,'" *Talking Points Memo*, April 17, 2015, http://talkingpointsmemo.com/livewire/donald-trump-hillary-cant-satisfy-america; Peter W. Stevenson, "A Brief History of the 'Lock Her Up!' Chant by Trump Supporters Against Clinton," *Washington Post*, November 22, 2016, www.washingtonpost.com/news/the-fix/wp/2016/11/22/a-brief-history-of-the-lock-her-up-chant-as-it-looks-like-trump-might-not-even-try/?utm_term=.94bd0ae67752.

8. Hillary Clinton, "Comments at LGBT for Hillary Gala," New York City, September 9, 2016.

9. Bonnie Berkowitz and Kevin Uhrmacher, "It's Not Just the Cabinet: Trump's Transition Team May Need to Find About 4,100 Appointees," *Washington Post*, December 5, 2016, www.washingtonpost.com/graphics/politics/trump-transition-appointments-scale.

10. Michelle Cheng, "Trump Still Hasn't Filled Top Jobs, and He Has (Mostly) Himself to Blame," *FiveThirtyEight*, July 3, 2017, https://fivethirtyeight.com/features/trump-still-hasnt-filled-top-jobs-and-he-has-mostly-himself-to-blame; Tal Kopan, "At 200-Day Mark, Trump Nominations Still Lag," CNN, August 7, 2017, www.cnn.com/2017/08/07/politics/trump-200-days-nominations/index.html.

11. Stephen N. Duncan, *Only the Most Able* (Lanham, MD: Rowman & Littlefield, 2013), 21.

12. Anne Joseph O'Connell, *Waiting for Leadership: President Obama's Record in Staffing Key Agency Positions and How to Improve the Appointments Process* (Washington, DC: Center for American Progress, April 2010), 11.

13. "Geithner Can't Keep Up, Critics Say," CBS News, March 5, 2009, www.cbsnews.com/news/geithner-cant-keep-up-critics-say.

14. Cheng, "Trump Still Hasn't Filled."

15. Lisa Rein, "Harvey Approaches During Leadership Vacuum in Some Crucial Agencies," *Washington Post*, August 25, 2017, www.washingtonpost.com/national/2017/live-updates/weather/hurricane-harvey-updates-preparation-evacuations-forecast-storm-latest/hurricane-harvey-approaches-during-a-leadership-vacuum-in-some-crucial-agencies/?u tm_term=.4b2a8a069ce7.

16. Dave Leventhal, "Want Honest Elections? Meet America's New Election Integrity Watchdog," Center for Public Integrity, February 24, 2016, www.pri.org/stories/2016-02-24/meet-nations-new-election-integrity-watchman.

17. Mark J. Oleszek, "'Holds' in the Senate," CRS Report R43563 (Washington, DC: Congressional Research Service, January 23, 2017).

18. Frank Bruni, "A Nominee's Crushed Hopes," *New York Times*, June 6, 2016, www.nytimes.com/2016/06/07/opinion/an-obama-nominees-crushed-hopes.html.

19. Will Doran, "James Comey Memo: Did the Former FBI Director Admit to Leaking Classified Information in Hearings?," *PolitiFact*, June 9, 2017, www.politifact.com/north-carolina/statements/2017/jun/09/north-carolina-republican-party/james-comey-hearings-did-former-fbi-director-admit.

20. Greg Jaffe and Greg Miller, "Trump Revealed Highly Classified Information to Russian Foreign Minister and Ambassador," *Washington Post*, May 15, 2017, www.washingtonpost.com/worldnational-security/trump-revealed-highly-classified-information-to-russian-foreign-minister-and-ambassador/2017/05/15/530c172a-3960-11e7-9e48-c4f199710b69_story.html?utm_term=.9373d77ba71d.

21. Peter Baker et al., "Israel Said to Be Source of Secret Intelligence

Trump Gave to Russians," *New York Times*, May 16, 2017, www
.nytimes.com/2017/05/16/world/middleeast/israel-trump-classified
-intelligence-russia.html.

22. C. J. Chivers, "Found at the Scene in Manchester: Shrapnel, a Back-
pack and a Battery," *New York Times*, May 24, 2017, www.nytimes.
com/interactive/2017/05/24/world/europe/manchester-arena-bomb
-materials-photos.html.

23. "British Police Suspend Intelligence Sharing with U.S. After Leaks,"
interview with Richard Clarke, *All Things Considered*, NPR, May 25,
2017.

CHAPTER 22: INCOME AND EDUCATION
INEQUALITY FAULT LINES

1. Data from Federal Reserve Board's "Triennial Survey of Consumer Fi-
nances," 2013.

2. For these purposes, upper-class households have incomes more than
twice the median household income; middle-class, two-thirds to twice
the median income; lower-class, less than two-thirds the median income. *The American Middle Class Is Losing Ground* (Washington, DC:
Pew Research Center, December 9, 2015), 1–7.

3. *American Middle Class*, 1–7.

4. *Indicators of Higher Education Equity in the United States: 45-Year Trend
Report* (Washington, DC: The Pell Institute and University of Pennsylvania Alliance for Higher Education and Democracy, 2015), 31.

5. Jennifer Giancola and Richard D. Kahlenberg, *True Merit: Ensuring
Our Brightest Students Have Access to Our Best Colleges and Universities*
(Lansdowne, VA: Jack Kent Cooke Foundation, January 2016), 5.

6. "Some Colleges Have More Students from the Top 1 Percent than the
Bottom 60. Find Yours," *New York Times*, January 18, 2017.

7. Derek Bok and William Bowen, *The Shape of the River: Long-Term
Consequences of Considering Race in College and University Admissions*
(Princeton, NJ: Princeton University Press, 1998), 49 (figure 2.12).

8. Mary C. Waters and Zoua Vang, "The Challenges of Immigration to
Race Based Diversity Policies in the United States," in *Diversity and
Canada's Future*, eds. Leslie Seidle, Keith Bantin, and Thomas Cour-

chene (Montreal: Institute for Research on Public Policy Press, 2007), 411–50.

9. The top socioeconomic half of the population was defined as a composite of income, occupation, and the education level of parents. Richard H. Sander, "Class in American Legal Education," *Denver University Law Review* 88 (2011): 651.

10. Lyndon B. Johnson, "To Fulfill These Rights," commencement address at Howard University, June 4, 1965.

11. Richard D. Kahlenberg, *The Remedy: Class, Race, and Affirmative Action* (New York: Basic Books, 1996), 15.

12. Kahlenberg, *Remedy*, 15.

13. US Department of Education, Institute of Education Sciences, National Center for Education Statistics, National Assessment of Educational Progress (NAEP), 2013 Mathematics and Reading Assessments; "Public High School Graduation Rates," National Center on Education Statistics, US Department of Education, figure 2, "Adjusted Cohort Graduation Rate (ACGR) for public high school students, by race/ethnicity: 2014–15," April 2017; Lauren Camera, "High School Seniors Aren't College-Ready," *US News*, April 27, 2016, www.usnews.com/news/articles/2016-04-27/high-school-seniors-arent-college-ready-naep-data-show.

14. Sarah Singer Quast and Lisa Castillo, *The State of College Readiness and Degree Completion in New York City* (New York: Graduate NYC, June 2016), 6.

15. Kurt Bauman and Camille L. Ryan, *Educational Attainment in the United States: 2015* (Washington, DC: United States Census Bureau, March 2016), 2, "Table 1, Educational Attainment of the Population Aged 25 and Older by Age, Sex, Race and Hispanic Origin, and Other Selected Characteristics."

16. "Concentration of Public School Students Eligible for Free or Reduced-Price Lunch, Figure 1," US Department of Education, National Center on Education Statistics, March 2017.

17. Michael Mitchell et al., "Funding Down, Tuition Up: State Cuts to Higher Education Threaten Quality and Affordability at Public Colleges," Center on Budget and Policy Priorities, August 15, 2016.

18. See "Exit Polls Data."

19. Betsy Cooper et al., "How Immigration and Concerns About Cultural Changes Are Shaping the 2016 Election," 2016 Public Religion Research Institute/Brookings Institution Immigration Survey.

20. Derek Bok, "Protecting the Freedom of Expression on Campus," *Boston Globe*, March 25, 1991.

21. William Galston and Clara Hendrickson, "The Educational Rift in the 2016 Election," Brookings Institution, November 18, 2016, www.brookings.edu/blog/fixgov/2016/11/18/educational-rift-in-2016-election.

CHAPTER 23: SINGLE-ISSUE FAULT LINES

1. Julie Rovner, "Abortion Funding Ban Has Evolved over the Years," NPR, December 14, 2009, http://www.npr.org/templates/story/story.php?storyId=121402281.

2. Rovner, "Abortion Funding Ban."

3. Michael Crowley, "Casey Closed," *New Republic*, September 16, 1996.

4. Hillary Clinton, "Address to the Planned Parenthood Action Fund," Manchester, New Hampshire, June 10, 2016.

5. Katie Glueck, "Trump Taps Top Abortion Foe to Chair Anti-Abortion Coalition," *Politico*, September 16, 2016, www.politico.com/story/2016/09/donald-trump-marjorie-dannenfelser-abortion-228252.

6. Scott Detrow, "Bernie Sanders Defends Campaigning for Anti-Abortion Rights Democrat," NPR, April 20, 2017, www.npr.org/2017/04/20/524962482/sanders-defends-campaigning-for-anti-abortion-rights-democrat.

7. Gabriel Debenedetti, "Megadonor Steyer Vows to Only Back Candidates That Support Abortion Rights," *Politico*, August 12, 2017, www.politico.com/story/2017/08/12/megadonor-steyer-abortion-rights-candidates-241563.

8. "Republican Candidates Debate in North Charleston, South Carolina," January 14, 2016, available online at the American Presidency Project, www.presidency.ucsb.edu/ws/index.php?pid=111395.

9. Jeb Bush (@JebBush), "America. [Image attached]," Twitter, February 16, 2016, 5:27 p.m.

10. Elena Schneider, "Gun Control Becomes a Litmus Test in Democratic Primaries," *Politico*, December 15, 2017, www.politico.com /story/2015/12/gun-control-democratic-primaries-nra-216764.

11. Louis Jacobson, "Hillary Clinton Correct That Bernie Sanders Flip-Flopped on Liability for Gun Makers, Sellers," *PolitiFact*, January 17, 2016, www.politifact.com/truth-o-meter/statements/2016/jan/17/hillary-clinton/fact-checking-gun-manufacturer-liability-bernie.

12. "Profile for 2016 Election Cycle: National Rifle Association," Center for Responsive Politics, accessed September 1, 2017, www.opensecrets .org/orgs/summary.php?id=d000000082.

13. Sam Roberts, "Bloomberg's Support Leads to Mixed Election Results," *New York Times*, November 8, 2012, www.nytimes.com/2012/11/09 /nyregion/bloombergs-campaign-contributions-yield-mixed-results .html.

CHAPTER 24: THE MILITARY/CIVILIAN FAULT LINE

1. "Veterans Population Projection Model," US Department of Veterans Affairs, 2014. See also Mona Cholabi, "What Percentage of Americans Have Served in the Military?," *FiveThirtyEight*, March 19, 2016, https://fivethirtyeight.com/datalab/what-percentage-of-americans -have-served-in-the-military/.

2. Karl Eikenberry and David M. Kennedy, "Americans and Their Military, Drifting Apart," *New York Times*, May 26, 2013, www.nytimes .com/2013/05/27/opinion/americans-and-their-military-drifting -apart.html.

3. Leo Shane III, "The Number of Veterans in Congress Will Likely Drop Again Next Year," *Military Times*, October 31, 2016, www.military times.com/news/2016/10/31/the-number-of-veterans-in-congress-will -likely-drop-again-next-year/.

4. James Fallows, "The Tragedy of the American Military," *The Atlantic*, January/February 2015, www.theatlantic.com/magazine/archive /2015/01/the-tragedy-of-the-american-military/383516/.

5. Fallows, "Tragedy of the American Military."

6. "After Paris Terrorist Attacks, Solid Majority of America's 18- to 29-Year-Olds Support Sending U.S. Troops to Defeat ISIS; Less Than

20% Inclined to Serve if Needed," Harvard Institute of Politics Fall 2015 Poll, December 10, 2015.

7. David S. Cloud and David Zucchino, "US Military and Civilians Are Increasingly Divided," *Los Angeles Times*, May 24, 2015, www.latimes.com/nation/la-na-warrior-main-20150524-story.html.

8. *Population Representation in the Military Services: Fiscal Year 2014 Summary Report*, United States Department of Defense, Office of the Under Secretary of Defense, Personnel and Readiness, 24; Bill Bishop and Tim Murphy, "Largest Share of Army Recruits Come from Rural /Exurban America," *Daily Yonder*, March 3, 2009, http://www.daily yonder.com/largest-share-army-recruits-come-ruralexurban-america /2009/03/03/1962/.

9. *Population Representation in the Military Services: 2015*, "Table B-10: Non-Prior Service (NPS) Active Component Enlisted Accessions, FY15: by Service, Gender, Race, and Ethnicity with Civilian Comparison Group," US Department of Defense, Office of the Under Secretary of Defense, Personnel and Readiness, 2016.

CHAPTER 25: WE THE PEOPLE MUST ACT

1. Lyndon B. Johnson, "Special Address to Congress: The American Promise," March 15, 1965.

2. Drew Desilver, "Turnout Was High in the 2016 Primary Season, but Just Short of 2008 Record," Pew Research Center, June 10, 2016, www.pewresearch.org/fact-tank/2016/06/10/turnout-was-high-in -the-2016-primary-season-but-just-short-of-2008-record.

3. "2016 November General Election Turnout Rates," United States Elections Project, www.electproject.org/2016g.

4. "Voter Turnout, National Turnout Rates, 1787–2012," United States Elections Project, www.electproject.org/home/voter-turnout/voter -turnout-data.

5. "Voter Turnout Demographics," United States Elections Project, www .electproject.org/home/voter-turnout/demographics. Note that the figures used are listed under "Census Weight."

6. "Voter Turnout Demographics."

7. Drew Desilver, "U.S. Trails Most Developed Countries in Voter Turn-

out," Pew Research Center, May 15, 2017, www.pewresearch.org/fact-tank/2017/05/15/u-s-voter-turnout-trails-most-developed-countries.

8. Madison argued, "The right of suffrage is certainly one of the fundamental articles of republican Government, and ought not to be left to be regulated by the Legislature." Debates of the Constitutional Convention, August 7, 1787.

9. Alexander Hamilton, "A Second Letter from Phocion," in *The Papers of Alexander Hamilton*, eds. Harold C. Syrett et al., 26 vols. (New York: Columbia University Press, 1961), 79.

10. Lyndon B. Johnson, "Special Message to Congress on the Right to Vote," March 15, 1965.

11. "Election Results: United States Representative," Indiana Secretary of State, accessed August 1, 2017, http://www.in.gov/apps/sos/election/general/general2016?page=office&countyID=-1&officeID=5&districtID=-1&candidate=.

12. "2016 State Election Results," Secretary of the Commonwealth of Massachusetts, accessed August 1, 2017, http://electionstats.state.ma.us/elections/search/year_from:2016/year_to:2016/stage:General.

13. See "Supreme Court of the United States Granted & Noted List Cases for Argument in October Term 2017," United States Supreme Court.

14. "National Assessment of Educational Progress (NAEP) 2015 Report," US Department of Education. The 2015 NAEP found that 28 percent of twelfth-grade students had reading levels "below basic," and 38 percent had mathematics levels "below basic." The current national dropout rate is around 17 percent. Thus, over 40 percent of twelfth-grade-age teenagers perform at "below basic" levels or have dropped out. For information on dropout rates, see "Public High School Graduation Rates," National Center on Education Statistics, US Department of Education, figure 2, "Adjusted Cohort Graduation Rate (ACGR) for public high school students, by race/ethnicity: 2014–15," April 2017.

INDEX

INDEX

INDEX

income inequality, xiv, 179–80, 206–7, 293n2
Indiana, gerrymandering in, 205
Internet. *See* social media
Iran, x, 6
  nuclear agreement, 27, 71, 72, 265n24
Iran-Contra affair, 6, 27, 32–33
Iraq War, 12, 14, 15, 27, 75, 76
ISIS, ix, 28, 75–76
Israel, 7, 71, 72
Israel, Steve, 59, 220
Issa, Darrell, 7

Jackson, Andrew, 237
Jay, John, 31–32
Jefferson, Thomas, 82, 83
Johnson, Andrew, 83
Johnson, Lyndon Baines, 127, 212
  affirmative action and, 181
  Califano in administration, xvi, 5, 20, 23, 28, 45–46, 112, 122, 177–78
  Civil Rights Act of 1964, 69, 112, 113, 166, 167, 263–64n15
  Congress and, 6
  earmarks and, 69
  executive orders and, 20–21
  on FBI director Hoover, 176, 178
  Fortas nomination, 87
  Great Society and, xvi, 17, 29, 29n, 87, 110, 112–14, 122, 199
  leaks during presidency, 177–78
  military draft and, 13–14, 246n22
  NSA for, 25
  on politics as war, 24
  power of federal funds and, 114
  presidential press conferences, 37
  public election financing and, 46, 46n
  racial voting blocs and, 165, 166–67
  staff for, 23–24, 32, 34
  Vietnam War and, 5–6, 10, 69, 73, 74n, 158
  Voting Rights Act of 1965 and, 204
  White House press corps and, 36
Joint Chiefs of Staff, 25
judicial branch. *See* federal judiciary

Judicial Conference of the United States, 102, 102n
judicial elections, 151–54
Justice for All, A (Eisler), 267–68n20

Kagan, Elena, 92, 98n, 99
Kaine, Tim, 76
Kasich, John, 145
Katzenbach, Nicholas, 32, 177
Kennedy, Anthony, 98, 134
Kennedy, Edward "Ted," 87, 175
Kennedy, John F., xvi, 25, 32, 34, 36, 37, 82n, 175
Kerry, John, 26
King, Martin Luther, Jr., 20, 21, 182, 212, 215
Kissinger, Henry, 14, 192
Koch, Charles and David, 60, 132, 145, 150, 207
Korean War, 10, 73, 244n3, 244n4
Kushner, Jared, 31

labor unions, 38, 90, 134, 136, 146, 153
Lansing, Mich., 118–19
Lear, Tobias, 22
legislative branch. *See* Congress
Levinson, Larry, 29n
Lewinsky, Monica, 33
LGBTQ issues and voters, 7, 168–69, 169n
  Obama's transgender bathroom directive, 18–19, 119, 249n10
Libya, 12, 13, 26, 33–34, 246n20
Lincoln, Abraham, 19, 83
Lippmann, Walter, 69
lobbyists, 45, 59, 62
  bundling appropriations and, 65–66
  business interests, 146–48
  former politicians or staffers as, 129
  Honest Leadership and Government Act, 262n19
  labor unions and, 146
  number of, 129, 146, 262n19
  single-issue supporters and, 129, 190–91
  for states and cities, 122
  See also special interests

INDEX

INDEX

INDEX

INDEX

INDEX

ABOUT THE AUTHOR

Joseph A. Califano Jr. was born on May 15, 1931, in Brooklyn, New York, where he grew up. He received his BA degree in 1952 from the College of the Holy Cross in Worcester, Massachusetts, and his LLB in 1955 from Harvard Law School, where he was an editor of the *Harvard Law Review*.

After military service in the office of the Judge Advocate General of the Navy and two years with Governor Thomas Dewey's Wall Street law firm, he joined the Kennedy administration in 1961. There he served successively as special assistant to the general counsel of the Department of Defense, special assistant to Secretary of the Army Cyrus Vance, general counsel of the Army, and special assistant and chief troubleshooter for Secretary of Defense Robert McNamara. In his Defense Department post he was responsible for the department's liaison with the Office of the President of the United States and was the Department of Defense representative on the President's Committee on the Economic Impact of Defense and Disarmament and the Federal Radiation Council.

President Lyndon B. Johnson named Mr. Califano his special assistant for domestic affairs in 1965, a position he held until the president left office in 1969. While in this post the *New York*

Times called him the "Deputy President for Domestic Affairs." In accepting his resignation, the president wrote, "You were the captain I wanted and you steered the course well."

From 1969 until 1977, Mr. Califano practiced law in Washington, DC. During those years, he represented the *Washington Post* throughout the Watergate affair, was counsel to the Democratic National Committee, and represented clients as varied as Coca-Cola and the Black Panther Party.

From 1977 to 1979, Mr. Califano was the US Secretary of Health, Education, and Welfare in the Carter administration. He created the Health Care Financing Administration to run Medicare and Medicaid; mounted major health-promotion and disease-prevention programs, including the first national anti-smoking campaign, an initiative that resulted in the vaccination of 90 percent of children, and the issuance of *Healthy People: The Surgeon General's Report on Health Promotion and Disease Prevention* (1979), which set health goals for the American people for the first time. He promulgated the first regulations to provide equal opportunity for the handicapped and to provide equal athletic opportunity to women under Title IX. Mr. Califano also funded the nation's first freestanding hospice in Branford, Connecticut, and made Medicare reimbursement available for hospice care. In 1979, he directed the US Public Health Service to eliminate its official characterization of homosexuality as "a mental disease or defect," which immigration authorities had used to deny individuals entry to the United States solely because of their sexual orientation.

From 1980 to 1992, he practiced law in Washington, DC, and New York. During that time he served as special counsel to the House Committee on Standards of Official Conduct (now the House Ethics Committee) and was the founding chair of the Institute for Social and Economic Policy in the Middle East at Harvard University.

ABOUT THE AUTHOR

In 1992, he founded the National Center on Addiction and Substance Abuse at Columbia University (CASA) and served as chairman and president of this independent think/action tank until 2012, when he was named its founder and chairman emeritus.

Mr. Califano is the author of fourteen books on a wide range of subjects, including student unrest in the 1960s, the presidency, and the media (with then–*Washington Post* managing editor Howard Simons); his years as Secretary of Health, Education, and Welfare; President Lyndon Johnson's White House years; several books on America's health care system and substance abuse and addiction; books for parents on raising drug-free kids; and a personal memoir.

Mr. Califano has written articles for the *New York Times*, the *Washington Post*, the *Wall Street Journal*, *Reader's Digest*, the *New Republic*, the *Journal of the American Medical Association*, the *New England Journal of Medicine*, *America*, *Washington Monthly*, the *Huffington Post*, and other publications.

Mr. Califano is married to the former Hilary Paley Byers. They have five children, Mark, Joseph III, and Claudia Califano, and Brooke Byers and John F. Byers IV; and nine grandchildren: Joseph IV, Peter, Brian, Russell, Olivia, Evan, Nicholas, Grace, and Patrick.